FF657190

TERRORISM TODAY

Aspects, Challenges and Responses

TERRORISM TODAY

Aspects, Challenges and Responses

Editors

Dhruv C Katoch

and

Shakti Sinha

INDIA FOUNDATION
ANALYSIS | ADVOCACY | AWARENESS

PENTAGON PRESS

TERRORISM TODAY: Aspects, Challenges and Responses
Editors: Dhruv C Katoch and Shakti Sinha

First Published in 2016

Copyright © India Foundation

ISBN 978-81-8274-880-4

All rights reserved. No part of this publication may be reproduced, stored in a retrieval system, or transmitted, in any form or by any means, electronic, mechanical, photocopying, recording, or otherwise, without first obtaining written permission of the copyright owner.

Disclaimer: The views expressed in this volume are of individual contributors and do not represent the viewpoint of the editors.

Published by
PENTAGON PRESS
206, Peacock Lane, Shahpur Jat,
New Delhi-110049
Phones: 011-64706243, 26491568
Telefax: 011-26490600
email: rajan@pentagonpress.in
website: www.pentagonpress.in

Branch:
Flat No.213, Athena-2,
Clover Acropolis,
Viman Nagar,
Pune-411014
Email: pentagonpresspune@gmail.com

Printed at Aegean Offset Printers, Greater Noida, U.P.

Contents

PART II
CONCERNS AND CHALLENGES

PART III
RESPONSE AND COUNTERMEASURES

Introduction

India Foundation in collaboration with Sardar Patel University of Police, Security and Criminal Justice, Jodhpur organised an international Counter-Terrorism Conference 2015 at Jaipur from 18 March 2015 to 21 March 2015; the first such conference that would be an annual affair. At Jaipur, there were delegates from 22 countries and also a large number of subject experts, analysts, members of the strategic community and students from India.

The conference was inaugurated by the Home Minister of India, Shri Rajnath Singh, while the Minister of State, Home Affairs, Shri Kiren Rijiju, delivered the Valedictory Address. There were Special Addresses by Smt Vasundhara Raje (Chief Minister of Rajasthan), Shri Ajit Doval (National Security Advisor), Dr Amrullah Saleh (Former Director of National Directorate of Security, Afghanistan), Dr Daniel Pipes (President, Middle East Forum, USA), Shri Shuja Nawaz (Senior Fellow, Atlantic Council, USA) and Shri Tarek Fatah, well-known author and weekly columnist for the *Toronto Sun*. The issues discussed covered the entire ambit of counter-terrorism across the globe: the New Caliphate in West Asia, its impact on the al-Qaeda, global jihad, cross-border terrorism, Islamism and Talibanisation, terror trade (weapons, narcotics and fake currency), chemical, biological, radiological and nuclear (CBRN) terrorism, intelligence-sharing and reforms, illegal migration and border security, cyberspace, social media and terrorism, technology and equipment for infiltration, modus operandi of terrorists, ethno-national terrorist groups (LTTE and Chechen rebels), and de-radicalisation.

The challenge of terrorism, particularly that inspired by the notion of jihad, is not going away. In fact just when it was felt that the threat posed by the al-Qaeda and its different local affiliates like the al-Shabab, Boko Haram and others was on the decline after the elimination of Osama bin Laden and the reverses suffered by the organisation in Ethiopia, Mali and Nigeria, the Islamic State (Daesh)—more popularly known as the ISIS—

burst on the international scene with the dramatic capture of Mosul on June 10, 2014. This was the first time that any jihadi group had actually defeated a regular army in a battlefield and held territory. What made it even more impressive was that the ISIS had fielded about 3,000 jihadis against 30,000 well-armed and trained soldiers of the Iraqi army, and yet the battle for Mosul lasted barely a day. Its next move was even more audacious—on June 29, it declared its emir, Abu Bakr al-Baghdadi, as the Caliph (Khalifa) of the global Muslim community (Umma) and called upon all jihadis to declare their loyalty (*bay'a*) to him. Even as this is being written, despite reverses, the ISIS runs a proto-state over wide swathes of western Iraq and eastern/northern Syria, which at its widest is almost 700 kilometres across.

Contrary to popular belief that it was the US invasion of Iraq in 2003 that led to the creation of the the ISIS (actually its predecessor, Jund al-Sham), its roots go back to 1999 when its acknowledged founder, Jordanian national Abu Musab al-Zarqawi, supported by al-Qaeda's money and Taliban sponsorship, opened a jihadi training camp in Herat (Afghanistan). Forced to flee the country when the US moved in to overthrow the Taliban, al-Zarqawi was sheltered in Iran by its government, facilitated by the Afghan jihadi Gulbuddin Hekmatyar. Post-2003, he moved to Iraq and his group morphed into the al-Qaeda in Iraq (AQI), changing its name a number of times. Though al-Zarqawi was killed in a drone attack in 2006, his group only grew in strength by merging with the other groups, making strategic alignments with the Baathists disenfranchised by the disbanding of the Iraqi army and by attracting jihadis from the different countries, often changing names to become the ISIS by late 2006.

The ISIS has attracted around 20,000 jihadis from around 90 countries to its ranks; the scope, scale and method of its operations makes it easily, the biggest challenge to the Westphalian system in West Asia, and a potential threat to the countries far from its shores. The ISIS has expanded in a limited way into the neighbouring Lebanon and Jordan and has affiliates in Saudi Arabia, Kuwait and Libya. However, the ferocity of its attacks in Paris and its claims of downing a Russian charter flight over Sinai, have dramatically exposed the vulnerabilities of countries located further afield, against both the 'lone wolf' as well as organised terror attacks by the jihadis.

The ISIS has moved out of the traditional jihadi framework established by the al-Qaeda. The latter declared that the tyrants ruling Muslim countries (near enemies) were sustained in power by the US and the West (far enemy); hence, the latter should be attacked. Till the Paris attacks, the

ISIS has ignored the far enemy and concentrated on displacing the near enemy. The al-Qaeda is all about Muslim victimhood and weakness; the ISIS stresses immediate change guaranteed by Allah and victory. Al-Qaeda uses individual acts of terror while ISIS conquers, holds and governs territory. Al-Qaeda's stand on Shi'ite Iran was practical; it made sense to have a tactical understanding with Iran. But for the ISIS, Shia's and all non-Sunni sects are apostates which must be destroyed. Al-Qaeda has independent affiliates; ISIS encourages *hejira*—the sacred duty of all Muslims to emigrate to 'safe' lands (the Islamic state) so that they could live in the correct manner and also help conquer more lands.

Four other facets of ISIS are significant. One, it glorifies brutality and extreme violence. This is both to demoralise the enemy and to inure the potential recruits so that they accept it as a part of their future lives. Two, the ISIS is not just a terrorist outfit or even an insurgency. It is both these as well as a regular light infantry. Its strength is surprise, mobility and long-term planning, as evidenced by its attack on Mosul—preparations for which started a year or so before the attack through targeted assassinations of the Iraqi army commanders there; attacks on the isolated check points and penetration of the Iraqi intelligence. Three, it is financially self-sustaining; at its zenith, its revenues from extortion, local taxes, sale of petroleum products and of antiquities fetched it $3 million or so per day till the recent collapse of oil prices. This allows it to run municipal services in the areas under its control, supply electricity and water, social services, schools and hospitals, subsidised bread for the elderly, rent control and a rigid enforcement of the Sharia. Four, unlike clunky propaganda videos of the al-Qaeda and other jihadis, the ISIS productions are slick, topical and ably exploit the social media. Despite efforts by the governments and media providers to limit such use, the ISIS has been able to use Facebook, YouTube and Twitter to reach out to potential jihadis besides actual tactical planning. An Indian, Mehdi Biswas, was running one of their twitter handles @ShamiWitness, out of Bengaluru. Their e-magazine, *Dabiq*—named after a village of that name in Syria where according to traditional belief the end-of-time battle will take place—is professionally produced; in all likelihood jihadis from Western nations are involved in the ISIS's media campaigns as it is tailored for the native speakers of English, French, Russian and other European languages.

It is not as if the al-Qaeda–ISIS brand of terrorism is the only, or even the most effective, one. It is, however the most extensive representation of what a terrorist organisation can do, and how it can morph into a regular insurgency using terror tactics. It is not just a cross-border phenomenon but a trans-national one too. Oil sales, including those across borders, as well as the sale of antiquities are an important part of its revenue-generating sources. It uses the social media extensively, and its slick, eye-popping and gruesome documentaries and short films are effective at creating fear and rallying potential supporters to its cause. Returnee jihadis are potential sleeper cells that can cause havoc in the future. Worse, whilst its presence has drawn in big powers like the USA and Russia into the fray, this has not been a smooth operation. Ties between Russia and Turkey, the West and Russia, and between various countries in the West Asia region have become frayed with suspicion being the predominant strain, instead of these outside powers aligning to take on and eliminate the ISIS. That makes the ISIS phenomenon an important reference to begin any discussion on counter-terrorism.

On the other hand, for many decades, India and Afghanistan have been victims of cross-border terrorism that is the Pakistani Army's weapon of choice, delivered through its strategic assets—the jihadi groups like Lashkar-e-Taiba, Taliban, Jaish-e-Mohammed, Haqqani network et al. While the November 26, 2008 attack on Mumbai got extensive international media coverage, it was neither the first sea-based terrorist infiltration, nor the worst in terms of the death toll; in psychological terms, Mumbai 2008 is a scar that won't go away easily. Cross-border terrorism has led to extensive civilian causalities in the Indian state of Jammu & Kashmir, as well as earlier in Punjab. And Afghanistan continues to bleed with no sign of stability.

This volume has three sections. The first section, 'Terrorism Sans Frontiers', introduces the reader to a full array of terrorism that is no respecter of boundaries, as the title makes clear. Yossef Bodansky ("The Rise of the Caliphate") locates the growth of the Islamic State to the deeply ingrained belief that the Caliphate, based on that of the first two (Rashidun) Caliphs, would be recreated. This idea and the hope for such a Caliphate is far bigger than what Abu Bakr al-Baghdadi, the self-proclaimed Khalifa Ibrahim, has been imagining and what has been in the making for half a century. The idea of a 'Muslim State' is deeply problematic, theologically speaking, but was legitimised by al-Qutb and later also by Hassan al-Turabi on very practical grounds. It is seen a 'as crucial and expedient phase in the restoration of the Caliphate under contemporary conditions'. Al-Turabi, and later Osama bin Laden, also encouraged other expedient measures—most notably, a close cooperation with Shiite Iran—as necessary and desirable in the pursuit of the triumph of jihad. Similar was the decision to let local, individual units get actively involved in the intifada against specific Arab states, aka the Arab Spring.

While the Liberation Tigers of Tamil Eelam (LTTE) operated overwhelmingly within Sri Lanka, apart from the horrendous attack at Perumbudur that killed Rajiv Gandhi and other targeted assassinations of the exiled Sri Lankan Tamil leaders in India, it drew on the support of a large Sri Lankan Tamil diaspora that allowed it to become a formidable fighting force for over two decades. Lt Gen A.S. Kalkat ("Ethno-National Terrorism: A Case Study of the LTTE") who led the Indian Peacekeeping Force (IPKF) in Sri Lanka, traces its origins to the harsh military crackdown on the civil unrest against the grievances of the Tamil population. This led to the formation of many Tamil terror groups; LTTE emerged as the sole terror group by ruthlessly eliminating all the others, in the process creating fear among the Tamils, who then could not go against it. While it did resort to looting and extortion, its primary sources of revenues were 'taxation' and remittances from the diaspora. Two clear messages emerge from his analysis. First, that such insurgencies, even one using terror tactics, need domestic political solutions, and there are limitations to what outside powers can do. Second, military efforts would need both 'bottoms-up' (counter-insurgency) and 'top-down' (counter-terrorism) approaches.

Natalia Tereshchenko ("The Chechen Rebels: From Separatism to Terrorism") introduces us to the long history of the Russian Empire's attempt to incorporate Chechnya, and the consequent counter-colonial insurgencies that followed. The recent conflict arose as a fall-out of the years of suppression following Russia's opening up in the late 1980s. The Chechen rebels have since crossed borders, carrying out horrific attacks in Russia, Ingushetia and Dagestan. Further, the propagation of extremism was a counter-reaction to the extreme pressure from the Russian state. The result is that Putin's ally Kadyrov, who has built a powerful security apparatus, and the Chechen rebels are fighting 'an extra-territorial civil war' in Ukraine. Chechens form the majority of the 1,000 or so Russian jihadis who are with the ISIS. While holding nationalism to be wrong, these Chechen jihadi terrorists retain an interest in the developments in Chechnya. The fear is that the returnee jihadis can bring back radical ideas leading to conflict on the borders of Europe.

India has long been a victim of cross-border terrorism (CBT), which Ata Hasnain ("Cross Border Terrorism in Jammu & Kashmir") tells us moved from Punjab to Jammu & Kashmir. The Pakistani agencies have been active in the southern states and are using Dhaka in the north-east as well. It was based on the 'exploitation of disaffected elements of minority community'. The J&K operations should be seen as part of the long-term strategic goal of the Pakistani Army's general headquarters (GHQ) to 'bleed India by a thousand cuts', aiming for not just the seizure of J&K but of India's disintegration. CBT is a war of deceit and opportunity, with deniability at its core. Like A.S. Kalkat, he too argues that CBT must be seen in the larger dimension and cannot be resolved through kinetic means only. In the continuum of conflict initiation-stabilisation-resolution-termination, India must not use yesterday's methods to be successful in moving the situation to the fourth phase.

Building on this, Ram Pradhan ("The 26/11 Terrorist Attack in Mumbai: A Critical Analysis of the Modus Operandi and Operation") who led the administrative enquiry into the 26/11 attacks, points to a systemic dysfunction that must be set right in order to avoid such incidents from happening again. One, there had been a number of alerts both about specific hotels being attacked and about terrorists using the sea route. Certain corrective steps were also taken but there was no one who was responsible for making an overall assessment. Secondly, while the response to the messages coming in was quick, it soon became haphazard since normal communications became clogged and policemen started using their mobile phones for communicating with each other. Third, the Commissioner of Police stayed at the scene for two days, leaving the control room to be led by a relatively junior official—a departure from the standard operating procedures (SOPs). Fourth, the Mumbai Police does not function under the state Director General of Police but its officers belong to the Maharashtra cadre of the Indian Police Service; in effect, there is a duality of control. The absence of a single chain of command meant that vital assets like the Anti-Terrorist Squad (ATS) and quick response teams (QRTs) were under-utilised. On a larger plane, the lacunae in intelligence-sharing and analysis must be set right.

Rajan Medhekar ("Mumbai Attacks: International Aspects and Impact—Failures to Detect Infiltration, Role of Media and (other) Stakeholders") argues that history would not repeat itself since 'we are committed to secure our freedom from terrorism and have faith in our commitment to succeed'. He also points to the need to look for systemic failures, and not individual scapegoats. The 26/11 attacks were 'conceived, planned and prepared in Pakistan' and the Laskar-e-Taiba enjoyed covert support from parts of Pakistan's intelligence and security apparatus. Unlike the insurgents and even extremists driven by ideology who are amenable to political and security solutions, terrorists are driven by blind hate, are uncompromising and driven by religious (and political) bigotry. Terrorism and the right of self-determination should not be confused. 26/11 was meant to humiliate India and cause economic damage, hence the resort to prolonged attacks and not the use of bombs that could have led to a greater loss of lives. The media has an important role to inform but must do it responsibly, and the people must be central to all the counter-terrorist efforts.

John Nomikos ("Illegal Immigration, Human Trafficking and Terrorism in Greece") alerts the reader to the fault lines in the European Union's immigration policies that leave Greece as a large host of illegal migrants; as per EU rules, member states return 'illegals' to the country that was the point of first entry into the Union. Paradoxically, these immigrants actually intended to use Greece only as a transit on way to the more developed countries. Greece's laws have also become more friendly to 'illegal' immigrants, and its population rise, points to the dangers of a demographic change. Such flows are also open to the possibility of terrorists and crime networks using this route: an al-Qaeda operative was arrested attempting to enter Greece. The European Union must rely more on human intelligence (HUMINT) to prevent traffickers bringing in illegal immigrants rather than trying to deal with them after they have entered the EU.

The next section, Concerns and Challenges, looks at different aspects of how terrorists networks operate, how they raise money, what types of instruments they are likely to use, what are the specific challenges that India faces in the maritime sector and how jihadism is getting entrenched through Talibanisation and the ISIS brand of Caliphate.

Amit Kumar ("Weapons, Narcotics and Fake Currency") alerts us to the dangerous intertwining that has taken place between the criminal and terrorist networks so much so that it often becomes difficult to distinguish one from the other. Both use trafficking in narcotics and weapons and money laundering and often rely on each other. The withdrawal of state support after the end of the Cold War and the need for deniability drives such local resource raising efforts. However, there is no fixed template and the specific instrument used is context-driven and dependent on core competencies. The 'factors that facilitate terrorism and its reliance on weapons, narcotics, and fake currency smuggling ... include porous and poorly policed borders and lack of governance in border regions.' Authorities should concentrate on pursuing money-laundering cases since these are the easiest to prosecute. This is necessary 'since terrorist financing takes place in much smaller amounts and is more difficult to trace and detect on its own'.

Attempted unconventional CBRN (chemical, biological, radiological and nuclear) acts of terrorism have been few, so should this threat be minimised? Jean-Francois Daguzan ("Unconventional Terrorism: An Assessment") argues for 'the need to assess the technical reality of a supposed threat and to see if recent technological developments have increased its potentialities...the link between the presumed technical threat and terrorism must be demonstrated'. Globalisation, easy access to knowledge of technologies, their dual nature, low visibility due to dispersal of production, 'mass impact' of any usage. etc., have made the world more vulnerable to its risks with a predictable augmentation of the panic effect. Though the actual threat is low—almost non-existent in the case of nuclear weapons—countries must be prepared to face other unconventional attacks. Global cooperation, better intelligence and targeted offensive capabilities with better civil defence would be needed.

For India, it is necessary to look at its local context; Ajay Lele ("CBRN Terrorism and South Asia") provides examples of Libya and Syria as examples that chemical weapons were produced, tested and actually used in the contravention of international law. However for decades, as the emphasis was on nuclear threats, the world lacks a regulatory framework banning the use of all types of CBR weapons. The absence of WMDs is Iraq was a setback to the efforts in highlighting such dangers but Libya's declaration of stocks of mustard gas and the use of chemical weapons in Syria alerted the world to its dangers. 'South Asian region today possesses all the ingredients for a potential geopolitical nightmare' even as 'there are emerging non-traditional security issues in South Asia that are of common concern to countries across the region'. The potential of Pakistan-backed groups using CBRN terrorism against India, or against Pakistani institutions itself because of deep fractures within the Pakistani state, cannot be ruled out, though the possibility is not very definitive.

Piracy has existed since time immemorial and though often destroyed, has not been eliminated. In fact, Shekhar Sinha ("Anti-Piracy and Maritime Terrorism") makes the point that this threat has often led to the establishment of strong navies, and even empires. Maritime security has become a key issue, particularly in the Indian Ocean which has many choke points and through which 1,00,000 ships transit annually. While international cooperation has reduced the menace of piracy, the threat of a hijacking dictated by criminal motives becoming an act of terrorism cannot be ruled out. A common agreement on defining maritime terrorism is therefore necessary. Somali pirates have adopted newer technologies allowing them to presently operate hundreds of miles away from their coast. India has been a part of international/regional efforts at combating this piracy including the provision of escort services. For India, a 'network of cooperative partnerships with Indian Ocean rim nations and extra-regional powers would serve to increase Indian influence in the region, create a safety cushion and provide more strategic space and autonomy'.

Continuing the discussion, Rahul Roy-Chaudhury ("Countering Maritime Terrorism against India: Challenges and Opportunities") argues that 'India continues to remain highly vulnerable to another maritime terror attack due to the growing complexity of the maritime security environment as well as continuing concerns over state-sponsored cross-border maritime terrorism'. The first maritime terrorist attack on India, and a very serious one at that, goes back to 1993. Though a Group of Ministers of the NDA government in 2001 had clearly listed India's maritime vulnerabilities, inadequate efforts and a lack of political leadership by the subsequent UPA government meant that 26/11 took place—an eerie reminder of the GoM's clear assessment. Subsequently, a number of steps have been taken—the Navy has been made the nodal authority; the Coast Guard and the coastal police strengthened; Joint Operations Centres established; an effective system of maritime domain awareness is in place, there is much greater regional intelligence-sharing, etc. The fact is 'that technological developments have made it possible for even a small group to acquire 'asymmetric' capabilities at relatively modest costs'. India therefore remains vulnerable and must be on the guard because 'criminal syndicates and sea-based smuggling routes have more links to maritime terrorism than piracy'.

Pakistan's policy of using Islam and non-state actors, while apparently successful in combating the Soviet occupation of Afghanistan in the 1980s, has come full circle, as Christian Wagner ("Talibanisation of the Pakistan–Afghanistan Region: State Sponsors and Non-State Actors") makes clear. Far from Afghanistan providing Pakistan with a 'strategic depth' against India, Pakistan has been forced on the back foot in that country while countering India's presence, besides paying a huge cost in terms of the domestic victims of the terrorists spawned by them. India is trusted as a reliable friend, the largest non-Western donor and emerges as the top liked country in different surveys. Though supporting the Taliban, Pakistan could not even sort out its boundary dispute with Afghanistan during Taliban rule and comes across as the most unpopular country. Pakistan's false distinction between the 'good' terrorist who targets India, Afghanistan and foreign troops and the 'bad' terrorists like the TTP who attack the Pakistani Army, stands discredited. In the wake of Operation Zarb-e-Azb and the Peshawar massacre, the Pakistani Army repudiated the distinction between 'good' and 'bad' terrorists but whether it has actually done so, is an open question.

Talibanisation, according to Marvin Weinbaum ("Confronting the Talibanisation in Pakistan and Afghanistan") is a success to the extent that many of its ideas and narratives have entered the mainstream national discourse of Pakistan and Afghanistan. Like Wagner, Weinbaum too makes the point that 'the threat of Talibanisation in Pakistan comes from an almost seamless alliance of militant groups, some of which are at least partially controlled by the state and others, like the TTP, which are at war with the state, attacking both civilian and military targets'. The Post-Peshawar course correction is patchy at best, with groups like the LeT continuing to operate openly. The Afghan Taliban emerged strong 'aided in no small way by the backing of Pakistan's premier security agency, the military's Inter-Service Intelligence'. A reconciliation between Pakistan and Afghanistan 'could go far in bringing the close cooperation needed to overcome their insurgencies' since this would allow Pakistan to 'feel freer to cut ties to its Afghan Taliban surrogates and may also be encouraged to confront those domestic extremist groups that the military and political leaders have increasingly come to admit are the chief sources of threat to the national security'.

Thomas Lynch III presented "The New Caliphate in West Asia: Impact on the al-Qaeda's Core, Global Jihad and Jihad in South Asia", his detailed research into the rise of the ISIS as a pernicious and durable terrorist organisation, how this represents a 'significant rupture in the global jihadist constellation' and how it affects South Asia, which is significantly different from its impact on West Asia or North Africa. He meticulously traces developments in Iraq and Syria, key characters like al-Zarqawi, al-Zawahiri, al-Baghdadi and the ISIS–al Qaeda split, thus dispelling simplistic, monocausal reasons for the rise of the ISIS. However, in South Asia, al-Qaeda has acted vigorously to prevent ISIS making inroads. It has established an affiliate for the Indian subcontinent, prioritised jihad in Afghanistan against the foreign troops, declared the Pakistani state as 'apostate' and spoken up for Muslim causes in India and Bangladesh and for the Rohingyas in Myanmar. There may be a number of reasons for the ISIS's relative failure to draw volunteers from South Asia including the existing jihad options, Indian pluralism and the Saudi/Gulf's anti-ISIS stance. Could this be replicated elsewhere?

Waiel Awwad ("The Caliphate and the Future of the Al-Qaeda and other Global Jihadist Groups") is firmly of the opinion that 'terrorism will continue to spread and to counter it will be a long haul process.' Large numbers of Saudis, Tunisians and Turks have joined the ISIS as it is seen in these countries as an organisation compatible with the Sharia and not as a terrorist organisation. Various factors like the artificial division of the Arab world by the Sykes–Picot Agreement, the destruction of feudalism, the creation of Israel, the rise of Pan-Arabism, the effects of the Cold War where all anti-Western forces were branded as communist, the Israeli occupation of Arab lands, the lack of political reform in Arab countries that left the mosque as the only alternative and the US 'policy of spreading anarchy, sectarian democracy and nourishing radicalism...led to the birth of the terrorist organisation, ISIS, a product of al-Qaeda that was itself created by the Saudi-ISI-USA nexus'. ISIS can only be defeated if there is political will among the leading powers, joint military operations, acceptance of Israel as a nation and the establishment of a Palestinian State.

This first piece in Section III: Response and Countermeasures, is by Lisa Curtis ("Counter-Terrorism Infrastructure and Capacity: The Need for Political Consensus and Preventive Steps—Administration, Security and Legal") who makes a case for an enhanced India–US cooperation on counter-terrorism, which would give the former greater access to technology and the latter, more information; better US appreciation, and follow-up, of the David Headley case would have helped both the countries. The 9/11 attack highlighted the need for bringing together inputs from different intelligence agencies, so that the full picture could develop. The US has taken many steps by establishing a Director of National Intelligence and changing the focus of FBI, among others. The most effective step has been the establishment of the National Counterterrorism Center (NCTC), which has 'resulted in an improvement in analysts' ability to connect the dots of the various streams of information'. Violent extremism has to be countered at all levels including the local, without 'alienating Muslim minority communities'; the US experience is that 'open communication between Muslim minority communities and local law enforcement has contributed to trust building and the disruption of terrorist plots through community informers.'

Intelligence is not about information alone; it is about knowledge, understanding and sharing. Andrea Margelleti ("Information-Sharing and Interconnection of Experiences: The Two Pillars of the Italian Intelligence Service Reform") informs us that Italy took the decisive step—'joining data, resources and efforts' based on its 'long history of fighting terrorism and criminal organisations inside our national borders.' The guiding principle behind Italy's effort at reforming its intelligence apparatus was 'the importance of the strategic information as a common good'. Its Strategic Anti-terrorism Analysis Committee (C.A.S.A.) brings together 'high representatives of the state police, of the Carabinieri, officials of the Italian finance police, representatives of the penitentiary administration department and the intelligence agencies'. Separately, both the internal and external intelligence agencies have been brought under the Prime Minister with a ministerial committee 'in charge of advising, proposing and approving the guidelines of the policies of the intelligence service'. To increase the people's faith, a parliamentary committee chaired by an opposition MP is 'charged with controlling all activities of security institutions upholding the principles of the Italian Constitution'.

Since traditionally the issues of terrorism and crime have been treated locally, hardly 'five per cent of the data about terrorism and organised crime in open sources is located in professional security service databases'. To overcome this, Darko Trifunovic ("Technology and Equipment for Counter-Terrorism") informs the reader that the 'Faculty of Science along with the Faculty of Security Studies, both from the University of Belgrade, formed a joint team to create such a database' called TOC. It subsequently got access to 'the reports on terrorism and organised crime on a global scale drawn up by graduate students of the George C. Marshall Center, which were based on various open sources'.' The TOC database 'contains information about terrorists and criminals, terrorist and criminal groups and organisations, their supporters, attacks, the locations of terrorist and criminal activities as well as the relationships between all of the above-mentioned categories' and is accessed by thousands of users globally including security agencies and has been used in global events like the Olympics, the FIFA World Cup, etc.

The changing geostrategic and geopolitical environment in South Asia, according to Shuja Nawaz ("The Regional Challenge and Cost of Terrorism") presents the countries with a 'clear opportunity to alter the traditional paradigms that have shaped the thinking in the region' for which 'economics needs to displace politics in the strategic calculus of governance'. These countries face challenges of terrorism and militancy. Rather than reshaping the environment that spawns and sustains terrorism and militancy, counter-terrorism operations are prioritised. Militarised approaches do not always work as Balochistan and Kashmir have shown. The nexus between state and terrorism is counter-productive. Political leaders should try to 'create the right kind of dialogue in the public sphere which remains critical to the success of the anti-terror efforts' and should 'distance themselves from any alignment with sectarian, religious or ethnic forces'. It is estimated that India and Pakistan lose 1.5% of their GDP annually as a result of the presence of conflict between them; instead, they should work to regionally integrate their economies and help create the millions of jobs that they require.

Rana Bannerji ("The Mumbai Attack: An Analysis") points out that though the intelligence had leads about the Mumbai attacks, the frequency of the alerts bred complacency. Pakistan's handling of the 26/11 case despite being given specific evidence like voice samples, details of the serving army officers' involvement, details from the Tahawwur Rana case, etc., has been unsatisfactory. Pakistan's judiciary and police come across as incapable of handling terrorism-related cases. It is troubling that Islamic extremism, concepts like jihad and the role of non-state actors have become institutionalised in Pakistan. The Lashkar-e-Taiba (LeT) serves the Pakistani state's explicit purposes, domestically now that its role in Kashmir has been neutralised; it however has become more active globally, training Rohingyas, tying up with Sikh extremists, etc. The Pakistani Army must understand that the country's main existential threat comes from its internal security situation, not from India. FATA needs both an economic development and an investing of political rights. On India's side, its needs to tighten up its domestic security apparatus, reach out to its Muslim community socio-culturally and its media must report responsibly.

Though the present Bangladeshi government has successfully demonstrated its zero-tolerance of terrorism, Farooq Shobhan ("Counter-Radicalisation and De-Radicalisation: Exploring the Approaches and Strategies for Bangladesh") explains that the real threat the country faces is radicalisation, which envisages a change in the systems of governance, locally or globally, or both. De-radicalisation programmes have been defined to 'reengineer an individual or a group of individuals in such a manner that they feel discouraged and lack any incentive to engage in radical extremist activities'. De-radicalisation programmes vary from country to country; however, they 'place great emphasis on addressing the economic hardship of the radicalised individuals, invest in education and religious scholarship, involve families and provide a suitable social life as the key approach to de-radicalisation'. Bangladesh has to develop its own de-radicalisation and counter-radicalisation strategies with different components including educational reform, countering the non-contextual misinterpretation of religious messages and involving civil society and families—in general, developing counter-narratives to counter the appeal of radical extremism.

This volume closes with Sultan Shahin ("De-Radicalisation: Use of

Media and Curriculum—The Way Forward") and takes the reader through how radicalisation takes place in mosques, madrasas, electronic media and cyberspace. Unfortunately, even the Barelvi madrasas have abandoned Sufi teaching and substituted Rumi and Sadi with Syed Qutb—the father of modern Islamic terrorism. In any case, 'Wahhabi–Salafi madrasas have, of course, been teaching Ibn-e-Taimiya, Mohammad Ibn-e-Abdul Wahhab, Qutb, Maududi and other extremist ideologues for a long time. While Islamic scholars now accept the link between Islamic teaching and terrorism, the export of radicalism and hate for all non-Wahabis, from Saudi Arabia continues. Wahhabis preach "hostility to any human practice that would excite the imagination or bolster creativity"'. Shahin posits the need to de-radicalise the ulema, reopen the *ijtihad* allowing for analytical freedom, question the sanctity of the Ahadees and Sharia (*fiqh*) as these are later additions and help 'evolve a truly Islamic and a coherent theology of peace and co-existence, moderation and modernity, to counter the very coherent theology of violence and xenophobia, intolerance and supremacism that the jihadi ulema have created over centuries'. A government funding of the present day madrasas should be conditional on their reforming themselves to produce scientists and philosophers, as they did in the past.

Shakti Sinha
Dhruv C. Katoch

Opening Remarks by Rajnath Singh*

It gives me pleasure to deliver the inaugural address of this International Counter-Terrorism Conference. It is also heartwarming that India Foundation and Sardar Patel University of Police Security and Criminal Justice are organising this conference. Today, when much of the world is trying to grapple with the menace of terrorism, this conference being held to deliberate on ways and means to counter terrorism is a welcome initiative.

A galaxy of counter-terrorism experts from several countries has gathered here. The timing of this conference is apt, since the world is witnessing an entirely new paradigm of terrorism in the form of the Islamic State (IS/ISIS). Never in the history of mankind, has a terror outfit controlled such a large geographical area, generated such huge funds and has been immune to world public opinion regarding its atrocities on innocent people. The appeal of the ISIS to the young, educated people, in spite of its medieval ideology, is a cause for concern to the global community. I hope this conference analyses this phenomenon and suggests policy prescriptions.

Terror outfits like the ISIS do not believe in a plural society and are extremely intolerant of a liberal and secular democratic order. They do not accept the fundamental fact that a diversity of faiths and philosophies reflects the inherent beauty of human beings. These terrorists unleash the worst forms of violence to erase the diversity and to destabilise the democratic order. Mass killings of people of other faiths and mass enslavement of women by the ISIS and Boko Haram—which belongs to this category of terrorists—are frequent occurrences these days. In their endeavour to shape a future for mankind according to their dangerous dreams, they do not even spare the past. They vandalise the secular

*Home Minister, Govt. of India, delivered on 19 March 2015 at the International Counter-Terrorism Conference held in Jaipur

heritage of mankind left in the various forms of art and craft. The destruction of Bamiyan Buddhas by the Taliban in Afghanistan and the pre-Islamic relics by the ISIS in Syria, and making a big spectacle of such destruction by posting their videos on the internet, reflect their utter depravity.

These terrorists are adept at using the latest technologies to propagate their beliefs and deeds. They extensively use modern technology to reach out to a wider audience with susceptible minds. Their online propaganda is causing online self-radicalisation among the youth. It is a matter of serious concern that they are seeding the minds of innocents with poisonous provocation and inspiring them to be brutally intolerant and violent with others. However, at the same time, I am happy to note that the influence of the Islamic State on the Indian youth is negligible. According to our intelligence agencies, just a handful of Indian youth have joined the ISIS. Some have also returned after being persuaded by their families.

The failure of ISIS to attract Indian Muslims, who constitute the second largest Muslim population in the world, is due to their complete integration into the national mainstream. Indian Muslims are patriots and not swayed by fundamentalist ideologies. Extremism is alien to their nature. Moreover, India, as a country is proud of all its diversities. I am happy to note that India has the second largest population of Muslims in the world after Indonesia. India is home to all 72 *firqas* of Muslims and it houses one of the oldest churches known to humankind in the world. We have been practising the philosophy of peaceful coexistence for centuries.

We also need to be concerned over the increasing possibility and opportunity to use available technology and cyber-space in a destructive manner. The computing power of your smartphone is greater than all the computing effort deployed to put a man on the moon in 1969. The menace of terrorism is greatly amplified in today's digital world. An incident in one corner of the globe can instantly spark a reaction thousands of miles away; where a 'lone wolf' or a 'DIY (Do It Yourself) terrorist' can go online and learn how to carry out an attack without ever leaving home. We have recently constituted an expert committee to look into all possible avenues of cybercrime and its linkages with the terrorist world.

The source of most terrorist activities in India lies across our borders. It is unfortunate that even after paying such a heavy cost for itself, Pakistan and its associates find it difficult to understand that there are no 'good terrorists and bad terrorists'. Differentiating terrorists into 'good' and 'bad' categories has failed miserably. If the ISI and the Pakistan Army stops their support to certain terror outfits, I have no hesitation in saying that the security situation in South Asia will improve significantly. I sincerely believe that Pakistan should seriously rethink its strategy of using terrorism as an 'instrument of proxy war' and it would be in its own national interest.

India has been a victim of cross-border terrorism for the last several decades. Terrorist organisations like the Lashkar-e-Taiba, Jaish-e-Mohammad, etc., patronised by those across the border, have inflicted several acts of terror on Indian soil. There are several instances of such proxies being used in other parts of the world. Terrorism knows no boundaries and doesn't respect nations' sovereignties. It has become transnational in character. The terrorists use modern technology to propagate their ideology and to perpetrate violence. They are exploring new frontiers to inflict terror such as cyber terrorism and the use of chemical, biological and radio-active nuclear devices.

Since terrorist outfits do not recognise national boundaries and acts of terror are executed often through networks spread over several countries, there is no alternative to the forging of international cooperation to effectively counter it. Such cooperation is required in the field of intelligence-sharing in order to preempt the terrorist threats. International cooperation is also an imperative among the law-enforcement agencies of different countries for post-event investigations to bring the terrorists to justice. It is also needed for building popular opinion and pressurising the countries that use terrorists as their strategic assets.

I understand that this conference is also discussing issues related to India's internal security like 'left wing extremism' and border management. I will keenly await your recommendations on these issues so that I get a non-governmental perspective for policy formulation.

This brings me to the next issue of the role of think tanks and non-governmental organisations in positively influencing policies of the government. It is my opinion that the government should benefit from as many strands of opinions as possible, in order to formulate policies. The inputs of the security experts and think tanks, at present, have little or no influence in policy formulation in India. I want this to change. I feel that the government should benefit from your expertise and knowledge. Also, the think tanks have an important role in developing a strategic culture in India by aiding an informed discourse on the issues of national security. Hence, I once again welcome this initiative of the Rajasthan Government in partnership with the India Foundation.

Finally, I am given to understand that one whole day is going to be devoted to the discussions on global terrorism. This is important since the lines of local terrorism and global terrorism are getting blurred. In many ways, international terrorism today is an unintended outcome of the process of globalisation. Hence, all countries should be aware of the developments in this area, which is bound to affect them in some way, sooner or later. Also, this brings me back to my earlier point that all nations should be on the same page to tackle terrorism and there cannot be any discrimination in this regard. With these words, I wish this conference all success.

Overview by Ajit Doval*

A watershed moment in the history of terrorism occurred on 11 September 2001, when terrorists attacked the United States. When looked at more deeply, the watershed moment was in reality 20 September of the same year, for on that date, The US President, Mr George Bush, while addressing the US Congress, declared war on global terrorism. That moment defines the genesis of the modern-day counter terrorism, in the international context. From that decision has flowed most of what we see happening at the international level and also at the regional and even the domestic level. The purpose of my talk today is to take stock of the situation from the time we entered the new paradigm of counter terrorism, until the present day, in terms of what has been done, the costs incurred, the strategy followed and what has been achieved.

The period witnessed international cooperation in terms of a slew of UN resolutions, on controlling terrorist financing, weapons and movement. Many joint working groups were formed at the bilateral level in different countries to address the problem. There was also a lot of domestic capacity building that was done.

An analysis was also carried out jointly by the Brown and Boston Universities, on the cost incurred by the US to fight this global war on terror (GWOT). On completion of the project in 2014, the study concluded that the US had, by itself, incurred a cost of USD 5.3 trillion. The global cost is estimated to be USD 8.8 trillion. In terms of comparative spending, for each dollar spent by terrorist organisations, the US is apparently spending roughly 75,000 dollars. The loss in human lives too has been substantial. There have been 2,25,000 fatalities and about 3,65,000 persons have suffered serious wounds. There have been over 3000 major incidents, a major incident being defined as one in which more than 15 person have been killed. While statistics do not matter, the cost has indeed been very heavy.

---

*National Security Advisor, Govt. of India

One of the objectives of the GWOT was to eliminate al Qaeda and to degrade capacities of such like groups which used terrorism as a tactic to further their aims. An underlying strategy in the GWOT was that preemption took precedence over deterrence, prevention and prosecution. Without getting into the rights and wrongs of the strategy, the underlying thought was that it was counterproductive to wait till the adversaries strike. While such a policy was not articulated, the manner in which events unfolded implied its usage. Thus, the intervention in Iraq was a preemptive action to obviate the use of WMD by the Iraqi forces, which that country was thought to possess. The fact that subsequently no WMD was found, was not of much consequence.

The second part of the strategy was capacity building to prevent attacks through intelligence collection and collation, development of technological capabilities, raising of special forces and enactment of special laws. The third was through international political and security management. This was done by convincing, cajoling, capacitating and coercing the states to participate in this international effort and eventually, about 136 countries fell in line, partially or fully. This led to international cooperation in terms of adopting UN resolutions, international cooperation in intelligence, forming of joint working group, technology transfers for security etc.

While the costs were high, the strategy needs to be seen in terms of its impact. Is the world safer now in March 2015, than it was when the GWOT began in 2001? Is the world today much more secure from the threat of terrorism? Are the gains commensurate to the number of lives lost? That is the yardstick with which the policy must be measured.

We see today that the geography of terror has become much more expanded than that which existed in 2001. At that point in time, while the term international terrorism was used, in fact, terrorism was confined to just eight or nine countries. While India and Afghanistan were affected, Pakistan was not. Yemen was affected, as were some parts of South East Asia. Then, some parts of Europe were affected as was the United States. Today, the entire West Asia is in turmoil as is Pakistan, which has now become the fountainhead of terrorism, being both a sponsor of terrorism, as well as its victim, where the second highest number of killings are taking place. Terrorism has also spread to various parts of Africa, whether it is Boko Haram in Nigeria or al Shabab in Somalia.

Next, let us see what was the capacity of the terrorists in 2001 and what is their capacity today. Their is an apparent surge in human resources as we find a large number of people from across the world, getting recruited and joining the ISIS. They have access to sophisticated weapons, and have huge financial resources, especially as they control a number of oil wells. This, despite the considerable amount of good work done in denying funds to terrorist groups, which was one of the main planks of the GWOT. Technologically too, the terrorist groups have upgraded their capability and it would be no surprise if some of them can get their hands on WsMD. Politically too, they have emerged stronger. In 2001, no one would have thought of engaging in dialogue with the Afghan Taliban. That is no longer the case as a decisive military victory has not been achieved. The net result is that the world today is more vulnerable than what it was in 2001.

This now leads to the obvious question: why has the GWOT failed to achieve its objectives? Are there any lessons to be learnt for us? I would like to share a few thoughts on this.

First, there is a need for the political management of terrorism. Counter terrorism is generally considered to be about tactics, weapons, force levels, intelligence gathering et al. All these things are important, but the most important aspect remains the political management of terrorism. This includes addressing issues of ideology and dealing with countries that sponsor or support terrorism. Here, the sponsoring states were not only not addressed, but were allowed to get away, despite the fact that they violated a number of UN resolutions on the subject. This was a serious lacuna in political management. Also, no sanctions were imposed on such states, and they remained protected, despite their support to terrorist groups. One of India's neighbours also uses these instruments of state power to further its national strategic security interest. This neighbour has differentiated terrorists into 'good' and 'bad' terrorists. Those sponsored by them to target India for achieving their strategic objectives are classified as 'good' but those that attack them are referred to as 'bad' terrorists. However, all types of terrorists have to be addressed if the GWOT is to be won. Such differentiation has cost the world very dearly.

Second, in such conflicts, civil society is both the frontier and the battleground which has to be protected and saved. Fragmentation of civil society rather than its consolidation is not a wise strategy. The former course leads to radicalisation, which thereafter leads to competitive violence. India's efforts at consolidating society has paid dividends, which is why despite various parts of the world being engulfed in violence, India was not caught in that cauldron. Civil society in India has the confidence that it would be protected and that trust has not been belied. This perhaps explains why so few people from India have joined the ISIS or al Qaeda or other such groups.

The third factor relates to inconsistent and unsustainable policies. Syria is an example. The regime in Syria is responsible and civilised, yet efforts are underway for regime change through supporting the opposition parties and promoting civil war. Such policies are unsustainable, because beyond a point, such opposition groups acquire the strength to operate independently, and thereafter, they become a bigger problem.

Another factor that needs consideration pertains to the defining of terrorism. In 1999, India had mooted a comprehensive convention on terrorism in the United Nations. This was debated in a conference in Kuala Lumpur, where the issue of defining terrorism arose. This was important, because victory cannot be achieved against an enemy that cannot be defined. The convention received tremendous support except from Pakistan and a few other countries on the question of the definition of terrorism. These countries wanted a clause stating that people should not be termed as terrorists who were fighting for a cause. We do not therefore, have as of now, a definition of terrorism. However, it is necessary to have a UN convention on terrorism in which terrorism is defined, for only then can sanctions be imposed on the defaulting countries. There is thus a need to define terrorism and what acts constitute terrorism. Once this is done, it will be possible to impose sanctions on a country which provides sanctuary to a terrorist. There are 13 different types of activities which could invite sanctions against a state, but terrorism is not one of them. While bilateral pressure can be applied against a country supporting terrorism, there is need for collective international action also. To that extent, we are worse off now than what we were in 2001. This however, does not mean that nothing has been achieved.

On the contrary, a great deal of progress has been made in enhancing internal security capability of a large number of countries, to include anti-hijacking mechanisms and laws, intelligence gathering capabilities, raising of special forces, technological upgradation, protection of vital installations, etc., which have led to both preventive actions and preemptive actions also. However, much more needs to be done.

Let us now take a look at some of the lessons learnt in the GWOT. The first lesson is that each country must develop its own internal capacity to fight terrorism and not overly depend upon multilateral or international support. The second lesson is that internationally, there should be zero level of tolerance to state sponsorship of terror. Countries indulging in such activities should suffer the consequences through UN mandated sanctions. There should also be a comprehensive convention on terrorism which defines the term and imposes costs on noncompliance.

The third lesson is that laws and procedures about dealing with the terrorists must be simplified and rationalised. This should relate to people arrested by a particular country on any offence, who are wanted by another country on charges of terrorism.

The fourth lesson is that the fight against terrorists cannot be won, unless the large overground base which provides the terrorists the ideological support is also addressed. While such support groups cannot be equated with terrorists, they would require to be dealt with, including those sponsoring overground organisations. A strategy is hence required to deal with such elements.

Today, the threat of terrorism has extended to a much larger geographical confine. The resources available with terrorists are much higher, they are better connected, have greater mobility, are equipped with sophisticated weapons and are well financed. They also have more supporters and an increased number of bases. So, we are heading for difficult times and even Europe, which is relatively insulated, is now threatened. Future attacks could come from groups or they could be lone wolf attacks.

There is a need for comprehensive strategies and greater international cooperation to ward off future threats. Our counter-terrorism effort has to be much more pointed, more focused, more objective and more professional. Let it not become an arena for politicking to achieve limited political objective. Let it really be a war in which we think objectively, because we also have to confront another dilemma - do we allow the action of the state to come into conflict with freedom of the society and its people. We do not want to make our society into a police state. We do not wish to curb the freedom of people; we wish to preserve our democratic values and freedom. Preserving the above and at the same time providing protection to the people is the challenge with which we are faced. This can be achieved through a concerted and integrated counter terrorist policy and through international cooperation.

PART I

TERRORISM SANS FRONTIERS

1

The Rise of the Caliphate

Yossef Bodansky

The Islamic Caliphate declared by Abu-Bakr al-Baghdadi is a most profound and defiant challenge of orthodox jihadism to the Muslim world, and, to a lesser extent, to the entire modern world. Throughout Islamdom, the reign of the first two Rashidun Caliphs—Muhammad's immediate successors Caliph Abu-Bakr (573–634) and Caliph Omar (577–644)—is considered as the apogee of human governance and a time of near-perfection that all humans must strive to attain. The crux of the message of Abu-Bakr al-Baghdadi in both word and action is "Yes, we can!" The Muslim world is capable of restoring the Caliphate of the first two Rashidun Caliphs, irrespective of the sensitivities and norms of the modern world.

Thus, the new Caliphate is a dream come true for the entire Islamdom. As such, the idea and the hope represented by the Caliphate will not go away, irrespective of the fate of Abu-Bakr al-Baghdadi and the jihadist state he has established at the heart of al-Jazira (eastern Syria and western Iraq in modern terms).

The establishment of the Caliphate in mid-2014 is the inevitable outcome of the evolution of political Islam in the last half-a-century. The Caliphate is the obvious culmination of the jihadist doctrine introduced by Osama bin Laden and his coterie with the sole profound deviation being over the relationship with Shiite Iran (where bin Laden encouraged expedient cooperation, while Baghdadi insists on irreconcilable Sunni–Shiite enmity).

Islam has always rejected the notion of a modern state and only legitimised the all-Islamic Sharia-ruled entity called the Caliphate. The rise and fall of a myriad of Islamic political entities throughout Islam's history is considered a necessary reaction to the prevailing circumstances, rather than a desirable or a legitimate solution. However, in the early 1960s, Said al-Qutb, the key luminary of modern political Islam, decreed that Islamism must accept the existing modern state with its fixed boundaries as an inescapable and unavoidable reality. The road to the utopian Caliphate, he wrote, starts with the transformation of the existing states into Muslim states and then using these states as the building blocks of the Caliphate. In the early 1990s, Hassan al-Turabi, the most important theologian of modern Jihadism, further legitimised the role of a modern Islamic state as a crucial and expedient phase in the restoration of the Caliphate under contemporary conditions. Al-Turabi also encouraged other expedient measures—most notably, close cooperation with Shiite Iran—as necessary and desirable in pursuit of the triumph of jihad.

The foundations of the current Caliphate were laid by bin Laden and his coterie in the late 1990s. Initially, bin Laden argued for the delinking of Islamdom from the West as a precondition for the establishment of a genuinely Islamic system of governance based solely on the Sharia. In 2001–02, Saif al-Adel, one of bin Laden's closest aides based in Iran, wrote a practical multi-phased programme for implementing the ascent of Islam called "The Working Plan Till 2020". Significantly, the fifth phase, to be implemented between 2013 and 2016, is the establishment of a Caliphate.

In 2005, the jihadist trend underwent its most profound evolution that was prompted by the changes in the post-9/11 world. While the jihadist supreme leadership gained theological permission to use weapons of mass destruction at the heart of the West—even though they would inflict immense casualties—it decided against their use for fear of Western retribution against the radicalised Muslim communities living in those areas. There followed a soul-searching cognisance of the growing diversity of othgr jihadist foci worldwide that led to the establishment of regional entities commonly known as the regional "al-Qaidas". The mere recognition of the diversity of the jihadist sub-movements challenged the viability of a global all-Islamic Caliphate.

In mid-2010, Saif al-Adel led a small group of jihadist thinkers from Iran to rejoin bin Laden's Shura Kabira in Pakistan. They argued that the jihadist trend can be sustained only if its doctrine became more prudent and pragmatic. With the Arab world on the verge of a major upheaval, the jihadist trend must abandon the quest for a utopian Caliphate and focus instead on supporting individual intifadas in specific Arab states. Bin Laden accepted the arguments of Saif al-Adel and ordered the establishment of the "Son of the Land" programme in order to launch, support and sustain these *intifadas*, known to the West as the "Arab Spring".

In Summer 2012, the jihadists interpreted their imminent triumph in Afghanistan and Pakistan, coupled with the ascent of Iran, as the beginning of the fateful "End-of-Time Battle" for the Middle East. According to the sayings attributed to Prophet Muhammad, the establishment of the Islamic Emirate of Khorasan (which encompasses the Central Asian republics, Afghanistan, Pakistan, Kashmir and Iran) would create conducive conditions for Islam's triumph in the "End-of-Time Battle". According to the Prophet's sayings, jihadist forces would then arrive in the Middle East from the East and wage the fateful victorious battle for the liberation of Bilad al-Sham and al-Jazira, and the establishment of the Mosque of al-Aqsa in Jerusalem (Islam's original Qiblah—that is, the direction of prayers—in CE 610–623) as the centre of a new Caliphate.

In early 2014, the jihadist leaders in al-Jazira concluded that the aggregate success of the Sunni forces provides for the expediting of the "End-of-Time Battle" by establishing a Caliphate that will spearhead the fateful jihad. In late April, they escalated the theological struggle by introducing "the Khorasan pledge" that focused on the pursuit of a Takfiri neo-Salafi jihad and the rejection of cooperation with Shiite Iran. Drastic steps were imperative because "al-Qaida deviated from the rightful course". Nine prominent al-Qaida Emirs from the Middle East, Afghanistan, Turkmenistan and Iran declared their allegiance to the new Emir of the Faithful—Abu Bakr al-Baghdadi al-Qurashi—the Emir of DI'ISH. Ultimately, the tenets of "the Khorasan pledge" amount to going back to the jihadist tenets as introduced by bin Laden a decade ago. This distinction is behind the great grass-roots popularity and acceptance of the calls for jihad and the Caliphate.

On 29 June 2014, DI'ISH announced the establishment of the Islamic Caliphate over the territories under its control as the first step in restoring the glory of all Muslims and the liberation of all lands ever ruled by Muslims. DI'ISH explained that one of their priorities is to smash the "partitioning of Muslim lands by Crusader powers" in the aftermath of the First World War in order to create a new Middle East. Only the abolishment of modern Arab states and the creation of an Islamic Caliphate in their stead will permit the restoration of Muslim glory and dignity. "The Jihadist Imam al-Baghdadi was designated the Caliph of the Muslims" and would be henceforth referred to as "Khalifah Ibrahim". Al-Baghdadi "has accepted this allegiance, and has thus become the leader for Muslims everywhere". Since then, the forces of the Caliphate have been on the offensive throughout al-Jazira and the neighbouring regions.

The best manifestation of the strength and popularity of the message of the Caliphate is the rapid emergence of localised Caliphates that swear allegiance to al-Baghdadi. The first followers were the Emirs of the Jama'ats in the Northern Caucasus and Crimea. They acted on the message and zeal brought back by the veterans of the jihad in Syria and Iraq. They brought a new enthusiasm to the anti-Russian jihad at the time when the Russian-supported revival of Sufism all but defeated the al-Qaida-affiliated Emirate of the Caucasus.

The most important development has been the impact of the establishment of the Islamic Caliphate, as reflected in the Maghreb, the Sahel and ultimately the areas controlled by the Boko Haram. Since early 2014, local leaders repeatedly tried to reconcile Ayman al-Zawahiri and Abu Bakr al-Baghdadi on the basis of a theological discourse about the relative merits of both the pursuits of jihadist orthodoxy and expedient pragmatism. Ultimately, they sided with the imperative to pursue a Takfiri jihad at all costs and gradually transformed their respective "liberated zones" into local Caliphates loyal to al-Baghdadi. The Boko Haram's Abu Bakr Shekau was recognised as a viable Caliph and his theological teachings have been cited by al-Baghdadi and his acolytes.

By early 2015, several other jihadist entities throughout the Middle East and South Asia had declared their allegiance to al-Baghdadi and the Caliphate. Significantly, the African Takfiri jihadists consider themselves devotees of the original teachings and the leadership of Osama bin Laden. This distinction was made clear when the Caliphate in eastern Libya was ready to surge forward on to the jihadist centre stage. On February 15, 2015, the Libyan Caliphate posted a graphic five-minute video titled "A Message Signed With Blood To The Nation Of The Cross". The video began with the marching and beheading of 21 Egyptian Copts who had been recently kidnapped in Libya. Dressed in Guantanamo-like orange jumpsuits, the Copts were lined up along a beach and abruptly beheaded by black-dressed mujahideen. The camera then focused on the sea water—red with blood.

A jihadist commander dressed in military fatigues delivered the message in American-accented English: "All praise is due to Allah the strong and mighty," he declared at the start of the video. "And may blessings and peace be upon the ones sent by the sword as a mercy to all the worlds." He connected the 'End-of-Time Battle' in al-Jazira with the decisive surge on Christendom to be launched from Libya:

> Oh people, recently you have seen us on the hills of ash-Sham and Dabiq's plain, chopping off the heads that have been carrying the cross for a long time, and today, we are on the south of Rome, on the land of Islam, Libya, sending another message.
>
> All Crusaders: safety for you will be only wishes especially if you are fighting us all together. Therefore we will fight you all together. The sea you have hidden Sheikh Osama bin Laden's body in, we swear to Allah, we will mix it with your blood.

After the jihadist leader finished his declaration, the line of mujahideen commenced the beheading of the 21 Copts kneeling in front of them. Once the slaughter was over, the commander stepped forward for a final statement. "And we will conquer Rome, by Allah's permission, the promise of our Prophet, peace be upon him," he declared.

2

Ethno-National Terrorism:

A Case Study of the LTTE

A.S. Kalkat

The LTTE's actions in Sri Lanka are an example of a civil unrest and militancy transiting to insurgency, leading ultimately to the organisation's own development as a terrorist one, which came to be listed by the US as the world's most dangerous terrorist organisation at that time. The genesis of the movement lay in the grievances regarding the deprivation and discrimination of the minority Tamils by a Sinhala-majority state. The Tamils were trying to protect their identity, language and the areas of inhabitation from a massive Sinhala influx which was occurring since 1956. The Tamil movement started with civil unrest and gradually escalated to an open confrontation with the state. The Sri Lankan response to this was to seek a military solution by launching military operations designated as a "War of Liberation" against the militant Tamil groups. The Tamil parties increased their demands for independence and a separate Tamil state (*Eelam*). The main militant Tamil groups were the Liberation Tigers of Tamil Eelam (LTTE), the Tamil Eelam Liberation Organisation (TELO), the National Democratic Liberation Front (NDLF), the People's Liberation Organisation of Tamil Eelam (PLOTE) and the Eelam People's Revolutionary Liberation Front (EPRLF). Amongst the militant groups, the LTTE led by Velupillai Prabhakaran achieved dominance. Ruthless military actions aimed at isolating and starving out the Tamil areas in the Northern and Eastern provinces led to a large-scale uprooting of the Tamils (who became IDPs) and over a hundred thousand fled to India in fishing boats and were housed in refugee camps in Tamil Nadu. Prabhakaran was highly ambitious and ruthless and dreamt of becoming the sole arbiter of the destiny of Tamils in Sri Lanka. As a result, he systematically eliminated the leaders of the other insurgent groups and used this to strengthen his cult and the LTTE. The large influx and presence of Tamil refugees in Tamil Nadu, which had a population of 45 million, had serious implications for India. India decided to engage with Sri Lanka for a political resolution of the issue which culminated in the "Indo-Sri Lanka Agreement to Establish Peace and Normalcy in Sri Lanka" (ISLA), popularly referred to as the Indo-Sri Lanka Accord. At the time of the signing of the Agreement, LTTE, PLOTE, TELO, ENDLF and EPRLF were the prominent insurgent groups. PLOT, TELO, ENDLF and EPRLF accepted the ISLA and surrendered their weapons; however, the LTTE refused to do so and resisted.

The Organisational Structure of the LTTE

The LTTE's group leaders were under their respective area commanders and it was effective in harnessing the seafaring traditions to form what was to become the Sea Tigers. Women cadres came up formally in ground operations around 1988. Prabhakaran was the supreme leader of the LTTE. He was assisted by Anton Balasingham, political commissar, and a military council comprising of Ajit Mahathiya a.k.a. Mahendra Raja the second in command, Sathasivam Krishnakumar a.k.a. Kittu, Kumarappa in Jaffna, Pulendran (later Karuna) in the East and Pottu Amman (head of the intelligence wing). The military council was assisted by Yogaratnam Yogi (head of the political wing), Sornalingam a.k.a. Shankar (head of the Air Wing) and Sivanesan a.k.a. Soosai (head of the Sea Tigers). The LTTE strength was assessed as 7,000 hard core fighters, 3,000 helpers (*podyan*) and an indeterminate number of sympathisers.

Early in its stage of competitive insurgency, the LTTE practised terrorist methods as well as summary execution, burning people alive and executing death sentences for ordinary offences. It terrorised other groups and the civilian population into submission. This gave it confidence to use the terrorist methods effectively for rising to the top. The other groups were unable to challenge the LTTE due to an absence of a matching charismatic leader as well as the internal power struggles among them. Sri Lanka's use of military force to quell the movement without a matching political strategy further alienated the masses and increased support for the LTTE.

The LTTE had a resilient system for garnering finances and enlarged its coffers from a variety of sources. Prominent among these were a taxation of the Tamil population and extortion from shopkeepers. Beginning from 1983 till 1997, almost all the major extremist groups including the LTTE had established overseas cells among the Sri Lankan Tamil diaspora, particularly in London. They became a major source of support, contributing in large measure to the cause. In addition, the LTTE resorted to looting banks and government treasuries, smuggling and trafficking of arms, people and drugs and hijacking maritime traffic to swell its coffers; the last being made possible due to Sri Lanka's strategic location on the international maritime routes. The Tamil diaspora was also used for media management and for providing real-time information. The LTTE also cultivated many media persons for propaganda, as also low-level government officials and political leaders overseas who were sympathetic to them.

The Indo-Sri Lanka Agreement (ISLA)

India's direct involvement in the civil war in Sri Lanka came about in July 1987 as a result of an agreement for a political resolution in consultation with the Tamil groups within the ambit of the Constitution of Sri Lanka, called the Indo-Sri Lanka Agreement to Establish Peace and Normalcy in Sri Lanka of 29 July 1987. It envisaged a ceasefire between the belligerent parties, the surrender of weapons by the armed Tamil militant parties and the amendment of the Constitution of the unitary state in order to create a federal structure, thereby ensuring a provincial autonomy for the Tamil-majority Northern and Eastern provinces. The Accord also envisaged the provision of an Indian Peace Keeping Force (IPKF), if asked for by the Government of Sri Lanka, for accepting the surrender of weapons by the Tamil militants and for ensuring security in the two provinces. The Sri Lankan Army was to be confined to the barracks in the Northern and Eastern provinces. Consequently, on the request of the Sri Lankan Government, India sent an infantry division to Sri Lanka in the last week of July for overseeing the surrender process by the militants. While most militant groups complied by handing over their weapons, the LTTE refused to do so. When coerced, it resorted to attacking the peacekeepers. Taken by surprise, the IPKF suffered large casualties and open fighting broke out between the IPKF and the LTTE.

By the time India got involved, terrorist attacks by LTTE had been on the rise. Initially, these attacks had been against the Sinhala population. However, early in 1987, Prabhakaran resorted to attacks on the other Tamil parties to wrest the leadership of all Tamils in Sri Lanka. The ruthless methods of the LTTE also instilled fear amongst the civilian Tamil population regarding obedience to the dictates of the LTTE leader. After assessing the situation, the Indian Government in consultation with the Sri Lankan Government, decided that the LTTE would have to be forcibly disarmed and while doing so, the safety of a vast number of innocent civilians would also need to be protected against the murderous attacks by the LTTE. Consequently, a force of five divisions (15 brigades and three para commando battalions [Special Forces]) was built up in North and East Sri Lanka under a headquarters designated as HQ IPKF. In addition, paramilitary forces comprising one Assam Rifles battalion, and one TA battalion and Central Armed Police Forces (CAPF) comprising two CRPF battalions, and one CRPF mahila (women) company were also inducted. Ad hoc complements of the Indian Air Force and the Indian Navy were also part of IPKF. I was appointed to command the Force, with an enhanced role and tasks as under:

- Conduct of offensive operations to disarm and neutralise the LTTE.
- Create normalcy and a secure environment in which elections could be held and the democratic process gone through in the Northern and Eastern provinces leading to a popularly elected Tamil-based provincial government being put in place in both areas.
- Relief and rehabilitation of the displaced Tamils. Over a lakh had fled to India and many were displaced within Sri Lanka.

By this time, the Northern and Eastern provinces had been ravaged by the civil war and civil administration of any kind was non-existent. The Northern Province which had the largest Tamil population concentrated in the city of Jaffna was very severely affected. There was no police force, neither were there any functioning public utilities like electricity, water, public distribution system, telephones, post, banking, etc. Consequently, the uprooted civilian population was undergoing extreme suffering.

Conduct of Operations

The LTTE had carried out its first suicide bombing with major success in Nelliady, well before the IPKF was inducted. The Black Tigers (suicide squads) were in their early formative stage. Their success was dependent upon the large-scale use of IEDs, booby traps and assassinations rather than on suicide bombings, though individual cadres committed suicide in order to escape capture. With the IPKF succeeding in weaning away the sympathy of the population from the LTTE to supporting a political resolution, the LTTE resorted to terrorist activities on a large scale in an effort to keep the population under their control.

The total absence of any kind of civil administration entailed a deployment of the IPKF under four divisional headquarters with the inter-formation boundaries conforming to the district boundaries for better coordination and control of both the military and the civil administrative role. I assessed that the first priority was to separate the LTTE cadres from the population centres and drive them into the uninhabited areas, away from the towns. This would enable the IPKF to use its superior firepower, including artillery. The clearing of population centres mainly consisted of "cordon and search" operations. A few LTTE cadres were caught in the net but the majority quietly slipped away. However, the purpose was achieved and the population centres of Jaffna, Trincomalee, Velvaturai, Killinochchi, Vavuniya and Batticaloa were by and large freed of the LTTE cadres and their threat. This enabled a semblance of normalcy for the population and the provision of basic facilities and medical aid. Thereafter, a major operation codenamed Operation Checkmate was launched. The aim was to militarily neutralise the LTTE (Checkmate I) and thereafter, neutralise it politically by ensuring free and fair elections without its interference and have a democratically elected provincial government in place (Checkmate II).

The Checkmate I operation commenced from the two extreme ends of the Northern and Eastern provinces; simultaneously rolling inwards. This resulted in all the LTTE cadres and their leadership getting holed up in the Wanni jungles at the centre of the two provinces. Thereafter, this thick jungle was cordoned off and clearing operations were launched (Battle of Nitikai Kulam). The LTTE suffered major casualties; however, the main benefit from this was the destruction of its command and control headquarters. Prabhakaran who was present, escaped through a series of long tunnels leading well away from the Wanni jungles. The clearance of the LTTE from the two provinces enabled us to restore normalcy in the Northern and Eastern provinces. The railway line from Colombo to Jaffna was made functional; the electric supply was restored; banks became operational and schools and essential supply outlets were re-opened.

On 18 September 1988, I was able to announce that the IPKF was now ready to ensure free and undisturbed elections in the two provinces. Operation Checkmate II now commenced and in response, the LTTE vowed to prevent and disrupt the elections. By maintaining tight security throughout the two provinces, the provincial elections were successfully held in December 1988 and the LTTE cadres were prevented from interfering with the electoral process. The turnout for that election was higher than the national average. This enabled the Sri Lankan Government to enact the 13th Amendment to its Constitution, which catered for a devolution of power to the provinces. This was followed by the country's presidential and parliamentary elections which also went off peacefully. Unfortunately, the new President was from the same ruling party that was opposed to the Indo-Sri Lanka Accord and held back the grant of devolution as envisaged in the 13th Amendment, which left the Tamil Provincial Government of the North-Eastern Province toothless (after the provincial elections, the Northern and Eastern provinces had been merged).

As part of the de-radicalisation process, widespread publicity was given of the benefits that would accrue to the Tamils from the Accord and the 13th Amendment. In addition, civilian contact and grievance redressal systems at various levels were established and interactions with the civic leaders and government officials through regular meetings were carried out. Community leaders and media persons were also regularly briefed on the various actions taken and appeals were made to the parents of the LTTE cadres to join the mainstream through leaflets and through group contacts.

Lessons

Most conflicts have a political dynamic and ultimately require a political resolution. At the politico-military level, only the government of a country can give a political dispensation to its citizens and not an outside power. Therefore, before intervening in such conflicts, the "intervening country" must ensure that there is a "cast iron" guarantee by the host government to grant the agreed political dispensation. If the host government reneges on its commitment, the only alternative left is a "regime change". Military planners must start with strategic guidance from the political leadership as to where they want to be strategically when the war ends. The test of a policy in war or conflict is "how it ends" and not "how it begins". When a conflict appears imminent, governments tend to avoid being distracted by the painful "what-if" scenarios such as the possibility of getting bogged-down fighting an entrenched insurgency. Expeditionary operations overseas however, should have clear strategic goals in order to be able to evolve tactical missions on a time-bound basis.

The Indian troops were not trained to set up public utility services, civil administration, police and judicial functions in Sri Lanka nor were they trained to undertake massive rehabilitation and reconstruction efforts across one-third of the country (the Northern and Eastern provinces)—a task they ultimately had to undertake. This should have been envisioned and planned for. Shaping perceptions is also an important component of such operations and should have been catered for, to ensure domestic and international support and for maintaining the morale of troops. It must also be remembered that in pluralistic societies, neither religion, nor ethnicity, nor language can be accepted as the basis for breaking away from a nation-state.

At the strategic level, post-combat stabilisation is the final stage of a war or conflict, i.e. the "end game of the war". Military planners tend to neglect the ultimate political goals and focus on winning engagements rather than on converting military successes into a strategic victory. Counter-insurgency (CI) has to be a "bottom-up" approach, which includes the battle for "winning hearts and minds" (WHAM) of the population while counter-terrorism (CT), which involves going for the leaders, needs a "top-down" approach. Very often, a combination of both is necessary. Public relations remain an important component of both the CI and CT operations. CI operations must be fought under a unified joint forces commander; especially in an overseas involvement. An institutionalised joint force HQ is necessary, not an ad hoc arrangement.

At the tactical level, air-mobile operations are basic to counter insurgency operations for quick response, surprise, for resupply and casualty evacuationand to avoid unnecessary casualties from roadside ambushes and booby-traps. This requires a sufficient complement of helicopters which must be catered for. CI operations—out of necessity—have to be decentralised, and thus demand a much higher standard of decision-making at the platoon, company and battalion levels. Sufficient "boots on the ground" are critical. Back-seat driving and trying to remote-control operations by chair-borne experts setting artificial benchmarks can be disastrous.

Strategic intelligence is important for back-channel talks, but is of little use to the troops on the ground who need tactical intelligence, which has to be fought for. The weapons and equipment available to the soldier must not be inferior to those available to the insurgents, which was the case in Sri Lanka. A greater integration of the civilian intelligence agencies with the army is also essential.

3

The Chechen Rebels:

From Separatism to Terrorism

Natalia Tereshchenko

Chechnya has recently fallen into the list of "forgotten conflicts" with more hotspots being prioritised by the international community. The historical battles with Russia have seemingly been forgotten, as attention has shifted to Ukraine and a more painful economic, rather than security, relation with Russia. Nevertheless, Chechnya and its hub of well-trained and experienced *boeviki* should be taken into high consideration, when looking at the conflicts in Ukraine and in Syria, the emergence of the ISIS and the ever-increasing threat of global extremism.

The Russian conflict with Chechnya has been continuing from around 1785—or even earlier—when Peter the Great followed his ambitions of annexation and expansion of the Russian Empire. Since then, the Empire tried to enforce peace in the region. Much later on, Chechnya became part of the former Soviet Union, and many Chechens were deported into Central Asia in order to lower the potential of counter-colonial insurgencies. However, the ethnic separatist conflict that we are witnessing today has its direct roots in the late 1980s–early 1990s. With the fall of the Soviet Union and as a result of many years of suppression, separatist and openly hostile and genocidal movements were born in Chechnya. Two full-scale wars ensued—with many deaths on both sides—before an agreement could be reached. The current ongoing low-level insurgency between Russia on the one hand and Chechnya, Ingushetia and Dagestan on the other, has quite frequently been sparked by terrorist attacks, directed by the Chechen rebels within Russia and abroad. To name but a few: the theatre hostage crisis, the school in Beslan, Domodedovo airport bombing, and further afield—the Boston marathon bombings.

How have the Chechen rebels transgressed the boundary from a right to self-determination, from separatism—even from war against Russia—to a more outspoken and evident terrorist action? It is difficult to trace the rise of extremism, but back in 2002, Russia already noticed more violence and more radical ideology in the Chechen rebel movement. One explanation of radicalisation is that it was a reaction to the high media attention the group had received and the politics of Putin, who heavily emphasised the danger Chechnya posed for Russia. Slowly, but steadily, this one-way policy gave rise to a counterproductive reaction—that of a propagation of extremist support through social media, with extremism-dedicated websites across Russia and the Commonwealth of Independent States (CIS).

The series of events in Ukraine and Putin's prolonged period of power have heavily impacted economic, political and social determinants of regional coexistence. Ramzan Kadyrov, the Chechen leader and a fervent ally of Putin, has been quite openly supportive of Russia, yet is outspoken about his own power aspirations. With internal tensions rising within Russia and in Chechnya, both Putin and Kadyrov find themselves in sensitive situations, with regard to their future power and the bi- and multilateral dynamics of regional relations.

So, what is the current situation among the Chechens and their power dynamics within the region? Recruiting from among the war veterans, as well as from among the rebels, Kadyrov has managed to establish a well-prepared governmental armed force. Determined to combat terrorism, Kadyrov, nevertheless, claims to have little power over the Chechens outside Chechnya. To date, Chechens have been fighting in Ukraine—ironically both on the Ukrainian as well as the Russian side. What we are witnessing is a conflict within conflict—an extra-territorial civil war—but not only, and perhaps not so much, between the hard-line Caucasus Emirate and the traditional moderate Muslims supporting Kadyrov's government but also between those that support Kadyrov and those that are combating his friendship with Russia. Ramzan Kadyrov has always denied the involvement of Chechen groups in Ukraine, stating that the Chechen diaspora is large and to control the activities of any national outside the borders of Chechnya is an impossible task.

However, it is impossible to deny the presence of the Chechens on both sides of the conflict. The battalion "Vostok", formed during the second

Russian–Chechen war at the initiative of the Russians, has been transformed and has been fighting on the side of the Russians. Earlier in February 2015, there had been some information that Kadyrov was calling back his forces due to the destabilised situation in Chechnya after the December terrorist attacks in Grozny. However, intense military activity continues within Ukraine, and the Chechens are becoming more openly involved in it.

At the same time, news has emerged about the existence of a new battalion "Dzhokhar Dudaev", under the leadership of Isa Munaev, made up of "volunteers" who deny being recruited by the Ukrainian government. Munaev's, and that of his successor Adam Osmaev who took his place after the death of the former, actions was motivated by the view of this being a fight against Russian imperialism, with Ukraine being an integral part in this combat and supporting the decolonisation of the Caucasus. This battalion comprises mixed numbers of those with prior experience in the Russian–Chechen wars, and those with no prior experience, yet having a more hard-line approach. Dubbed by the Russians as *boeviki*, the battalion may be seen as having a directly terrorist approach towards Russia, which does not however mean that its extremism is exclusively directed towards Russia.

Going further afield from Ukraine, it is essential to briefly consider the case of the Chechen rebels in Syria. Of ISIS's 15,000 or so foreign fighters, about 1000 are from Russia—more specifically from the Caucasus. An eminent figure is Omar al-Shishani, one of the toughest military leaders of the ISIS, who has Chechen roots. Ironically, al-Shishani is not a follower of any religious ritual, making him an "unpopular Muslim" among the fighters. This minor fact is quite revealing in discovering the motivation of the Chechens in their fight for separatism or extremism. Apart from a presence in the ISIS, the Chechens form part of other rebel groups such as the Jaish al-Muhajireen wal Ansar, which calls itself the official group of the Caucasus Emirate in Syria and whose emir, Salakhuddin Shishani, is of Chechen origin.

The Syrian "jihad" began as a sort of proxy conflict for fighters who could not go home to fight in Chechnya or Dagestan. In time, that ideological trend has developed with the rise of the ISIS. The majority of the Chechens in ISIS argue that the concept of global jihad is important and that the fighting in Chechnya is "nationalism" and therefore wrong. Yet, at the same time, individuals like al-Shishani support both causes and do not allow for a religious interpretation of their actions.

On the other side, even though national ethno-separatist movements like the Caucasus Emirate have had, up to now, a very clear line of ideology, and have even proclaimed that allegiance to ISIS is an act of "treachery", splinter movements or rather, ideologies, have also been forming in the Caucasus. At the same time, the sense of belonging to the Chechen nation and the root cause of the current engagement is taking its toll. The recent attacks in Grozny, apparently staged by the Vilayat Nokchicho, the Chechen wing of the Caucasus Emirate, have been praised by the Chechen militants in Syria, demonstrating a continuous interest in domestic "politics" and the fight for separatism as well as a certain engagement between the different parties across the borders.

Whereas the ideology or political stance of ISIS may not always be aligned to that of smaller regional organisations, it forms a solid backbone for limited-resource groups that may serve as a stepping stone towards the propagation and expansion of individual or coalition terror organisations upon the return of the jihadists home, or on their expansion regionally. Apart from that, being part of a group that is being widely covered by the media is undoubtedly prestigious. By far, not all the Chechen fighters in Syria form a military "elite", as the West likes to portray. Yet, the overblown attention that the jihadists get from the media plays well for them, as it boosts their image and, perhaps, even their cause back in Chechnya.

Finally, what is the implication, if any, on the activity of the Chechen groups in the region? The presence of the Chechen rebels in Ukraine, their links with Chechnya and, potentially with the networks in Syria and Turkey is a direct, destabilising factor due to the proximity of such forces to Europe. As soon as the fighting in Syria and Ukraine is over, a new and a much stronger old generation of Chechen fighters would occupy the Russian borders, where pro-ISIS and extremist social networks and propaganda have been steadily increasing. Beyond this, with human, financial and weapon resources, the "war front" and the influence of rebels has expanded to the very borders of Europe. The potential of Syrian, Turkish and other jihadists from the Middle East to migrate to Ukraine, obtain false identity documents for a sum of around $15,000 and immigrate to Europe is increasing. This poses a threat not only to Russia and its direct neighbours, but also to the wider Europe.

Even though Chechnya and Chechens are on the low radar today within the international community, there are several points of concern that raise alert. Intense conflicts in Ukraine and Syria, the emergence of ISIS and the proximity of hotspots within the Middle East may account for a rebirth of the Chechen question, or its transition to a more dangerous phase of terrorism. In the current situation, it remains to be seen whether nationalism would prevail over jihadism, and whether the localisation of conflict would prevail over a globalisation of the same, with the former being the lesser of the two evils.

4

Cross Border Terrorism in Jammu & Kashmir

Syed Ata Hasnain

Cross Border Terrorism (CBT) has been a byword in the lexicon of India's security for over twenty-five years. It came into prominence during the Punjab-based militancy and terrorism in the eighties, with the sponsorship that Pakistan extended to such terror activities. However, it matured as Pakistan withdrew its hand from Punjab and extended it to Jammu & Kashmir (J&K), where a more serious situation arose in 1989–90. Over the last twenty-five years, the term has come to be associated with a range of activities all over India, in which Pakistan has assiduously extended its support to the various anti-national groups in India's heartland, extending to even the southern Indian states and North-East India using Bangladesh as the base for the latter. In Central India, most of that sponsored terrorist activity has come from the ISI bases in Nepal. Such activity has been sponsored through an exploitation of the disaffected elements of the minority community. However, CBT assumed the proportions of proxy war through the sponsorship of the separatist movement in J&K where violence has been calibrated by Pakistan to achieve long-term strategic goals of bleeding India by "a thousand cuts", wresting the state of J&K and promoting disintegrative trends all over India. In this paper, I will delve on Pakistan's CBT campaign in J&K.

A few aspects of CBT as an element of irregular warfare need to be known. It is a war of deceit and opportunity with denial at the core of the concept. It is usually a war by the weak, shrewd and clever and includes activities across the spectrum of irregular warfare. Usually associated with the use of violence, it also encompasses aspects such as counterfeit currency, gunrunning, narcotics, media manipulation and even cyber terrorism. It is a great conflict initiator but as conflict situations progress and the handlers of CBT feel more and more empowered, they tend to become the obstacles to conflict resolution. CBT cannot be an effective finisher in a sponsored campaign to achieve certain ends.

With regard to India's problems with CBT, the armed forces, central armed police forces (CAPFs) and intelligence agencies have done a marvellous job in securing India. The fact that there has been no major terrorist strike since 26/11 and that the number of terrorists in J&K is dwindling, are measures of the success of the Indian state. Pakistan, as a weaker and once defeated and divided nation, chose to use CBT as the ideal means of asymmetric warfare to firstly wreak revenge for the past and secondly, attempt to weaken India's hold over J&K through a proxy war employing all methods of irregular warfare. These include terrorism and subversion. While India has engaged Pakistan's proxies for twenty-five years and more and seen the ups and downs of such an internal conflict, it has successfully stemmed the offensive and taken the situation over the hill. However, India needs to understand the current situation in the larger dimension of conflict management. Fighting such conflicts cannot resolve the problem in your favour if only the kinetic realm is adhered to. Much more needs to be done for conflict resolution, as succinctly stated in theories of conflict management. CBT is a subset of the internal conflict brought on by proxy war and needs a fresh look to nudge the counter campaign beyond the static situation at which it is stuck.

While examining afresh, a few observations may add weight to subsequent arguments. Firstly, India's intelligence agencies have demonstrated their coming of age, with their relative control over the activities of Pakistan's proxies; this is evident from the inability of the proxies to execute actions within India. However, in this game, a single successful act can offset all their gains. Secondly, there is high frustration among the proxies with the LeT, JeM and Al Badr being the prominent Pakistani groups based in West Punjab. This is due to Pakistan's inability to simultaneously handle internal security, Afghanistan and J&K. In the priority of things, Pakistan's establishment treats J&K as the lowest in relevance because it perceives that it can keep the situation simmering while it handles the other two. It doesn't always work like that. The jihadi groups targeting India have been at it for twenty-five years and feel that their relevance will dilute over time if nothing seems to happen at their behest. The low strength of terrorists in J&K and a lack of effective leadership in the terrorist ranks force them to up the ante from time to time; the manifestation is felt in the hinterland and in recent times equally at the LoC, IB and its vicinity.

The situation demands that we fight smart in the present-day environment and not use the methods of yesteryears. The dynamics of conflict management indicate that the situation has travelled through the usual process of conflict initiation to conflict progression to conflict stabilisation, and is now moving towards conflict resolution before it gets to conflict termination. Each stage has its own characteristics and needs to be dealt in its own unique way. Obviously, there are no fixed dates or specifics to bracket these stages as they merge into each other and sometimes it is difficult to discern the exact stage at which the conflict is. However, it is good to examine one or two instances which exemplify the movement process.

The period 2003–04 were crucial years when the then NDA government, on the advice of the then Army Chief, Gen. Nirmal Vij, took the landmark decision to construct a fence along the LoC. The near-impossible task of fencing the LoC gave the army the means to handle counter-infiltration with a greater focus and professionalism. It further led to the reversal of the mathematics of terror in J&K with the army eliminating more terrorists in its kinetic operations than the number which could infiltrate. This effectively reduced the terrorist presence by 2010. In 2011, a decision was taken to focus on the terrorist leadership in the main urban centres leading to the terrorists becoming leaderless. This assisted in the two good years of tourism and the absence of any high-profile operations before Pakistan and its proxies decided to commence targeting the LoC, IB and the areas in the vicinity such as Kathua, Samba and Uri. The conflict stabilisation stage, having been in place for some time, now needs a nudge towards conflict resolution to prevent a resurgence of CBT. For this, the following are essential:

- The correct identification of the centre of gravity (CoG) of the adversaries. Usually, a generic CoG is identified for most asymmetric and irregular conflicts; "People" being the usual notion. However, intellectual application reveals that the CoG is beyond generics and must be positioned on the idea of *Azadi*, because this drives the psyche and thinking of the people—the thought that such an *Azadi* is achievable. It must be replaced by the idea of "One India". In fact, in many ways the slogan *Sab ka Saath, Sab ka Vikaas* is an apt theme to follow towards the mainstreaming and integration of the errant minds in J&K.

- The presupposition is that the army will prevent all infiltration or limit it to inconsequential proportions; the Intelligence Bureau (IB) will control all financial conduits and aim to dry up the coffers of the separatists.
- All surrendered terrorists who came overboard through the various surrender schemes and who have not been integrated due to the failure of the schemes, must be engaged and the unfulfilled promise be delivered in order to prevent their angst later flowing the anti-national way.
- The radical extremist belief being spread through the medium of the mosques run by the Ahl-e-Hadith through foreign funding be monitored; the mosques be handed back to the Sufis and the imported clergy from Central India be excluded from J&K for bringing a resurgence of the Sufist belief as a counter to the rampant radical Wahabism.
- Bring a professional campaign of perception management to the fore, even as kinetic operations to contain and defeat the terrorists continue. This must be conceptualised, taking the advice of academics, clergy, politicians, army officers, intelligence and police officers, educationists and skill developers. Exploit the proliferating social media networks along with an appeal to the national media to join the campaign and contribute positively to the transformation. National soft power should progressively replace hard power as the mainstreaming process moves ahead.
- Follow the British example of setting up a social media brigade to fight disinformation while educating and informing the public. This is not propaganda nor psychological warfare but professional perception management.
- Take the Armed Forces Special Powers Act (AFSPA) as a test case where the perception game was lost by the establishment because of its inability to counter the campaign against it. The army's presence, to hold the hard positive situation on the military front, is mandatory as long as the region to the west is turbulent. To be functional, it needs a just empowerment to operate without reference and a legal protection for its men against manipulation or inadvertent errors. Steps taken by the army to prevent the law being exploited for excesses, must be placed in the body of a new law which must remain broad based and limited to two sections.

> The Supreme Court's "Dos and Don'ts", the standard operating procedures (SOP) for functioning drawn up by HQ Northern Command, the "Ten Commandments" issued by the Army Chief and the guiding principles of the WHAM campaign (Sadbhavana), must all find place in the body of the new law. This will offset all unfair criticism against the army which has been the key functionary in the countering of CBT.

CBT is not restricted to J&K nor is Pakistan its sole sponsor. It has happened from other neighbours as well. The test case of J&K, which appears as a successful model, could be considered for other border areas. The last word is simply related to the longevity of the threats arising from CBT. This has to be a sustained campaign as Pakistan and any other inimical neighbours will continue instigating problems in India to prevent it from rising to its rightful place in the comity of nations.

5

The 26/11 Terrorist Attack in Mumbai:
A Critical Analysis of the Modus Operandi and Operation

Ram D. Pradhan

In the backdrop of several terrorist attacks in Mumbai, the November 26, 2008 attack was altogether of a different nature. This was almost a military operation carefully planned, precisely executed and supported by intelligence, sophisticated weaponry, and above all, almost a minute-to-minute direction from a distant hideout. I propose to elaborate on the failure of the intelligence agencies in stalling that attack; likewise, on the failure of the coordination between the state government authorities and central authorities in frustrating the terrorist attack. In the light of inquiry conducted, I would like to briefly spell out the action programme for dealing effectively with such operations.

This attack was not the first attack that took place in Mumbai. Previously, the city had witnessed 12 serious incidents of bomb attacks between March 1993 and July 2006 resulting in the deaths of 516 persons and injuries to 1952 persons. All these attacks involved improvised explosives devices (IEDs). Some of these were so powerful that in March 1993, 257 persons were killed. In the attack in August 2003, there were 50 deaths and in July 2006, serial train blasts resulted in 181 casualties.

When I and my colleague Shri V. Balachandran were asked to undertake an enquiry into 26/11, no one knew the dimensions of the attack that I have spelt out. Moreover, we were also given terms of reference that we found—as the enquiry proceeded—rather restrictive. We were asked to look into:

- (Lapses) To act on intelligence inputs provided by the Central Intelligence Agencies.
- (Lapses) To promptly act or react to the various terrorists act perpetrated on 26/11 in Mumbai in order to save lives and safeguard property.
- The Committee may make appropriate recommendations to deal with such acts in future.

Our Committee, known as the High Level Enquiry Committee (HLEC) was not a Commission of Inquiry. It was an administrative committee and we had to devise our own method of enquiry. Not being under the Commission of Inquiry Act, we did not consider it necessary to record statements or go in for a cross-examination of the witnesses. Instead, we identified officers in the Mumbai city and elsewhere who could contribute and decided to interview them informally. For that, we obtained first the written statements from each one of them about his/her own role with reference to the points indicated by the HLEC. We then interviewed these officials and closely examined each one with reference to their own statement and what we came to learn as the enquiry proceeded.

We examined several aspects related to our task, but I propose to cover only four specific areas, namely:

- Intelligence and handling of security intelligence at operational levels.
- Action to handle the attack.
- Means to face the terrorist attacks.
- Command and Control.

Intelligence

There were several intelligence reports beginning 7th August 2006, indicating that LeT (Lashkar-e-Taiba) was making preparations to infiltrate fidayeen (commando terrorists) into India by sea. There were six alerts on the possibility of a seaborne attack, while eleven were on the possibility of multiple and simultaneous attacks and three on the possibility of attacks by commandos.

Some intelligence alerts pointed to a possibility of Taj and Oberoi—two luxury hotels—as well as CST (Chhatrapati Shivaji Terminus) being the likely targets of some terrorist violence. There was however no specific intelligence that seaborne terrorists would target Hotel Taj (now Taj Palace) or Oberoi Sheraton. There was no intelligence whatsoever on the Cama Hospital (specialised in treating women and children) and the Nariman House (that provided shelter to the Jewish nationals visiting Mumbai) as being the possible targets of attack.

The attacks took place in almost the southernmost area of Mumbai city that faces the Arabian Sea in the West and the Mumbai port area on the East. The Island city is narrow at this point and it starts spreading east–west as one travels from the south to the north. The place where the attackers landed and the first place of attack—namely the Leopold Restaurant—is hardly 500 metres as the crow flies. Beyond that was the Taj Hotel, which is hardly 400 metres from Leopold. Hotel Oberoi is hardly 700 metres away. The Chhatrapati Shivaji Terminus was north of the landing place and about 2 km away. Likewise, the Cama Hospital was also the same distance. The Nariman House was hardly 500 metres from the place of landing.

So far as the intelligence was concerned, there were three alerts—two in the month of May 2008 and one in August 2008—that mentioned certain targets including the Taj Hotel and the Oberoi Hotel. We found that in the case of these two hotels, while the local police authorities did take some action to alert the hotel authorities, there was no mechanism within the state government to make an overall assessment. In any case, there were several inadequacies in doing that. Since counter-terrorism action must be based on careful intelligence inputs, no action could be planned in the absence of such intelligence.

Action to Handle the Attacks

The suddenness and enormity of the task facing the Mumbai Police is evident from the sequence of events. The first call regarding Leopold came to the police control room (C/R) at 21.48 hours and was about foreigners being injured. At 21.50 hours, Tourist Mobile opposite Leopold was shot at and at 21.54 hours details of the Taj firing emerged. At 21.56 hours, the Oberoi shooting report came in and at 21.59 hours, the CST firing was reported. Then came a report of a taxi being blown up at Wadi Bunder at 21.56 hours and at 22.53 hours there was a report regarding another taxi exploding at Vile Parle. Both places are at a considerable distance away from the Taj. Apparently, the terrorists who had travelled in taxis to Leopold and CST had planted bombs under the driver's seats. Later examination showed that they had used RDX. In fact, two bags were found by alert citizens, one on the road from Leopold to Taj and another one hardly one hundred feet from the main entrance of the Taj. But for that, the death toll may have been in thousands.

These simultaneous incidents sparked off panic all over the city, leading to the control room (C/R) receiving as many as 1,365 calls between 21.00 and 02.00 hours among which 267 were terrorism-related calls (4.5 calls per minute). There were rumours that 60 terrorists had entered the city. The C/R was flooded by panic calls from the outnumbered police units facing actions at different spots.

The overload of wireless (O/T) communication system made the officers and the control room utilise personal cellular mobiles/alternate channels for communication with each other. It was apparent that the simultaneous attacks and calls from the field units for more manpower made on cellular phones did result in the deployment of striking reserves in a haphazard and helter-skelter manner. The control room did not function as it was expected to.

Regarding the handling of these attacks simultaneously at multiple targets, we found that the initial response from the police stations and the senior officers was quite prompt. However, by the time the police units reached a specific spot, the terrorists had already moved on. While the attackers were equipped with the most modern weaponry including grenades, the policemen had to rush in with their usual equipment meant for performing normal duties.

There were some exceptional acts of bravery by different individuals while performing their duty. Sadanand Date, IPS, Additional Commissioner, Central Region on learning of the attack volunteered to go to the scene. He was asked to go to the CST. On reaching there, he learnt that two terrorists—Abu Ismail and Kasab—had gone towards Cama Hospital. He, with a small armed contingent, entered the hospital and went up to the fourth floor when he learnt that the two terrorists had gone to the terrace. When the terrorists found their passage blocked by Date and his men, they came down the stairs, shooting with their AK-47s. Though Date was hit on his thigh and lay injured, he continued to guide his men. In another incident at the Girgaum Chowpatty, Assistant Inspector (ASI) Tukaram Omble tackled the two terrorists Abu Ismail and Kasab when they came at high speed in a car down Marine Drive to proceed towards the Raj Bhavan. He killed one (Abu Ismail) and physically held on to the other (Kasab). In that brave act, Omble laid down his life. But for his apprehending Kasab alive, the knowledge of the conspiracy hatched in Pakistan in launching the attack would not have been known. There were several acts like this in which a number of police personnel laid down their lives.

Before delving on the fourth important aspect, command and control, the very special and peculiar manner in which the Mumbai Police functions needs to be highlighted. The Commissioner of Police, who is the head of the Mumbai Police, has full command and control over his force. The Director General of Police (DGP), Maharashtra, whose headquarters is also in Mumbai, has no direct control over the Commissioner. Their working arrangements depend on a good sense and relationship between these two senior police officers. This results in a dual control of the IPS officers working in the Commissionerate. They have to maintain a proper relationship with the DGP and the senior officers in the DGP's office while working under the City Commissioner. This is an untidy situation that is a historical legacy from the British times. No government has found it possible to do away with the dual control of the Mumbai police and establish a single line of control under the Director General of Police as in the other states of India.

We went into the "dual control" aspect in the light of the operations. We found that the control exercised by the Commissioner of Police, through the operations of the CP's control room, were untidy. This was made worse by the Commissioner, who instead of taking command of the whole force at the control room, decided to go on the spot near the Oberoi Hotel and station himself there for the two following nights. In his place, a senior officer, of a Joint Commissioner of Police rank, who was in fact in-charge of the Crime Branch, was put in charge of the control room. Although this Joint Commissioner of Police had been tracking some individuals suspected to be planning attacks in Mumbai and is one of the most efficient officers of the Maharashtra IPS, and did his work efficiently and tried his best to deploy the manpower effectively, it was a wrong man working at the wrong place. The one lesson that has to be followed in facing such terrorist attacks is thus not to tamper with the standard operating procedure (SOP) that has been carefully worked out, drawing upon the experience and lessons learned from the past.

I can only very briefly mention the modus operandi of the terrorists and the operation against them. Well-informed and trained terrorists—ten in number—knew the targets and the role each had to play. The Taj and Oberoi hotels, the two main targets, had superficial security arrangements. At the Taj, the terrorists could nonchalantly enter through the main entrance. At the Oberoi, there was some resistance by the hotel's security set-up. In general, in the absence of a single line of command, the police officers and men could not give their best. This was obvious in the manner in which the Anti-Terrorist Squad (ATS) functioned. Similarly, the quick response teams that were formed were not used properly.

I do not think it necessary to go into many details about our recommendations that involved coastal security, modernisation of the police, reorganisation of the anti-terrorist squad, setting up flying squads, etc. But I do wish to come back to the working of the intelligence agencies. By the terms of reference, we were restrained from examining the central intelligence officers. As the enquiry proceeded, we almost came to the conclusion that there were lacunae in the handling of intelligence by the IB itself.

We are now dealing with terrorist activity planned and organised by agencies across the borders of India. We have also witnessed such activities perpetuated by the citizens of India living within our borders. Increasingly, outside forces are using Indian citizens to perpetrate terrorists act after motivating the individuals, training them to commit such acts and also providing the means for this purpose. Human life has almost no value when a terrorist is willing to sacrifice his life and engage in mindless slaughter. How do we deal with these activities? How do we face—if not forestall—such acts?

Till 1985, we were only relying on the CrPC and the Indian Penal Code to deal with acts of terrorism. These were dealt with as serious crimes and the police followed the usual investigating tools. But it was soon realised that the persons who committed such acts were ruthless, armed with sophisticated weapons and chose their targets with a view to create panic and induce an atmosphere of insecurity and fear amongst individuals and instability in the political system. We found that the people in general did not like what was being done by certain individuals but they had no means to either voice their protests or to resist these extremists. In fact, even the police found that it was impossible to carry out a normal investigation because none would come forward to identify the perpetrators or to give any kind of evidence. Often, no one even reported such acts.

The only primary instrument at our disposal are the police and various agencies at the central and state levels involved in obtaining intelligence of such activities. In the course of our 26/11 Report, my colleague V. Balachandran and I found that there were many weaknesses in our system. With the federal structure and somewhat compartmentalised working of the central and state police agencies, we found that often, prior information that is available at the Centre did not properly percolate to the state police agencies. Moreover, such information that may be available in abundance cannot be of practical use unless the instruments that receive such information analyse it for operational purposes. Only then can they counter the activities of individuals, planning and executing the acts of terrorism.

The legal and constitutional means to address the situation, apply only after the perpetration of the acts. But what about the rights of the ordinary citizens—for peaceful conditions for carrying out their daily life and vocation—without being the targets of terrorist acts? All these have made the situation far more complex and difficult for the police to deal with.

Unfortunately, we are also facing another dimension of terrorist activities within India. Till a few months back, it was taken for granted that such acts were being carried out by individuals from a minority community. But now, it is evident that persons from the majority community are also carrying out such acts. Thus, the scope and the persons to be covered under the system of surveillance have widened. The task of policing has become more complex. Without the society and the people in general playing their role as "police", it may be impossible to tackle terrorism.

This calls for a consideration as to what is the role of the citizens in general to help the police and other agencies to identify and report the activities of individuals planning terrorist acts. What kind of legal and constitutional protection should be given to such individuals? Generally, one finds that an individual communicating information to the police finds himself/herself as a likely target of investigation. Several "whistle-blowers" have been killed. I am aware that the subject is far too complex and that there is no easy answer. It is not merely a question of the rights of the individuals versus the right of the state but also one of defending constitutional rights and duties that are enshrined in the Indian Constitution.

6

Mumbai Attacks: International Aspects and Impact:

Failures to Detect Infiltration, Role of Media and (Other) Stakeholders

Rajan K. Medhekar

We are sufficiently removed in time from the horrible sequence of events of 26/11, and yet not too far removed to treat the events as a mere historical fact. I have no doubt that we would have to face more such attacks in the future, no matter how well we are prepared to pre-empt or prevent them from happening. We therefore need to analyse and discuss what happened in Mumbai, so that we are better prepared to face such an attack in the future. I will attempt to express certain thoughts on the subject at hand, under three headings:

- 26/11 Mumbai terrorist attacks: their international aspects and impact.
- Failure to detect infiltration.
- Role of media and other stakeholders.

Edmund Burke famously said, "Those who don't know history are destined to repeat it"; we all know how true this is! But what is history? History itself is part fact, part projection and interpretation and part fiction! And mostly, it is an account constructed from this heady mix of fact, fiction and interpretation by non-participants, people who are far removed from the times and the circumstances in which the events occurred. Then are we destined to repeat our failures and forget our successes? I don't think so. I say this because I am convinced that we are committed to secure our freedom from terrorism and have faith in our commitment to succeed; Mahatma Gandhi said, "A small body of determined spirits fired by an unquenchable faith in their mission can alter the course of history". We must take inspiration from these words for while we, all hard-headed realists, do not easily believe that we, security specialists, can alter the course of history—we could in our fields of specialisation contribute towards reducing this scourge of terrorism.

President Eisenhower once said, "The hunt for the scapegoat is the easiest of all hunting expeditions". It would thus be more productive to finding the faults in our systems rather than indulging in the usual fault-finding and indulging in a blame game that helps no one but destroys teamwork and erects barriers of suspicion and turf-guarding. One thing I must make clear—26/11 will forever be etched on our collective minds and memories for the extent of its diabolical and cynical nature and for the indiscriminate and unprecedented violence against innocent members of the public. We can neither forget nor forgive those who planned and perpetrated these vile acts that had no other motive than to inflict a body blow on an unsuspecting people who had in no way harmed those who had committed these wanton and criminal acts.

I would begin with the international aspects and impact of 26/11. The entire operation was, as we now know, conceived, planned and prepared on foreign soil, in Pakistan. There is little doubt that this was the direct handiwork of Pakistan's Lashkar-e-Taiba (LeT) and its votaries. There are few who would believe that the LeT did not have the covert support of some sections of the intelligence and security apparatus of Pakistan. For the Pakistan government to talk of "non-state actors" is neither here nor there, for it then commits itself to admitting its acts of omission—a crime equally grave as that of commission for a state is duty-bound to prevent the use of its soil or resources or manpower to wage a proxy war against a neighbour.

As for Pakistan, given the continuance of the infiltration of terrorists from its soil into India, it is yet to learn from the words of the former Secretary of State, Hilary Clinton—"When you breed poisonous snakes in your backyard you cannot expect them to bite only your neighbours". But, that is Pakistan's problem.

But, it is from these words that the international community must take heed for the terrorists are no respecters of international borders or the rights of the sovereign nation-states. While ideologies drive insurgents and extremists, they are amenable to political and security solutions, but the terrorists are driven by blind hate and sustained by an uncompromising, exclusive and discriminatory form of religious and political bigotry. Those who make the mistake of presuming that terrorists can change their minds or hearts are only fooling themselves.

Terrorism is like a malignant growth, a cancer that cannot be cured by "medication" alone but needs to be exorcised; freeing the healthy cells from its malevolent, self-destructive effects. The by and large, peace-loving, law-abiding international community must take a stand on this and not confuse the acts of terrorist crime with the right of a people to self-determination. Terrorism is wrong—whatever its motivation.

The Impact of 26/11

Not only were a large number of Indians killed, maimed permanently or seriously injured (and these included NSG commandos and police personnel) but foreigners too were killed; nationals of the US, UK and Israel were specifically targeted. This latter aspect needs to be kept in mind when analysing the international aspects of these crimes.

Tourism was adversely affected and so was trade and commerce. FDI inflows slowed down and exchange rates fell. In fact, economic initiatives designed for the welfare of the common man too were subjected to an adverse impact directly and indirectly. These are matters for the experts in the fields of economics and finance to study and work out but suffice it to say, acts such as these—and they can happen anywhere as 9/11 and 26/11 have shown—can and do have adverse impacts and consequences far beyond the ground zero where they are actually perpetrated.

There are other links and aspects that need careful analysis—the David Headley connection, and the not-so-full sharing of timely intelligence inputs gathered by the various international intelligence agencies and institutions. The terrorists coordinated their act far better than the security agencies of the democratic world and one lesson that we cannot afford not to learn is that without close-knit and coordinated action, we would only succeed in pushing our local problems across our borders into other states, which in turn would become victims of a similar action by our neighbours.

One fact, more than others, stands out in proving the international impact or intended impact of the 26/11 attacks. This is that while the direct objective seems to have been to humiliate India based on the perceived wrongs at its hands or because of envy or hate or all three combined, the terrorists had bigger aims—to impact the international community. Here, it is instructive to note the following facts:

- It was planned to be a prolonged attack.
- It targeted certain foreign nationals in a big way.
- It was an attack not on any security or political establishment but on the financial and business hub of India—Mumbai.
- Hotels, hospitals and railways stations were attacked.
- Bullets were used more than bombs.
- Infiltration was via the seas and not across the Line of Control or any land border.

These facts must be examined in conjunction with these other details: Specifically, in the 1993 bomb blasts in Mumbai, 257 Indian nationals were killed by 13 strategically placed bomb blasts. Later in 2006, Mumbai witnessed an attack on its local trains in which five bombs killed 209 people. So, if the body-count of the Indian nationals was the only measure of success sought by the terrorists who participated in 26/11, then they would have used bombs—but they didn't. This time, they wanted targeted killings at specially selected places over a prolonged period, long enough to attract a wide and adverse international reaction, intense media coverage on TV and the electronic media. All this was to send a message to the international community regarding their prowess, their capabilities and intentions in an unmistakable way. In fact the 'heroic' manner in which all the terrorists (except one) of 26/11 died fighting as 'martyrs', was meant to motivate the other terrorist groups all over the world to act similarly and without fear. These facts alone are enough to establish the international impact of 26/11.

Failure to Detect Infiltration

The attack on 26/11 witnessed not the first but the second infiltration via the sea. Explosives and weapons used in the earlier 1983 blasts were smuggled in via the western Maharashtra coast. It is one thing to talk of, and sometimes even expect, "fool-proof" security but we know that nothing can be perfect. We can always improve and remove the deficiencies in our system. But this will always be work-in-progress, as it should be.

To prevent infiltration from across such a vast sea border is an almost impossible task. But with new technologies and due diligence, protection levels can always be enhanced. There are three areas that require quantum improvements; there is no time for incremental change.

- Enforce the standard operating procedures (SOPs) that have been meticulously drafted. This is possible only through sustained practice and course corrections derived from experience and not armchair criticism from non-professionals.
- Induct new technology and systems including big data analytics, digital encrypted communications, airborne and satellite surveillance and fast-interception land, air and sea craft.
- Coordinated and focused intelligence and intelligence-sharing based on a sense of national security and not driven by credit garnering or by turf-guarding.

In the context of 26/11, the question to be asked is, could the infiltration have been prevented? First, merely blaming it all on an "intelligence failure" is totally counterproductive, for no intelligence is omnipresent and all-knowing. In fact, we would have to fear such perfect intelligence services more than the terrorism itself! This does not mean that matters could not have been better. If there was more trust and there were systems of intelligence exchange, we would have had the information that was available with the UK and US intelligence, and investigation agencies, among others. Apart from that, despite forming the Multi-Agency Centre (MAC) and the Subsidiary Multi-Agency Centres (SMACs), intelligence-sharing within our country still leaves much to be desired. The recent interception by the coast guard of a fishing vessel suspected to be carrying terrorists into Indian waters from Pakistan, based on the inputs from one of our own intelligence agencies, has started a debate as to which other intelligence and security agencies should have been involved, etc. The point is that apart from better-quality intelligence, a higher level of sharing and trust would have yielded better results in preventing such an infiltration.

Having said that, I would also like to add—and without attributing blame or imputing incompetence on either the Indian Navy or the coast guard—that the only time the infiltration and thus the attacks could have been neutralised was on the high seas or the territorial waters when the terrorists or at least their hit-team were isolated at one place and thus vulnerable. Once the terrorists landed on terra firma, they spread out, which made their containment exponentially more difficult.

Preventing infiltration will always be a difficult proposition and we must continue with our efforts in dealing with this problem. In this, we must realise that in the final analysis we would have to depend on ourselves and not hope that somehow we would receive help from outside.

The Role of Media and Other Stakeholders

The role of media in any democracy cannot be overemphasised. Notwithstanding the allegations of "paid media", increased TRPs, competitive journalism, commercialisation, etc., the advantages of an alert and fearless media far outweigh its negative—and sometimes outright—harmful effects.

But as India matures as an open and secular democracy, we expect a more mature media; a media that clearly balances its duty to inform public opinion as fairly as possible and its responsibility towards the security of the people it so informs. It is a fine line, often obscured by competing interests—including commercial interests—but that distinction must be made if the rights of the media are to be balanced by proportionate responsibilities and duties towards the general public that it serves and depends upon.

It is heartening to note that SOPs and informal guidelines have been evolved after 26/11, in order to ensure that security agencies and media don't work at cross-purposes like they appeared to be during 26/11. Let us remember the thumb rule—if it's not good for the National Interest, it (whatever it is) should not be done.

As for the other stakeholders, we have a long way to go. Our firefighting forces, medical and emergency civil services like power supply and water, our municipalities and panchayats also must gear up to face the challenges of terrorism; so also our disaster management systems and organisations. We are experts at setting up special task forces, writing SOPs, bringing out schemes and enquiry reports, but unfortunately we are not ready to put them into practice. Also, our reports and schemes are often drawn up by those who are not responsible on the ground for their implementation. The results are skewed and this gives rise to blame and counter-blame. In fact, it often seems that our SOPs and other interventions are often templates to fix blame after the incident as against assigning responsibilities before the incidents even occur.

Eventually, the biggest and, in a sense the ultimate, stakeholders are the people. We must not feel that our security is totally outsourced to the government and security agencies. If we retain a right to demand and criticise, we also must share the responsibility to observe restraint and remain alert to the dangers posed by the misuse of media and social media as well as be discriminating enough to realise that political manoeuvring and caste politics are not the real issues but only attempts to misguide and misrepresent so as to grab power.

In the final analysis, "a chariot is a successful partnership between two or more wheels—a one-wheeled chariot is not only unbalanced and unstable but mostly useless". It is, therefore, in the interests of all stakeholders—the media included—to work in a spirit of cooperation rather than competition, particularly in times of an emergency such as 26/11. Democracy is to be practiced both in peace times and in war; we must subjugate our own opinions and desires to those of the collective—the Nation.

7

Illegal Immigration, Human Trafficking and Terrorism in Greece

John M. Nomikos

During the 1990s, the immigration problems in Greece began to exhibit explosive dimensions due to not only the political and economic developments in South-Eastern Europe but also to the continuing conflicts in the Middle East and North Africa. An important factor which played a relevant role in shaping these developments was the 1991 collapse of Ramiz Alia's regime in Albania and the subsequent flow of illegal immigrants into Greece from Albania and the other Balkan states (mainly Serbia, Romania, Bulgaria, and the Former Yugoslav Republic of Macedonia—FYROM), due to the political unrest that had taken place in the region during that period.[1]

In Greece, the national immigration policy today faces a bureaucratic inflexibility, functions in a fragmentary way and makes no substantial effort toward solving the problem. Dealing with illegal migration as a national security threat is a strategic option. The formation of national immigration policies which will prevent the flow of illegal immigrants is absolutely necessary, as is giving direction with regard to the integration of legal immigrants into the Greek society in coordination with the European Union Member-States Common Immigration Policy.

The European Commission in Brussels (Belgium) must pay attention to the strategic added value of the human intelligence (HUMINT) component in the European Immigration Liaison Officers (ILO) Network.

The officers need intelligence in dealing with illegal immigration instead of trying to manage immigrants after they have already entered Greece, a member of the European Union.

Greek Immigration Policy and Legal Structures

After the fall of Europe's communist regimes, there was a massive influx of illegal immigrants into Greece, mostly from the neighbouring states. The influx consisted not only of ethnic Greeks from those countries, but also of Albanians, Bulgarians and other Eastern Europeans. A later wave of illegal immigrants arrived from the Middle East, South Asia and Africa, which increased considerably between 2005 and 2014 and now constitutes about half of the annual flow.

The census of 1991 indicated that the population of Greece was 10,260,000. A decade later, by March 2001, the population had increased to 10,964,020 of whom 797,091 were foreign citizens. Among the foreigners, 47,000 were citizens of the European Union member states. According to the latest official data, Greece's immigrant population is about 1,150,000. Around 300,000 are ethnic Greeks from neighbouring Albania and the former Soviet Union. This leaves about 850,000 non-Greek immigrants, of whom 600,000 have a residence permit acquired through consecutive regularisation. Notably, though, recent unofficial estimates indicate that more than 140,000 regularised immigrants are unable to meet the criteria for the renewal of their current residency permits.

The immigration policy implemented by Greece has been mainly repressive, aimed at restricting the flow of illegal immigrants at the respective national borders, but with varying results. Greece must study the past and current situations in 2015, note the weaknesses of its legal frameworks and design realistic and sustainable long-term immigration policies along with a Common European Union immigration policy. This is because the problems of immigration—legal and illegal—will become more visible in the coming decade with serious repercussions for national security and employment in Greece (with a 26 per cent unemployment rate at present) and other European Union member states, especially of those on the Mediterranean (Portugal, Spain, France, Italy along with Greece).

Regarding the Greek legal structure, the first law dealing with the issue of foreigners living in Greece was enacted in 1929 (Law 4319/1929).[2] It lasted until 1991 when it was replaced by Law 1975/1991, according to which residence permits were given only to foreigners who had labour contracts. During the following years, the number of illegal immigrants entering Greece increased rapidly due to the dissolution of Yugoslavia and the resulting social, economic and political unrest in the rest of the Balkans. In a perverse way, this situation led to a relaxation of the deportation policy regarding the immigrants living in Greece and those who were coming from the Balkan states.

Since 1991, Presidential Decrees (PD 358/1997 and 359/1997) led not only to relaxation but also to the first programme of legalising the illegals which was implemented in 1998. Moreover, the new Law 2910/2001 replaced the word "deportation" contained in the previous laws with "legalisation" and other measures. Then it introduced the concept of family reunification as part of the process of permanent residence in Greece.[3] Unfortunately, instead of setting goals which would strictly tackle the issue of illegal immigration, it inaugurated a practice of legalising illegal immigrants with the fewest possible preconditions required of them. This led in subsequent years to the increasing flow of illegal immigrants, especially from Africa (Nigeria, Kenya, Sudan, Algeria, Egypt, Morocco), the Middle East (Iraq, Kurdistan, Syria) and Asia (Bangladesh, Pakistan, Sri Lanka, and Philippines). Thus, potential illegal immigrants are attracted to Greece since the prospect of acceptance, integration and permanent residence in that country is so easy.

Furthermore, in 2005, a new Law 3386/2005 emphasised the concept of integration and hinted at a policy of integration of illegal immigrants into Greek society. A National Committee for the Social Integration of Immigrants (Law 3536/2007) was created under the supervision of the Ministry of Interior. The National Committee issued a report regarding developments related to the social integration of immigrants at the national and international levels. The report submitted to the Greek Parliament included policy recommendations regarding the necessary measures to be taken to tackle this problem of social integration.[4]

The legal structure of the Greek immigration policy leaves open several questions that can be answered only by the Greek law enforcement officers who deal operationally with the problems of illegal immigration. The illegal immigrants are overtaxing the capacity of the detention cells of the law enforcement agencies including the Greek police and coast guard. The overcrowding occurs because in many cases the deportation procedures (depending on an immigrant's nationality and country of origin) take a very long time. The procedure involves the identification of illegal immigrants who, most of the time, possess no document validating their identity. When this happens, the Greek authorities must contact the diplomatic missions of the countries to which the immigrants declare that they belong in order to obtain the travel documents needed for the completion of the deportation procedures. Problems also arise when the declared country of the arrested individual does not recognise the illegal immigrant as its citizen. As a result of this bureaucratic dead end, illegal immigrants are detained illegally for months in the detention cells of Greek law enforcement agencies, with serious consequences for their health and general well-being. What is usually happening is that the illegal immigrants who come from the states not represented diplomatically in Greece are released and ordered to leave Greece within 30 days (Law 1975/1991) at their own expense!

Terrorism, Organised Crime and Human Trafficking: A Threat to Stability in Greece

In the last decade, Greece has become the recipient of an indefinite number of illegal immigrants from Asian and African states. Half the illegal immigrants arrested by the Greek law enforcement agencies are Albanians. Most of the illegal immigrants enter Greece mainly through the Greek–Turkish border; such action is tolerated if not assisted by the Turkish state authorities, regardless of the bilateral agreements that have been signed on this matter since 2003.[5]

Notably, many immigrants who enter Greece illegally prefer to seek asylum in other European Union member states and use Greece as only a transit to such other member states. Therefore, the Dublin II Arrangement has proven to be rather insufficient for two main reasons: a) while Dublin II apparently sets the basis for regulating a rather chaotic phenomenon, in fact it constitutes a convenient way for the European Union member states that are not in the front line of illegal immigration to deal with the problem. As a consequence, asylum seekers having passed through Greece are transferred back to Greece, which in 2010 undertook the heavy burden of coping with 90 per cent of all illegal immigrants entering the European Union member states. b) A flaw of the Dublin II Arrangements is that it does not take into consideration the fact that no equivalent standards and practices for the protection of asylum seekers prevail in the European Union member states. In fact, Greece has one of the lowest refugee recognition rates.[6] As a consequence, illegal immigration is actually an asymmetrical threat that destabilises the Greek state.

Of special importance is the study of the causes of Turkey's violation of the Readmission Protocol for illegal immigrants that was signed with

Greece. The Turkish authorities do not comply with the terms of the Protocol and do not cooperate on the issues of readmission. Therefore, they create many problems, particularly during the procedure of the surrender of illegal immigrants on the borders with Greece. The Turkish government effectively implements the former Turkish President's "Ozal Doctrine" which states that "we do not need to make war with Greece. We need to send them a few million illegal immigrants from Turkey and finish them."[7] The uncontrolled flow of illegal immigrants poses multiple dangers to Greece's national security because it can destabilise social cohesion through demographic change and the encouragement of the spread of organised crime and terrorist networks. An illegal immigrant, a high-level operative of the al-Qaeda, passed the Greek border and was arrested by the Greek law enforcement agencies after he tried to receive political asylum with forged documents![8]

Conclusion

The Greek government must now finally understand that the time in which the issue of illegal immigration could be solved by arid discussion and confrontation between politicians has long passed. The intensity of the phenomenon is "ante-portas", judging from the overpopulation of many Asian and African states, along with the continuing (last six years) Greek economic crisis. Greece must declare to the European Commission and especially to the international community that it can no longer serve as the ideal geographical area through which illegal immigrants seek to pass in order to reach other European Union member states—perhaps more attractive destinations.[9]

In order to efficiently and operationally confront the problems of uncontrolled illegal immigration into the European Union member states, the European Commission has established a Network of Immigration Liaison Officers to prevent the traffickers from bringing illegal immigrants into the European territory, and not limit itself to dealing with the problem after the illegal immigrants are already there (Greek land).[10]

In conclusion, preventive strategies must be developed and implemented by each European Union member state within the framework of a New Common European Union Immigration Policy. The European Union member states should shift their efforts from law enforcement repression operations to human intelligence (HUMINT)-led preventive activities. However, all these depend on the development and maintenance of a strong political and coordinated will at both the national and European Union levels.

NOTES

1. John M Nomikos, "Illegal Immigration and Organized Crime in Greece", Research Paper, No. 144, August 2010, pp: 6-10, Research Institute for European and American Studies, Athens, Greece.
2. Law 1975 (12 April 1991) clarifies explicitly the Police responsibility for controlling the borders (Article 3, Paragraph 4), the entrance of immigrants (Article 6), the stay of immigrants (Articles 12, 13, 14), work permits of immigrants (Articles 21, 22, 23), and restrictions and deportation procedures (Articles 26, 27, 28, 29).
3. Law 3386/2005 (Article 3) refers to the process of social dialogue in order to shape policies which are promoting the integration of immigrants in all spheres of society according to International Law and the European Vest.
4. Law 3536/2007 refers to the foundation of the National Committee for the Integration of Immigrants in the Greek Ministry of Interior. Articles 3 and 4 refer to the general prerequisites for the renewal of the residency permit of immigrants.
5. Since 2003, Greece has been implementing the Dublin II regulations, according to which the responsibility for handling illegal immigrants from the European Union belongs to the country through which they first entered.
6. United Nations High Commissioner for Refugees (UNHCR), Greek Chapter Report, at http://unhcr.gr/exec/BOSTAT%20table2009EL.pdf, Athens, Greece
7. Theodoros Katsanevas, "Nobody is Worrying", *To Paron* (Greek Newspaper), 3 August 2009.
8. "An Al Qaeda High-Ranking Operative was Arrested among Illegal Immigrants", *To Paron* (Greek Newspaper), 3 August 2009.
9. "Joint Law Enforcement Action to Tackle People Smuggling Network in Greece", *Europol*, http://www.rieas.gr/research-areas/2014-07-30-08-58-27/balkan-studies-5/2392-joint-law-enforcement-action-to-tackle-people-smuggling-network-in-greece, (Retrieved on 23 March 2015).
10. European Commission, Regulation No. 377/2004 of the European Council of 19 February 2004 explained the basis for the creation of a Network of Immigration Officers. *Official Journal of the European Union*, March 2004. L.64/1.

PART II

CONCERNS AND CHALLENGES

8

Weapons, Narcotics and Fake Currency

Amit Kumar

This article examines the relationship between terrorism and its financing by criminal methods and means like weapons smuggling, narcotics trafficking and fake currency circulation. What motivates and necessitates terrorists to use these modes of criminal finance and the benefits thereby that accrue to terrorist organisations is also examined. The article also explores the comparative scale and scope of these criminal activities and their relative importance to terrorists, using various examples of terrorist enterprises and their use of these methods.

First, money, fake currency, narcotics, and weapons all have a monetary value and are used to finance terrorism. The proceeds of illicit arms sales, narcotics smuggling, and the proceeds of the circulation of fake currency are used to fund terrorist operations, set up and administer terrorist organisations and for the recruitment and radicalisation of terrorists. For example, the Taliban has relied on drug trafficking, the Irish Republican Army used weapon smuggling and the Lashkar-e-Taiba has used fake Indian currency to finance their operations.

Second, terrorists tend to rely on criminal sources of income and criminal methods to obtain that income to finance their activities. This is due to the squeeze on licit sources of funding and the need for plausible deniability on the part of the terrorists to dissociate themselves from criminal methods. Another factor is the proliferation of terrorist affiliates and cells that require local sources of income to survive. In addition, the loss of state support, post-Cold War collapse of the Soviet Union and the

Warsaw Pact countries and the subsequent lacunae in governance structures are contributory factors. Terrorists and criminals both need weapons. Narcotics can be exchanged for money and weapons by criminals and terrorists. Criminals possess expertise to print and circulate fake currency and terrorists use fake currency generated by the criminals to finance their operations. The relationship between terrorists and criminals becomes so neatly intertwined that often it is difficult to distinguish a criminal organisation from a terrorist group and vice versa.

Third, due to the attractiveness of the proceeds of crime, terrorists switch to criminal methods either partially or fully. Arms trafficking is lucrative; trafficking in narcotics is the most lucrative criminal enterprise; fake currency is a classic criminal/terrorist tactic employed to subvert the economies of states in addition to financing terrorism as mentioned; though, in comparison to weapons smuggling as well as narcotics trafficking, it may be the least lucrative monetarily.

Fourth, terrorists use criminal routes to traffic arms, narcotics and fake currency. Fake currency smugglers use the same routes as those used by arms traffickers and narcotics traffickers. In fact, criminals and terrorists use the same routes; thus, very clearly and distinctly showing how and why the criminal–terrorist nexus is so widespread and strong.

Fifth, there are certain factors that facilitate terrorism and its reliance on weapons, narcotics and fake-currency smuggling. These include porous and poorly policed borders and a lack of governance in the border regions which makes it easier to smuggle weapons, narcotics, fake currency, criminals, terrorists, etc. alike through the border regions.

Sixth, the choices of revenue streams for terrorists depends on the core competencies of the criminal/terrorist group in question as well as the expertise of its criminal/terrorist partners in weapons trafficking, narcotics trafficking and fake currency circulation. It also depends on the geographical locations of their criminal partners. A typical example is the reliance of the Taliban on the D-Company for drug trafficking out of Afghanistan; the dependence of the FARC on IRA for weapons supply and training and the support of the D-Company in helping Lashkar-e-Taiba transport fake Indian currency across the Indian borders with Pakistan, Nepal, Bangladesh, Myanmar, etc.

Seventh, the need to launder funds on the part of the terrorists is also an important variable that factors into the terror financing–criminal nexus calculus. Like criminals, terrorists have to disguise the sources of their criminal income from the final destination that such income is headed for, i.e. the financing of terrorist infrastructure and operations. This laundering exercise serves one all-important purpose—it makes it difficult to trace terrorists' funds since these are co-mingled with the proceeds of crime. The proceeds of weapons trafficking are huge; the proceeds of narcotics trafficking the largest in absolute amounts and the proceeds of fake currency trafficking are the least in absolute amounts. This difference in magnitude is also reflected in the total amounts laundered by these criminal methods and activities. Since laundering is a profitable income-generating exercise in itself, criminal organisations that possess core competency in laundering end up laundering funds for themselves as well as for terrorist outfits. A notable case in point is the Los Zetas drug cartel in Mexico laundering funds for Hezbollah—itself a terrorist organisation as well as a global criminal syndicate.

Eighth, terrorist funds are laundered eventually through banks and terrorist organisations typically rely on criminals to launder funds. Proceeds of weapons trafficking are laundered through banks or used to buy drugs; proceeds of narcotic trafficking are laundered through banks or used to buy weapons and proceeds of weapons trafficking and narcotic smuggling are used to manufacture and transport fake currency which is then laundered through banks. In all the above, laundering provides an extra income to the criminals.

Ninth, money laundering follows three stages: Placement, Layering and Integration.[1] In terror financing, the funds are channelised to finance terrorism after the Placement and Layering stages and Integration is not required.

Tenth, since money laundering is more widespread and in much greater amounts, it is easier to gain convictions for money-laundering crimes. The investigating authorities may then scratch the surface, go back and stumble across terror-financing activity as a predicate activity to the money-laundering activity. This investigatory strategy is helpful since terror financing takes place in much smaller amounts and is more difficult to be traced and detected on its own.

Eleventh, terrorist groups can and do rely on the misuse of charities/ offer social services to fund their activities. Criminals engaged in the smuggling of drugs, weapons and fake currency rely solely on crime for financing their operations.

Twelfth, given the intersection of terror financing and money laundering discussed in the preceding paragraphs, combating both requires sanctions, investigations and enforcement, regulation, outreach to banks and international partners and anti-money laundering/countering the financing (AML/CFT) controls in banks.

Finally, of special relevance to India and its neighbourhood, is the fact that Lashkar-e-Taiba is a terrorist organisation that relies on D-Company for financing and laundering activities. D-Company is a criminal organisation that relies on the smuggling of drugs, weapons and fake currency. Members of D-Company have also been designated as terrorists; hence, it also can be counted as a terrorist organisation.

NOTES

1. For a description of the three stages of money laundering, please see http://www.moneylaundering.ca/public/law/3_stages_ML.php

9

CBRN Terrorism and South Asia

Ajay Lele

The terminology CBRN terrorism refers to chemical, biological, radiological and nuclear terrorism. This expression is similar to what is also known as Weapons of Mass Destruction (WMD) terrorism. Nuclear weapons have great destructive capability—causing damage to both life and property. On the other hand, the actual devastation caused by chemical and biological weapons could vary and is dependent on the lethality of the weapon used and the nature of the target. Also, while the actual destruction to human life could be more, the destruction of property could be far less compared to a nuclear attack. Radiological weapons could be considered more as weapons of mass disruption. Hence, in literature, particularly in the context of terrorism, the term CBRN terrorism is found to be more frequently used than WMD terrorism. Also, it may be noted that from the point of view of defining structures for protective measures against such threats, the term CBRN offers a greater clarity of purpose.

The United States (US) invaded Iraq in 2003, on the pretext that Iraq had a stockpile of WMD. The absence of WMD on Iraqi soil, however, changed global "sensitivity" towards the issue of WMD. However, the issue of CBRN weapons came back into focus in 2004, when Libya formally disclosed that it had produced and stored a stockpile of over 20 tonnes of deadly mustard gas. The mustard gas had been made in the Libyan desert and had been kept along with a variety of chemical precursors intended for nerve agents at two storage facilities. The gas had also been tested as a weapon and thousands of bombs had been made for delivering the lethal agents as part of Libya's secret chemical weapons programme, which had begun in the 1980s.[1] The Organisation for the Prohibition of Chemical Weapons (OPCW), the agency responsible for the destruction of the chemical weapons under the United Nations mandate, successfully destroyed these weapons by 2014.

In Syria, the first report of the usage of the chemical weapons came in 2013; evidence also emerged in March 2015 about the usage of chlorine gas. While the UN has confirmed that chemical weapons have been used in the ongoing Syrian civil war, (some reports indicate that they are still being used as of April 2015), the problem of determining who is using these weapons has become complex. Both the government forces and those fighting the Assad regime claim that the other side is using the weapons against them. In the claims and counter-claims that abound, it is difficult to determine who the actual user is. That notwithstanding, this issue clearly highlights the dangers of CBRN terrorism and also demonstrates that the threat is real.

The subject of CBRN is vast and could be viewed from a variety of viewpoints. During the early years of the Cold War, the possibility of conventional conflict escalating to nuclear exchanges was very real. Consequently, the world was sensitised to the dangers of nuclear war. This period did not see much talk about chemical and biological weapons. Post-Cold War, many states and individuals across the globe started raising concerns about issues like human rights, global warming and climate change, as well as the use of heinous weapons in war, like vision damaging lasers, permanent disability causing landmines etc. The probability of the usage of CBRN weapons in future as a form of warfare is therefore low, but cannot be ruled out. Presently, no acceptable global norms exist towards banning all types of CBRN weapons. Besides the five declared nuclear powers, some others too have stockpiles of nuclear weapons, which they are loathe to abandon. In addition, some states are working to develop nuclear weapons. On the other hand, there is a growing danger that non-state armed groups could use CBRNs in some form or the other, especially terrorist organisations, which seek to use such weapons not only as "weapons of destruction" but also for "mass disruption", exploiting in full the "fear-factor" and psychosomatic impact the use of such weapons can cause.

The South Asian region today possesses all the ingredients for a potential geopolitical nightmare. State failure in any one of the region's most vulnerable countries could prove potentially devastating for the region's stability on the whole. Agreements on traditional security concerns are often hampered by the conflicting domestic political and foreign policy priorities of the South Asian states. However, there are emerging non-traditional security issues in South Asia that are of common concern to countries across the region. The twenty-first century is beset with such "non-traditional" challenges as the looming food and water resource crises, the often devastating environmental impacts of climate change and the threat of pandemic diseases that cut across geographic boundaries. All of these, as witnessed in recent years, have an immediate human impact on the South Asian countries, with implications for future stability, both domestic and regional. Calamities in any one of these areas bear the very real potential to exacerbate conditions, contributing to traditional security threats in the region.[2] Another very important non-military threat which demands attention is terrorism. There are various terrorist outfits which are operational in parts of South Asia. They include organisations like the Afghan and Pakistani Taliban, Lashkar-e-Taiba (LeT), Harkat-ul-Jihad-al-Islami (HuJI), Jaish-e-Mohammed (JeM), etc. For many years, the Sri Lankan dreaded terror outfit LTTE (Liberation Tigers of Tamil Eelam), operated in Sri Lanka and in India. States like Bangladesh and Nepal also have serious internal security concerns. In addition, there are issues like cross-border terrorism and state-sponsored terrorism. Various acts of terrorism in the region demonstrate that terrorists use various approaches to spread terror and hence, there exists a possibility that acts involving CBRN terrorism could also happen in the region.

No state is overtly able to support any usage of CBRNs because since the end of the Second World War, various treaty mechanisms have been put in place to stop the usage and spread of such weapons. Also, the development, sale and purchase of various weapon platforms which could be used for delivering such weapons to the target are being monitored regularly. This is particularly so in respect of nuclear weapons where mechanisms such as the Nuclear Non-Proliferation Treaty (NPT) exist to limit, reduce, and eliminate such weapons. Two remaining categories of WMD—biological and chemical weapons—have also been outlawed by international treaties, namely the Biological and Toxic Weapons Convention Treaty (BTWC) that came into being in 1975 and the Chemical Weapons Convention Treaty (CWC) in 1997.

The September 11, 2001 attacks have particularly forced the various states facing the dangers of terrorism to rethink their security policies, e.g., the anthrax attacks in the US immediately after 9/11—though a relatively less number of people (five) were killed but major panic was created and a substantial loss to the economy was caused, raising concerns about CBRN terrorism. Today, in general, the use of CBRN agents by terrorists as a terror tool cannot be completely ruled out.

South Asia is a region where the security landscape is totally different from that of the rest of the world. In this region, India and Pakistan are nuclear weapon states as is China. All these nuclear weapons states share geographical borders. India and Pakistan have fought four wars during the last sixty years and one of these (Kargil) was fought under the shadow of nuclear capacities. In general, India's relations with nuclear Pakistan have remained strained for most of the period since independence over the Kashmir issue. Pakistan's attempts to settle the border issue by the use of force have not borne fruit and now, in a change of tactics, Pakistan is covertly supporting terrorism within India, waging in effect a proxy war against it. Hence, a possible use of CBRN terrorism by such groups sponsored by Pakistan exists in the region.

Politically, Pakistan remains unstable. Many groups, that are supported by Pakistan in their proxy war against India, are now also attacking the Pakistani state. In the recent past, they have attacked military installations, airports, schools and the like, demonstrating a deadly ability to launch major attacks using modern technology. The danger lies in such groups getting access to WMD. Technically, Pakistan's nuclear arsenal is overseen by a National Command Authority (NCA) which was set up in 2000 and is headed by the President with the Prime Minister as its vice chairman. Key cabinet ministers and the heads of the army, navy and air force are also members of the NCA, which controls all aspects of the country's nuclear programme, including deployment and, if necessary, the use of those weapons.[3] There is no nuclear arsenal kept available in a ready-to-use form. Also, to use nuclear weapons, delivery platforms like fighter aircraft, ballistic missiles or submarine-based capabilities are required. Under these circumstances, there exists a very limited possibility that any terror organisation could be able execute a nuclear attack. Obviously, when the terror groups are aware that conventional attacks are beyond their reach, they could look for other options. One possibility is that they could sabotage the nuclear installations. The Chernobyl accident and the Fukushima meltdown owing to the impact of the tsunami, indicates that a very well planned and properly executed sabotage operation could make a major impact. At the same time, it needs to be noted that an attack on a nuclear installation on the lines of 9/11 may not provide them with the desired output. This is because the design and construction of nuclear installations are carried out by factoring various possibilities of accidents and adequate precautions are undertaken while constructing such installations. Under these circumstances, a sabotage attempt inside the factory could be considered as a most desirable option by the terror groups. There also exists a possibility that a terror organisation could manage nuclear disaster by undertaking cyber attacks.

Radiological weapons are offshoots of nuclear weapons. Any usage of such weapons may not lead to a catastrophe as in the case of nuclear weapons. Radiological material is easily available in any laboratory where X-rays are taken. Such material could be used in the preparation of a small bomb or IED, etc. The detonation of such a bomb could create moderate damage but would also spread radiation which could have a long-term impact on the human beings in the vicinity. Such bombs are usually referred to as dirty bombs and could be preferred by terrorists as a weapon, more to create fear than to actually cause any major damage.

For many years the Asian region has been the sufferer with regards to CBRN attacks. The recent Syrian attacks indicate that the trend continues. Japan has been both a victim as well as an attacker. The Second World War ended with the dropping of two nuclear bombs over Japan. But in the late thirties, Japan had used biological weapons in China. In 1995, a Japanese cult Aum Shinrikyo had successfully used a chemical agent "Sarin" in a Tokyo subway, killing 15 people. On another occasion, followers of Osho (Rajneesh) had attempted to poison salad bars in Oregon, US. Fortunately, CBRN has never been used in the South Asian region till date. However, the absence of such weapons as a terror tool does not indicate that such attacks cannot occur in the future.

Pakistan is a signatory to CWC and BTWC and has stated that it does not have any such weapons. Hard evidence to prove Pakistani interest in biological weapons and chemical weapons programme is scarce but certain circumstantial evidence raises doubt on the issue. It is possible that Pakistan has the potential and the intention to develop and produce offensive CB systems and a few reports have indicated that it probably has an interest in the acquisition of technology related to biological and chemical weapons programme. Some assessments based on intelligence inputs indicate that Pakistan has manufactured weapons for blister, blood choking and nerve agents. It is believed that China could have been a possible supplier of the technology and equipment in this regard. Pakistan has numerous munitions systems which could be used to deliver chemical warfare agents, including artillery, aerial bombs and missiles. Baloch nationalists have often accused the Pakistani security forces of using chemical weapons—namely, phosphorus gas—against the Baloch rebels and civilians. India believes that Pakistan used chemical weapons against its soldiers in Siachen in 1987. However, officially there is an agreement between India and Pakistan on the complete prohibition of chemical weapons, which was signed in 1992. According to US reports (1996), Pakistan had been conducting research and development activities with potential biological warfare applications. It is not known whether this potential has since been realised.

Broadly, it could be argued that there is a lesser possibility of (covert) state support to terrorist groups operating in South Asia for undertaking CBRN attacks. This is particularly so in regard to chemical and biological weapons. However, this does not mean that terrorist groups would not be able to attempt to indulge in this form of terrorism. After the US invasion of Afghanistan in the mountains of Tora-Bora, various calculations and drawings towards designing a system constituting of weather balloons (helium-powered) to deliver anthrax spores on pre-designated targets were found. Could this have been related to the attempts by forces antithetical to India, which could use the westerly wind flows to burst such balloons over a target area in India in order to spread the spores? Such anthrax spores inhaled by large populations would undoubtedly create panic, fear and death.

While CBRN attacks have not taken place in South Asia, the changing nature of terrorism gives ground for concern about the possibility of the usage of these weapons.First, the global community as a whole is more worried about CBRN terrorism because of the phenomenon of new forms of terrorism, which is fundamentally different from the earlier versions. Second, the behavioural patterns of the present generation of terrorists have changed. In South Asia, terrorism is politically motivated and the various terrorist groups operating here adopt violent means only to a limited extent. They essentially use violence as a bargaining tool. Be it Kashmir, Nepal or Sri Lanka, they are fighting for a piece of land. But, at the same time, the Islamist groups are getting support from the global terrorist networks like al-Qaeda/ISIS. Such groups are religious fanatics and have been found to be more interested in mass casualty terrorism and total destruction. Such terrorist groups are expected to be more likely to use CBRN tactics. It is also important to note that terrorist groups operating in Afghanistan and the adjoining regions could target troops from the US or their allies. Also, in the Indian scenario, it could be argued that for the last couple of decades though various terrorist groups have executed a few successful attacks, they have not gotten much mileage out of it. Their ultimate motive has not yet been achieved and they have actually been pushed much further away from their objectives. Under such circumstances, there is a likelihood that they could opt for CBRN terrorism owing to their frustrations and to demonstrate that they exist. They could hence go to any extent to achieve their objectives.

In conclusion, it could be said that though the CBRN terror threat to the South Asian region is not very definitive, the prospects for future attacks should not be ruled out.

NOTES

1. Judith Miller, "Libya Discloses Mustard Gas Program and Stockpiles", *The New York Times*, March 5, 2004
2. http://www.nbr.org/research/initiative.aspx?id=39, (accessed on April 20, 2015)
3. Zeeshan Haider "Pakistan's Nuclear Command Stays Unchanged: Official", Apr 8, 2008, http://www.reuters.com/article/topNews/idUSISL28991220080408, (accessed on April 15, 2015).

10

Unconventional Terrorism:
An Assessment

Jean-François Daguzan

A new terrorism related to structural changes in the post-Cold War world?[1]

The threat of nuclear, radiological, biological and chemical (unconventional) terrorism is a paradox and a problem for both governments and states. It represents the dilemma between the theoretical highest risk for the population and a very low scale of occurrence. Statistically speaking, unconventional terrorism represents nothing. From 1968 to 2005, the Memorial of Oklahoma City and the Rand Corporation Terrorism database indicated 20,781 terrorist acts. Real unconventional terrorism acts or attempts, match around a dozen! Why has such a concern emerged in the strategic minds in the last 20 years? What does it really mean?

The final throes of the Gulf War and the discovering of Saddam Hussein's NRBC programmes (1990–1991) brought into focus the threat of chemical and biological warfare. Some international events confirmed this concern: Aum Shinrikyo and the gas (sarin) attacks in 1994 (Matsumoto) and 1995 (Tokyo); the discovering of a radiological bomb in a park in Moscow in 1995 and of course, the major biological attacks with the anthrax agent in the United States (Autumn 2001), following 9/11. Moreover, at many times, the al-Qaida's leading members have expressed their own interest in these means. These affirmations were confirmed in 2002 with the discovery of plans and training books in Afghanistan and

Europe. Further, the Saudi Sheikh, Naser Bin Hamad al-Fadh, published a fatwa in 2003, legitimising the use of WMDs against the enemies of Islam.[2] Novelists such as Tom Clancy (*The Sum of All Fears*) and Larry Collins (*The Fifth Horseman*) had, in their day, highlighted the risks of nuclear terrorism. Along the way, the question of WMD terrorism became a major issue. Some events in the last ten years make us conscious of this new threat. Many have written on this topic, but what really lies behind this literary or even sensationalist treatment?

Once addressed, the question resolves itself into a twofold problem. On the one hand, there is the need to assess the technical reality of a supposed threat and to see if the recent technological developments have increased its potentialities. On the other, the link between the presumed technical threat and terrorism must be demonstrated. In other words, the first question is: has terrorism and its links with the weapons of mass destruction changed since the end of the Cold War? And the second question: has the nature of terrorism changed in such a significant way that the relevant groups or individuals now seek to use large-scale means of creating terror, hitherto reserved for violence between states?

This second question is fundamental because it is based on an essential premise: traditional terrorism is always based, in principle, on a rational approach on the part of the individual who indulges in it, even if the goals which inspire him are seen as pre-ordained. The terrorist, with very few exceptions, acts not for the pleasure of terrorising but with a precise aim of protest. It is the judgement of the society which suffers the consequences and which brands him as irrational. So what are the factors of conventional terrorism—political and sociological—which enable us to attribute to it a certain rationality, and which of them are susceptible to change?

The means for non-conventional terrorism (mainly chemical and biological weapons) have always been available since many years, but were exclusively held by states. Over the past 20 years, the situation has changed dramatically.

Open Access

The globalisation factor: With an increase in the effect of publicity engendered by globalisation, a local terrorist can benefit from global repercussions. The accessibility of technical knowledge now permits any group—governmental or otherwise—to profit from the readily available knowledge, often considered as declassified by the Western nations, but potentially dangerous when it is diverted to terrorist uses (the Iraqi nuclear programme or the existence of terrorist sites on the Internet). Moreover, the actions of groups can be rendered less visible thanks to the fragmentation of tasks and dispersed production. In addition, the globalisation of the means of communication, most notably the media, equally contributes to the growth of the terrorist risk, to the extent that disadvantaged populations can follow world events via satellite channels and witness a display of opulence from which they feel totally excluded. The phenomenon of exclusion is true for each country—as much internally (intra-state) as externally (extra-state). The coexistence of this set of factors nowadays renders the advanced societies more vulnerable than in the past to wide-ranging and more reactive terrorist attacks, with a predictable augmentation of the panic effect.

The technological factor: Is there a substance more "terrorisable" than others or is simply more terrorising? The real new development would seem to be the availability of means, formerly reserved to the state, to non-governmental groups or indeed individuals. The spread of knowledge has had much to do with this, as well as the increase in the level of education of much of the world population; combined with these, globalisation has done its work. Finally, the dual nature of a good number of technologies (especially chemical and biological), access to powerful computers and sometimes the availability of a mercenary work force, have shattered the sphere reserved for the state. Nonetheless, not all these means are easily accessible—by virtue of their nature and the different disciplines of massive destruction involved. Nuclear terrorism is considered by many specialists to be the least likely option at the moment. The technological hurdles and miniaturisation pose problems which have to be overcome; this can only be done with national-level resources, which would imply "remote control" terrorism by a "godfather" state (described as a sponsor by the Anglo-Saxon analysts, and in the French eyes, largely unlikely in terms of retaliation). On the other hand, the dispersal of radioactive substances seems, a priori, more easily achievable.

So, if one believes the specialist literature, chemical and biological terrorism appears, along with radioactive dispersion, as the "way of the future".

Motivations and actors: does the nature of terrorism change as a function of the means? Once the technical credibility has been established, the question of the potential perpetrator and his motivations must be considered, in all respects, as central. The technical dimension is, of course, fundamental. The discussion of unconventional terrorism would make no sense, in the eyes of most authors, if it did not include the new accessibility of the technologies formerly reserved for the exclusive military use of states, and henceforth subject to use by the non-governmental groups. The term "terrorism by massive destruction" has been widely used by American writers. It deserves to be critiqued. Certainly, there is a new "requirement" on the part of certain terrorist groups for more lethal weapons (Oklahoma City, World Trade Center, Nairobi, 9/11, Mumbai, etc.). Today, the Islamic State (IS or ISIS) or Taliban groups have a wide reach and have been engaged in a mass slaughter of people, assassinations, burning of villages, etc. (for e.g., actions by the Boko Haram). But this does not necessarily imply the dimension of "massive destruction"—a term which current writers use in excess and mostly for reasons more political than analytical. It is, perhaps, necessary to speak of a quest for more media-worthy weapons, or of "mass impact"—a term which is becoming more and more current among specialists. This is why the term "unconventional terrorism" seems more appropriate in this respect, since it corresponds better to the different hypotheses of use, which run from the "image" of an attack of mass destruction, to its acknowledged execution (probably the least likely option). The term "unconventional" refers, from our point of view, less to the military sense of conventional or non-conventional weapons, than to a new approach to terrorism on the part of the groups (one could also say "non-conformist").

Now, we come to the identification of the new means available for a terrorist act and, above all, the assessment of their degree of feasibility. To set out the subject clearly is already a way of responding to this crucial problem which threatens our security. It also begins to envisage the right answers.

Which is the Most Foreseeable Threat?

To develop nuclear weapons (even rustic) is a very complicated path. The Iraqi example has shown that research into the production of uranium only (not to mention plutonium), enriched for military purposes (UHE 235 at 93 per cent) is a very difficult process taking into account the problems posed by the technical hurdles and the rigour of international controls. So, given that a terrorist group succeeds in procuring the necessary fissile material (a dozen kilos), it means taking a long road to arrive at the stage of attack. In fact, the production of a bomb—even a rudimentary one—poses the problem of design, and then of detonation.

The nuclear option also involves the problem of transport. Depending on its size and weight, the bomb could be non-transportable, transportable by ship, by cargo aircraft, by truck, droppable, or finally, if a certain level of militarisation and miniaturisation is achieved, projectable by gun or ballistic missile. (These last two methods being possible, in this sense, if the group has acquired a warhead, its fusing and its codes, which constitutes a lot of "ifs".)

The other big question is that of detonation. The possession of the fissile material counts for nothing without a conventional capacity to compress it for creating a chain reaction. As far as the highly enriched uranium is concerned, a relatively simple detonation system can be put together. For plutonium, the detonation system is much more complex and requires the possession of both the technical tools, and the knowledge to achieve a set of simultaneous detonations in the order of a nanosecond. Such a technical barrier leaves little prospect of success even to a group with significant technical and financial resources.

The idea of time must be taken into account as a central factor when speaking of nuclear terrorism. With all the resources of a rich state, Iraq took about ten years to bring its nuclear programme to a head (but uranium enrichment was its stumbling block); it was not complete at the time of the Gulf War.

In conclusion, the steps leading to a nuclear attack seem to be complicated, burdensome and uncertain (this option had also been studied and rejected by the Aum cult). It may be classified as of a very low probability.

The hypothesis of an attack by means of radioactive material is a more dangerous case since it combines a facility in concept, assembly and execution with a guaranteed media and psychological impact. Its concept is simple: it involves propagating radioactive material in sufficient quantity in an urban area. Very many radioactive products can be used. A whole range is available (irradiated fuel, cobalt, nuclear waste, cesium137 and others: strontium, etc.). These products exist in many places by virtue of their medical and industrial uses. As for the militarised products, theoretically they may be bought, stolen or handed over by a foreign power.

These products can be dispersed by explosion. The phenomenon of an explosion approaches the image of a nuclear weapon. But dispersion from the air is also possible, as is the contamination of drinking water supplies. The only real risk run by the terrorists during their preparations is that of contamination by contact with the material or its container—it will certainly be highly radioactive (one example of its terrific effect could be found in the Goiâna accident [Brazil] in 1987 where children found a "golden powder" lost in a waste plant [in fact cesium 137] and played with it. Four of them died and two hundred and forty five persons were very seriously injured).

Chemical and biological agents possess their own characteristics which make them more attractive for terrorist use. On the one hand, the ratio of lethality to volume of these agents could be very high, which allows for significant results to be achieved with limited quantities of agent. On the other hand, the process could be cheap, essentially because the terrorists do not focus on quality. This characteristic permits the costs of production of the agent to be reduced and to dispense with a large scientific and industrial infrastructure, which reduces the risk of detection during the manufacturing stage. Regarding a chemical threat, there is also the risk of terrorists exploding existing capabilities close to or inside cities (fertiliser plants, chemical tanks trains, vessels, etc.) Moreover, a biological threat could specifically play on the anxiety of the populations confronted by images of the great pandemics of the past (plague, cholera, Spanish flu, etc.), which could raise the prospect of real panic effects, whatever the nature of an agent released in a major urban centre or during a major international event (the Olympic games, for example). Urban areas are the most vulnerable zone for such types of threat and, within these, places where the concentration of people is the most dense, e.g., metros, shopping centres, tower blocks, sport stadiums, theatres, etc.

Other characteristics which make these weapons particularly suited to terrorist actions are:

- The absence of reliable detection systems for some chemical and biological agents.
- The minimal "traceability" of some agents.
- The relative facility with which it is possible to make such substances, especially when compared with the difficulty of the same for a nuclear weapon.
- The delay, which varies with the agents, between their dissemination and the moment when they produce their first effects on the victims, which enables the perpetrators to make their escape.
- Their capacity to spread terror and panic amongst the civil population.
- The possibility to do serious harm to a potentially more powerful adversary by inflicting heavy civilian or military losses, or disorganising his economy.

Geostrategic considerations can explain the fact that chemical and biological weapons constitute an attractive alternative for small terrorist groups. Hence, the concept currently in vogue in the United States of an "asymmetric war", born of the Gulf War, appears pertinent, and seems to be able to justify the theory according to which the Western countries—

and particularly the United States—by accentuating their conventional military superiority, incite their potential enemies to use such weapons. Unable to match their adversaries on the conventional military field, terrorist movements may place their hopes on the possibility of using a sufficiently credible threat.[3]

Many states, and not the smallest ones (one thinks obviously of the United States), now consider unconventional terrorism (essentially through chemical means) as one of the principal threats to international security and place this question at the heart of their strategic preoccupations. But other "candidates" could seriously compete for the use of such arms as the table below shows. The main ones are the cult terrorists, as Aum Shinrikyo demonstrated; but also political/religious group as the al-Qaida and now Daesh, which have largely used chlorine assaults notably in Iraq. Last but not the least, one cannot ignore the lone wolves and other "Mad Scientists" as proved by the "Amerithrax" attacks in 2001.

Groups Liable to Commit Acts of Unconventional Terrorism[4]

Group	Act
Political	Seek gain and/or psychological impact. Have an agenda and a code of negotiation. Execution of acts of mass destruction is difficult except in a situation of despair (rare).
Religious and millenarial, anarcho-rightists.	Seek the total destruction of adversary (Aum, Radical Islamists). AQ or Daesh are on the knife-edge between politics and sect—high probability.
Amateur, Lone Wolf (eg: Unabomber) and Mad Scientist (eg: Amerithrax)	Works over time and in secret. Very difficult to detect **Low probability—very dangerous.**
Venal	Blackmail of a state or an industry (frequent cases in Germany and Japan). Numerous cases.
Pariah state acting under cover of a third party.	Runs major risk of massive reprisals if discovered. Probability of identification high owing to long and porous chain of command. Exceptional.

How States and Societies Should Respond

On the issue of unconventional terrorism, political decision-makers and security forces are on the horns of a difficult dilemma. The events anticipated are categorised at a very low level on the scale of possibilities, whilst this potential threat must, all the same, be taken into account. Strategy is always the fruit of the consideration of a given threat and the available means. How can non-conventional terrorist threats be integrated into the order of priorities?

The good response seems to be the most appropriate as far as civil defence is concerned. The integration of emergency plans for such a threat into the general plans situates it as a serious event like all others, and thus treatable as such. Of course, as for all catastrophes, a threshold effect can lead to the disorganisation of the resources. Nevertheless, one would suggest that every system can be improved:[5]

- Reinforcement of the collective resources for rapid detection and for training.
- Improved capacity of the emergency teams to protect.
- Increased decontamination capabilities.
- Considerably reinforce the awareness and training of the hospital personnel involved.
- Improved capacity for the treatment of victims.
- Reinforce coordination and organisation of all the means available in the territory in order to maximise the impact of the national reaction.
- Develop, on a large scale, training and manoeuvres for testing the procedures and try to reduce the delay between aggression/identification and response.
- Give the population clear and comprehensive information (ignorance could lead to panic reactions).
- Increase R&D expenses.[6]
- Develop European and international cooperation which at present is not satisfactory. The risk of mass impact implies a mass response and certainly, the cooperation of allies in an emergency crisis would be necessary.

Globally, an effort should also be brought to bear on the development of the capacity of the states for the management of this type of crisis, on the ability to communicate effectively at the time of crisis and on an appropriate level and content of prior information.

At the international level, enhanced efforts have been made to reinforce cooperation against WMD terrorism. These include voluntary initiatives such as PSI (on maritime security and smuggling), G8 global partnership and global initiative to combat nuclear terrorism (2006) and specifically for addressing various facets of these composite threats. But the most interesting effort is the UN-1540 resolution which forbids the facilitation by any sponsor state for the production, development and use of WMD for use by terrorists. Moreover, this global prohibition is within the ambit of Chapter VII of the UN Charter which authorises the use of force in cases of non-compliance of this obligation by member states. This unique resolution has been extended for ten more years by resolution UN-1977. Another important step that was reached has been the adoption of the International Convention for the Suppression of Acts of Nuclear Terrorism (13 April 2005).[7] There are some technology control regimes such as the Nuclear Supplier Group (NSG), Australia Group (Chemical and Biological) and the Missile Technology Control Regime (MTCR) which now include the survey of unmanned vehicles which contribute strongly to global vigilance. Two, disarmament treaties play a role in the efforts against unconventional terrorism: Nuclear Proliferation Treaty (NPT), through the development of the International Atomic Energy Agency (IAEA) capabilities; Chemical Weapons Convention (CWC), which unfortunately does not have constraining measures and the Biological Weapons Convention (BWC). Every convention, which at the beginning was dedicated exclusively towards the military, has seen its mission extended to defend against unconventional terrorism.

Intelligence would be the essential element of all action plans, both national (including local) and international, which would have to rely on cooperation by specialised services. And in this matter, the development of autonomous intelligence capabilities is an absolute necessity.

Finally, one cannot end without standing up for the idea of having specialised offensive capabilities, not only for destroying terrorist groups wherever they may be, but above all, to cope with the "treatment" of NBC capabilities or installations (destruction, dismantling, removal). A specialised force would be required for the latter, as an ad hoc force could suffer harmful consequences (contamination, for example).

Conclusions: Prevent the Unspeakable and Anticipate the Improbable

In the range of non-conventional terrorism, it helps to distinguish two distinct approaches which will probably necessitate two types of reactions:

- The methods of terrorists who would use non-conventional means for traditional ends, with the aim of reinforcing their psychological and media impact.
- Those who would choose this approach in the hope of obtaining the maximum lethal effect; these would be very rare but also the most dangerous.

For the first category, of the three modes of terrorism described (chemical, biological and nuclear), chemical and radioactive dispersion appear as the two "ideal" methods. They bring together a limited lethal effect and maximum impact. The crisis which they would provoke can be managed, as much by the government attacked as by the terrorists themselves (limited consequences, possible negotiations, crisis bounded in space and time, media management).

The nuclear and biological options relate more to cults, religious fanatics and cranks of all kinds. These are the supposed weapons of mass destruction, even if their effects are not totally guaranteed. However, public opinion considers them as probable threats. Their use would result in the heaviest of reprisals. Although the nuclear option is very difficult toaccess, the biological one is much less so. Evidence of a smuggling market has been proved. The revelations of the former chief of the Pakistani nuclear programme, Dr Abdul Qadeer Khan, showed that the risk of dissemination of military or terrorist-used technologies has arisen from the companies involved.

While it does seem that the psychological barrier has not yet been crossed, nothing suggests that it would not be so in the future. As Ranstorp and Normak said, "We need to gain a better understanding of how the terrorists themselves perceive CBRN pathways, not as we perceive the technical revolutions and their impact on opportunities to commit mass-impact attacks (terrorist-cost-benefit calculations)."[8] As a matter of fact, most American authors consider such capability as a threat.[9] It could be a misperception. A key element in the appreciation would be the suicidal character of its potential users. Thus, the twin cases of nuclear and biological must be placed in the category of events of low probability of occurrence, but which cannot be totally discounted. This is a paradox in the case of biological weapons, which is that its execution is easy while the probability that it would happen is low. Would this paradox endure?

On the other hand, most experts place the highest probability on the use of chemical weapons by terrorists. The precedent of the Aum cult supports this analysis. And the evidence of the use or attempts to use against non-combatants have been identified (through chlorine barrel explosions) in the Chechen War, Iraq, Jordan (attempt), and now in Syria. The attacks on chemical plants or trains are also a credible hypothesis. Unfortunately, we have a good knowledge of the effects with the catastrophes of Bhopal (Madhya Pradesh, Union Carbide plant) in December 1984 (between 8000 and 20,000 estimated casualties); Toulouse (AZF plant in France) in October 2001 (35 fatalities, 2500 persons injured) and for trains, the catastrophe of Lac-Megantic in Quebec (Canada) where a 72 wagon-tank petrol train exploded on 6 July 2013, inside a small city (45 casualties).

An informed policy of prevention of unconventional terrorism cannot be conceived without a coordinated and concomitant action of the government actors involved. This action must bring together several approaches which should consist of:

- Preventing, or limiting as far as possible, terrorist access to technologies most likely to be used. This could only be achieved in the framework of an international policy of cooperation and coordination.
- Developing prompt methods of detection and ensuring their dissemination through the civil defence structure.
- Alerting civil defence personnel to problems through training methods and exercises. This step has widely begun in the United States and to a lesser extent in France.

Two, biological terrorism is a threat which must not be underestimated. However, terrorists need to overcome a large number of obstacles before being able to successfully conduct this type of operation. First, the difficulty in procuring an agent, then in its cultivation, packing for dissemination, deciding on the dose required to produce the desired effect and, finally, dissemination. Mastering the whole chain of competencies is not an easy matter and necessitates considerable financial resources. The difficulties inherent in the specific characteristics of biological agents render the concrete and efficient achievement of such an operation tricky. The vain attempts to disseminate biological agents by the members of the Aum cult in Tokyo in 1995 demonstrated this. But Daesh could be a good candidate for such an attempt because this organisation seeks the most ghastly means for terrorising.

Anyway, the hypothesis of an attack using biological agents remains plausible. The most dangerous case is the "Amerithrax" 2001 affair in the United States. At it seems clear now, the author was a former military scientist from the Fort Detrick laboratory who had been a military agent. This is the case of a mad scientist—well known in movies—who effectively uses his knowledge for terrorist aims. Terrorist groups would more likely turn to chemical weapons. Nonetheless, the perspective could change as a result of the spectacular development of techniques of molecular engineering and their increasing spread around the planet. This could only reinforce the idea of a biological threat growing by the day, so that it would be unreasonable to totally dismiss the possibility of a new biological attack.[10] Fortunately, response systems are evolving too as demonstrated by the control of the African Ebola epidemic in 2015 and the use of new medicines and the large development of P4 laboratories (with the capacity to manage the most dangerous virus or bacteria) and the training of civil security professionals and procedures. At present, with the development of numerous vaccines and procedures, there is reasonable confidence in the capacity to control a smallpox epidemic, which was absolutely impossible in 2001. But the same cannot be said about a pandemic of flu.

Therefore, our countries must prepare to confront a threat which, if it became reality—however small the probability—would nonetheless represent an intolerable blow to the social body and the state.[11] This low probability, and its high level of potential destruction, makes it one of the most difficult challenges for the services charged with the responsibility for the security of every country. Moreover, terrorists have time and (as proved by Daesh) no limits. To keep the guard high and to develop resilience are the key issues in the ability to tackle these dramatic challenges.

NOTES

1. This paper is a synthesis of various works issued by the FRS for the last 20 years. A first summary has been published: Jean-François Daguzan and Olivier Lepick, *Le terrorisme non conventionnel*, PUF, Paris, 2004, p. 152.
2. See the paragraph: "Al Qaida et les armes de destruction massive" (Al Qaida and the WMD Weapons) in Jean-François Daguzan, Terrorisme(s) abrégé d'une violence qui dure, CNRS Editions, Paris 2006, pp. 154-159. Gary Ackerman and Jeremy Tamsett (eds.), *Jihadists and Weapons of Mass Destruction*, Boca Raton, FL: CRS Press, 2009, 494 pages.
3. Benjamin Cole, *The Changing Face of Terrorism: How Real is the Threat from Biological, Chemical and Nuclear Weapons?* New York: I.B. Taurus, 2011, p. 320.
4. See, Brad Roberts (ed.), *Hype or Reality? The "New Terrorism" and Mass Casualty Attacks*, The Chemical and Biological Institute, Alexandria, VA, 2000.
5. Regarding the biological terrorism threat, between 2006 and 2009, FRS developed a European Union programme named BIO3R (Research, Reaction & Resilience) in order to address the solutions for enhancing the resilience of the society and organisation and the R&D pathways. We led a consortium of 19 European research centres and companies from 9 countries. Some recommendations come from the results of the study.
6. Stephen M. Maurer (ed.), *WMD Terrorism: Science and Policy Choices*, Cambridge, Mass., The MIT Press, 2009, p. 619.
7. http://legal.un.org/avl/ha/icsant/icsant.html
8. Magnus Rasntorp and Magnus Normak (eds.), Unconventional *Weapons and International Terrorism: Challenges and New Approaches*, Routledge, London & New York, 2009, p. 199.

9. See Michael Levi, *On Nuclear Terrorism*, Harvard Univ. Press, Cambridge Mass., 2007, p. 210 & Brian Michael Jenkins, *Will Terrorists go Nuclear?*, Prometheus Books, New York, 2008, p. 457.
10. See Andreas Wenger and Reto Wollenmann (eds.), *Bioterrorism: Confronting a Complex Threat*, Lynne Rienner Publishers, Boulder Col. & London, 2007, p. 203.
11. See R.J. Ursano, A.E. Norwood and C.S. Fullerton (eds.), *Bioterrorism, Psychological and Public Health Interventions*, Cambridge Univ. Press, 2004.

11

Anti-Piracy and Maritime Terrorism

Shekhar Sinha

Piracy and maritime terrorism on the high seas are not a new phenomenon. The scourge of piracy has been active, in varying measures, in every historical era. Whether it was piracy in the Mediterranean in the first century BCE, the dreaded *Vitalienbruder* in the Baltic and North Seas in the fifteenth century or the Barbary Corsairs of the eighteenth and nineteenth centuries, the activities of pirates have ebbed and flowed as a wave-like or cyclical phenomenon through the ages. The historical response to piracy has also varied from an initial neglect of the issue to a subsequent realisation of its severe implications; and finally, to the concerted "wars on piracy". Ultimately, pirate-hunting navies have been formed and have managed to successfully destroy and defeat the activities of the pirate organisations in every era. Yet, piracy has never been fully eradicated and tends to be a recurrent phenomenon.

History is also replete with examples, when efforts by the maritime powers of the time in curbing piracy, laid the grounds for those powers to establish their presence in the region. In most instances, this "presence" was followed by a subsequent subjugation of the regional powers. Roman operations against the Mediterranean pirates of the first century BCE led to the establishment of the Roman Empire in Cilicia (modern-day Turkey). French operations against the Barbary Corsair pirates laid the foundation for the subsequent occupation of Algeria. Closer home, the nationalist operations of Kanhoji Angre along the Konkan coast necessitated the British Navy to maintain a sustained presence; a subsequent reluctance to part with the assets acquired in those operations contributed to the rise of colonial India.

Presently, the Indian Ocean is viewed as a more "active" ocean than the Atlantic and Pacific oceans, as it hosts a spectrum of activities ranging from extensive trade and transportation to important energy transfers which are quantitative as well as qualitatively much larger in scope and size than in the other two oceans. Given that nearly 1,00,000 ships transit the expanse of the Indian Ocean annually, it is a very trade-busy ocean. It is perhaps the only ocean through which the SLOCs (Sea Lines of Communication) reach out to the entire world.

Significantly, some of the world's most important choke points and narrow passages provide access to the Indian Ocean, and these can have associated vulnerabilities. As such, the current accent on increasing globalisation has brought the attendant maritime security concerns to the fore. Thus, with a rising trajectory of seaborne trade which compliments this ascent, there seems to be a corresponding increase in asymmetric threats as well.

Incidents of transnational maritime crime such as modern piracy, maritime terrorism and drug running in their ever-evolving manifestations have emerged as the bane of the seafarer. As these maritime security challenges are essentially asymmetric in nature, there have been strident calls for effective law enforcement and maintenance of maritime order by all stakeholders.

This growing importance of seaborne trade, and the attendant rise in transnational threats, has also led to the adoption of enhanced cooperative approaches between the navies of various littoral countries in the form of numerous anti-piracy patrols that have resulted in the eventual decrease in the number of piracy attacks. But the challenge remains as attacks continue to take place at further ranges due to the usage of sophisticated technologies by the pirates and other non-state actors.

The concept of maritime security is one of the most recent additions to the vocabulary of international security. If security at sea used to be discussed within the framework of concepts such as seapower, maritime safety, or less frequently maritime terrorism, maritime security offers a new umbrella term, which to some degree replaces the older terms and discussions. The salience of maritime security is related to significant challenges such as maritime terrorism, and, perhaps most prominently, the challenges piracy poses to the maritime community.

Piracy is not the same as maritime terrorism. Piracy is mere robbery, and is unlikely to harm national interests. However, the moment a ship gets hijacked, the possibility of a terrorist act cannot be ignored. That it may not turn out to be so is not the issue; rather, it is that hijacking has the potential to become a terrorist act. Related to this, India remains very concerned about the proliferation of weapons of mass destruction (WMD). Some years ago, a North Korean ship was intercepted and arrested whilst carrying centrifuges to Pakistan. This highlights the need for an internationally accepted understanding of what is meant by maritime terrorism. India is also concerned about drug trafficking, as it is also clearly linked to arms smuggling, which is in turn linked to terrorism.

Geopolitical changes are reshaping the nature of the maritime commons. The global shift in maritime power thus harbours a strong potential for conflict and confrontation between regional powers and could slip out of control if caution is not exercised. The main reason for this scenario is the global diffusion of maritime power as a result of the "Rise of the Rest", which is above all, changing the geostrategic maritime balance. It would result in enabling new entrants to project power beyond their territorial waters. Inevitably, neighbouring countries would respond by strengthening their own power projection. The deep linkages of maritime terrorism and of "container security" were realised only after a search of a vessel by the US naval forces which yielded a group of al-Qaeda terrorists, who had been hiding inside a well-equipped shipping container.

A dramatic increase in containerised cargo and inadequate infrastructure to check all sealed containers led to the Container Security Initiative (CSI) and the requirement to make ports compliant with the International Ship and Port Facility Security Code (ISPS). But, a robust foolproof method against security lapses has yet to be arrived at. In the years to come, maritime terrorism is likely to manifest and evolve itself in many unique ways. The use of the seas as a supply-chain link for terror attacks on land-based targets is likely to be the chosen methodology of the terror outfits. While the seas ensure the easy passage of men and material for the attack, land provides them with the publicity and numbers of victims that are not available at sea. Hence the constabulary functions of maritime agencies are likely to see an enhancement with the growing demand for foolproof coastal security systems.

The recent years have seen an upsurge in piracy emanating from the Somalian waters into the Gulf of Aden. With its roots in the lack of governance and extreme poverty prevalent in the Somalian hinterland, this phenomenon has progressively expanded in geographical expanse as well as in its nature over the previous 5–6 years. As in the past, the initial international response to the incidents was, at best, muted with some sporadic anti-piracy efforts by the forces operating in the region. However, the increasing frequency of attacks, increasing capabilities of the pirates and the significant economic implications of the phenomenon have forced nations to take proactive measures to try and curb this menace.

While piracy is presently active in South East Asia and Africa, a key characteristic of Somali piracy is that, in a short amount of time, it has experienced a significant technological evolution. Initially, pirates operated dhows or fishing boats to assault vessels that came too close to the Somali coast. As commercial vessels improved their defences and stayed away from the Horn of Africa, pirates acquired better arms and faster and more powerful boats, which allowed them to seek targets further afield.

As operations became more organised and better funded, pirates invested in a mothership strategy involving a large pirate ship, located deep in the open ocean, serving as a base for a number of speed boats. Upon finding a suitable target, pirates would board speedboats and quickly approach and attempt to hijack the target ship. If captured, the vessel would then be directed to a pirate safe haven in Somalia, where it remained while ransom negotiations took place. The result of this technological and organisational evolution is that piracy increased dramatically in intensity, violence and geographical spread. Starting in 2004, attacks took place between 300 and 600 nautical miles from the coast and, after 2005, some attacks have taken place up to 800 nautical miles from the Somali coast. As the reach of piracy extended further and further into the Indian Ocean, ships were increasingly spending more time transiting in pirate-infested waters.

Piracy imposes two types of costs on maritime carriers. Direct cost is incurred in the event of pirate capture. Once a ship is captured, it is taken to the Somali coast where the cargo, crew and ship are taken hostage, often for long periods of time, while ransom is negotiated. Most hijacking cases are resolved with the ship, crew and cargo being returned to the owner once the ransom has been paid. Sometimes, captured vessels are retained and turned into pirate mother ships, or crew members are killed or die in captivity. It is estimated that at the peak of piracy, only 0.2 per cent of the ships passing through the Gulf of Aden were boarded by pirates. Nonetheless, the substantially high costs of capture have imposed increased operating costs on all transiting ships. These include a higher risk premium on insurance as well as on increased wages and benefits to crews as a result of the risk of being attacked, taken hostage, or even killed. They must also engage in other defensive measures such as hiring security forces, increasing travel speed in pirate waters with the consequent increases in fuel use and modifying ships to make them less likely to be hijacked. It is estimated that shipping costs through the Gulf of Aden have gone up by 8–13 per cent following the increase of pirate activity.

Maritime piracy emanating from the Gulf of Aden is thus now a constant irritant for merchant traffic in one of the world's busiest international shipping lanes (ISLs), which sees over 24,000 ships navigating the Gulf of Aden annually. The international response to piracy has included multinational efforts by the US-led forces in the region (CTF 151), NATO Standing Maritime Groups and EUNAVFOR operations (Operation Atalanta). The UN, on its part, has passed several resolutions against piracy in the region and has authorised foreign powers to operate in consultation with Somalia's Transitional Federal Government, and to take measures as required to curb the activities of the pirates. The UN Resolution 1851, passed in December 2008, has permitted countries to enter the Somalian territorial waters to chase pirates with the sanction of the country's transitional government. However, to date, no UN-led Anti-Piracy Force has been formed in the region.

In addition to these multinational efforts, there are several anti-piracy and escort operations being conducted independently by various navies to effectively safeguard their respective merchant marine. This includes the navies of countries such as India, Russia, China, Japan and the Republic of Korea (ROK), which, due to domestic political compulsions or other factors, have chosen not to join the international coalition forces. This has resulted in an upsurge in the presence of foreign navies in the Gulf of Aden, attracting concern from the Indian strategic thinkers about the long-term impact of this phenomenon.

The Contact Group of Piracy off the Coast of Somalia (CGPCS) was set up in January 2009 to "foster closer international cooperation to address the scourge of piracy off the coast of Somalia", following the adoption of the UN Security Council Resolution, 1851. However, it was established outside the formal UN framework to maintain a high degree of flexibility. It presently includes over 80 participants including states, international organisations and representatives from the industry and seafarers.

India has been a founding member of the CGPCS. Brazil, China and Russia are also member states of the CGPCS. Indian naval officers have participated in the working group meetings for military coordination and regional capacity-building and the plenary meetings. The forum has given India an opportunity to present its efforts in sustained counter-piracy operations. These operations led by the Indian Navy (IN) and the Indian

Coast Guard (ICG) have resulted in shrinking the piracy-affected areas to primarily off the coast of Somalia.

Regional Cooperation Agreement on Combating Piracy and Armed Robbery against Ships in Asia (ReCAAP) is a government-to-government agreement to promote and enhance cooperation against piracy which came into force in September 2006 amongst ten Asian countries, including India. The ReCAAP Information Sharing Centre (ISC) was established in 2006. The Maritime Rescue Coordination Centre at Mumbai is the focal point for ReCAAP in India. The role of ReCAAP ISC is to serve as a platform for information exchange with the ReCAAP focal points, facilitate capacity-building efforts and cooperate with organisations and like-minded parties.

The Indian Navy also has periodic dialogues with the European Union–EUNAVFOR on the issue of counter-piracy. The first dialogue took place in India in December 2011 and the second dialogue was held at Brussels (EU HQ) and Northwood (OHQ EUNAVFOR) in September 2013.

Another initiative to counter piracy has been the introduction of group transits where vessels are coordinated to transit through high-risk areas under escort, in suitable time-windows. The naval presence in this region is driven by economic imperatives as well as an underlying desire to establish the emergence of the European Union as an effective concert of nations, capable of delivering a coordinated military effect when required. Given the huge financial costs of the operations and the specific tasking, the presence of the EU forces in the region may reduce once the piracy is brought under control.

The threat of piracy in the Gulf of Aden has also spawned the rise of private maritime security companies (PMSC), privately contracted armed security personnel (PCASP) and floating armouries. These oceangoing armouries are the by-product of global trade, high-seas piracy and national arms restrictions. Shippers traversing the dangerous waters off Somalia want armed guards to protect their cargo and crews, but most countries do not permit private security forces to bring guns into their ports. Ships have now appeared to cache weapons offshore for the security companies and ferry guns and guards to the vessels needing protection. The shipping industry once regarded armed guards on vessels as too dangerous. But the spate of Somali pirate attacks has changed that thinking.

Every month now, thousands of weapons pass through the Indian Ocean and hundreds of security teams rotate on and off ships in the Gulf of Oman. A similar trade goes on in the Red Sea and off Sri Lanka. It is estimated that the international shipping industry spent around $1 billion on armed guards and equipment in the Indian Ocean in 2014. There is no official record of how many armouries exist or who operates them, nor are there any regulatory bodies overseeing such enterprises in international waters since international standards for the private security firms do not address floating armouries.

The armouries themselves could be targets for attack by pirates or terrorists. In India's view, these armouries present a security risk, and it is thus pushing the International Maritime Organisation (IMO), a United Nations agency, to develop guidelines for regulating the industry. The IMO has issued circulars stipulating the guidelines in this regard and ISO standards have also been promulgated. In addition to the MV Enrica Lexie incident of the shooting of Indian fishermen in 2012, the MV Seaman Guard Ohio, a floating armoury was operating in the Indian EEZ since July 2013 till its detention on 12 Oct 2013.

In 2010–11, incidents of piracy extended to new areas in the East Arabian Sea. In order to counter this trend, the Indian Navy and Indian Coast Guard substantially increased their anti-piracy deployments in the East Arabian Sea. The Indian Navy apprehended four pirate mother ships in 2011. A total of 120 pirates were apprehended and 74 fishermen were rescued in these operations.

Due to the concerted efforts of 49 Indian naval ships deployed in the Gulf of Aden since October 2008, the Indian Navy has now established itself as one of the leading navies in the fight against maritime terrorism and piracy. In addition to escorting Indian flagged vessels, ships of other flags have also been escorted by the Indian naval ships. Till January 2015, a total of 3,066 ships have been escorted by the Indian Navy in the Gulf of Aden. During deployments for the anti-piracy operations, the Indian naval ships have so far thwarted 40 pirate attempts on merchant vessels.

India's Maritime Military Strategy, aptly titled "Freedom to Use the Seas", highlights the tenets of maritime cooperation and increased inter-operability with regional as well as extra-regional navies. It explicitly states: "(E)xercising linkages with countries located astride the maritime choke points in the IOR is an important goal for Naval foreign cooperation." It further states that "(A)nother important factor of foreign cooperation is the need to standardise procedures and achieve inter-operability in maritime areas ranging from disaster relief to anti-piracy missions and non-combatant casualty evacuation operations. These imperatives demand close engagement with advanced regional navies as also extra-regional ones." The Indian Navy therefore needs to proactively follow this aspect of its maritime strategy by evolving an innovative plan that blends joint military exercises, security agreements and intelligence-sharing. A network of cooperative partnerships with the IOR nations and extra-regional powers would serve to increase India's influence in the region, create a safety cushion and provide more strategic space and autonomy.

The Indian Ocean Rim Association for Regional Cooperation (IOR-ARC), which was set up in 1995, was not able to address the maritime security issues in our region. The "security vacuum" within the IOR-ARC has now been effectively addressed by India's initiation of the Indian Ocean Naval Symposium (IONS) in 2008, which could be used for consolidating the IOR maritime security and anti-piracy institutional mechanisms. This is an important initiative which could be vital for the Indian Navy's role in the region. While the IONS has been envisaged primarily for fostering the informal navy-to-navy interactions, it could also serve as a medium to facilitate a greater military cooperation between the IOR navies, without forming a dedicated military bloc. The challenge for the IONS would be to cooperate and collaborate to ensure the establishment of a maritime security framework for this region, which could function effectively at the "ground level", despite the political limitations or differences between the regional stakeholders. Some key initiatives for the success of the IONS initiative would include the preparation of the necessary legal instruments for a regional anti-piracy cooperation, confidence-building measures (CBMs) between member navies, collaborative capacity building and the establishment of a shared Maritime Domain Awareness.

Given its existing infrastructure, the Indian Navy could take the lead in emerging as q "hub" for sharing the comprehensive Maritime Domain Awareness in the IOR between India and IONS navies and the multitude of forces operating in the region, with an aim to ensure an effective monitoring of the region and the conduct of coordinated anti-piracy operations. The Indian Navy already enjoys a favourable international reputation for effective anti-piracy policing and operations. This confidence is reflected in the noticeable shifting of the traffic patterns in the IOR. Ships transiting towards Malacca from the Gulfs of Aden and Hormuz are now sailing close to the Indian coast before heading southwards, despite the financial implications of this detour. Robust, proactive and effective actions in anti-piracy operations would further serve to cement the standing of the Indian Navy in the international community. A proactive media campaign about its successes in anti-piracy operations would also help to further this aim.

Presently, the initiative in anti-piracy operations has, to a large extent, been seized by the Western navies. The US-led CTF 151 includes over twenty ships from NATO countries and other US allies, while Operation Atalanta under EUNAVFOR involves 5–10 ships, auxiliaries and maritime patrol aircraft from thirteen EU and non-EU nations. Domestic political compulsions preclude India from joining a NATO or US-led coalition. The Indian Navy could take the lead in setting up regional mechanisms that ensure coordinated escort and anti-piracy operations in the open waters of the Western Arabian Sea; if necessary, under the aegis of the UN.

A Counter Piracy Shared Awareness and De-confliction (SHADE) Meeting initiative was taken to "bring together" the naval forces operating in the support of anti-piracy operations in the Gulf of Aden with the prime objective of building a shared awareness and a de-conflicting deployment of surface and air assets in the international anti-piracy efforts. As part of the de-conflicting charter, convoy coordination is undertaken during the quarterly SHADE meetings. The origin of the meeting was the need for communication/information-sharing amongst the forces deployed in the region. SHADE meetings are being held since Jan 2009, and Indian naval representatives have been attending since April 2009.

In view of the overall improvement in the pirate situation since 2011, there has been a progressive reduction in the numbers of ships being escorted in the International Recommended Traffic Corridor (IRTC) by the national convoys. A SHADE analysis of Convoy Coordination has highlighted that in November 2014 only 9 per cent ships chose to use national convoys as against 17 per cent in November 2011. During September 14–November 14, Indian naval ships have on an average undertaken about 12 escorts per month, with an average of about 25 ships being escorted.

The UNCLOS states that all states are duty-bound to "cooperate" and do their best to counter piratical attacks. However, there is no legal obligation on the part of the individual states to prosecute the captured pirates under universal jurisdiction or under their domestic laws. The UNCLOS does not lay down any stipulation regarding the adoption of criminal laws by states and leaves it to the states to lay down anti-piracy laws. As a result, many states treat piracy cases as certain ordinary criminal acts. At present, the prosecution of captured pirates is a serious challenge to the nations worldwide. It is reported that around 85 per cent of the pirates encountered are not prosecuted. A lack of adequate and stringent laws is the primary reason for the discharging of pirates. In light of the recent requirement for an anti-piracy law, an anti-piracy bill was tabled in the Indian Parliament in April 2012, which is still in the pipeline.

The best management practices (BMP) for protection against piracy, promulgated by a consortium of stakeholders operating in the Gulf of Aden, defines a high risk area (HRA) as an area where pirate activity or attacks have taken place. The HRA has presently been defined as an area bound by the Suez and the Strait of Hormuz to the North, 10ºS and 78ºE. The eastern limit of the piracy HRA was extended to 78ºE longitude in June 2010. This expansion was done considering the extended reach of pirates in the Central and Eastern Arabian Sea, using mother ships, which converted the existing "Reporting Areas" East of 65ºE Longitude also into a "Piracy High Risk Area". The extended HRA now covers the entire Arabian Sea, including the Indian EEZ and coast.

Consequent to the assertive actions by the IN and ICG, there have been no piratical attacks east of 65ºE since April 2012. The last pirate incident, which was successful in the East Arabian sea, was of MV Eglantine on 26 March 2012 which was 280 nm from Male (440 nm from Thiruvananthapuram). The present HRA, which extends to areas within which no piratical activity has been recorded since May 2012, i.e. east of 65ºE till 78ºE, has resulted in the re-routing of the east-bound merchant shipping close to the Indian coast. It is pertinent that ships transiting in these areas continue to be governed by the permissive ROE (rules of engagement), thus endangering local fishermen. It has also given rise to higher costs to the shipping industry in terms of insurance, hiring of private security, transit at "uneconomical" speeds and floating armouries.

Although the HRA extends till 78ºE, the current deployment of multinational forces off the coast of Somalia, the Gulf of Aden and off Oman and Yemen clearly indicates that the military assessment of a pirate risk is limited to the western areas of the current HRA. As a result of no piratical attacks east of the 65ºE line, India has regularly taken up the issue of the revision of the HRA in various international forums since 2012. At an ad hoc meeting to discuss the HRA, under the aegis of the CGPCS on 26 October 2014 at Dubai, India has found support from Bangladesh, Egypt, France, Mauritius, Russia, Saudi Arabia and Seychelles.

The Indian Navy is one of the instruments of state policy for meeting India's strategic aims in this region. Within the parameters of the envisaged Indian Grand Strategy, the Indian Navy needs to take bold and proactive initiatives to *Engage and Assert* itself in the region, and to leverage the advantages that it enjoys by virtue of its geographical location and force levels. An effective employment of the Indian Navy's sustained reach and operability in the region would be the most effective demonstrator of India's natural maritime leadership in the Arabian Sea and the Indian Ocean. Instead of an undue alarm over the maritime security scenario in the region, a dynamic leadership, proactive engagement, increased maritime domain awareness and an effective deployment of Indian maritime assets for maritime security operations, would further enhance India's influence in the region. A central agency is the need of the hour with all stakeholders being under one organisation. At the moment, the navy, coast guard, shipping customs, revenue intelligence, port authorities and marine police apart from the intelligence agencies, all tend to operate in their own silos leaving large gaps in the implementation of the directives of the Cabinet Committee on Security (CCS). There is a need for a mechanism to control all the multifarious agencies under one umbrella—that of the National Security Advisor (NSA); maybe he should have a Maritime Assistant to help him run this mechanism.

12

Countering Maritime Terrorism Against India:

Challenges and Opportunities

Rahul Roy-Chaudhury

Maritime terrorism relates to the use of the sea to carry out a terror attack on land or a terror attack at sea against a ship or an offshore site. The aim is to maximise casualties and publicity. This is quite distinct from piracy, which relates to the hijacking of a ship in international waters for financial reasons. Maritime terrorism is politically driven whereas piracy is essentially criminally motivated.

Indeed, criminal syndicates and sea-based smuggling routes have more links to maritime terrorism than piracy. Smugglers can be given assistance and facilities in exchange for the infiltration of terrorists and the landing of explosives, arms and ammunition on the target coast.

India's Maritime Terror Attacks

India's first maritime terror attack took place in Mumbai on 12 March 1993. This has also been India's deadliest terror attack to date, with 13 bomb blasts killing 257 people and injuring 713 others. This attack was masterminded by the noted crime chief Dawood Ibrahim and his criminal syndicate. This took place through the illegal smuggling of a large quantity of arms including AK-56 rifles, pistols, hand-grenades and RDX explosives into India through the sea. These were landed at the Dighi jetty and the

Shekhadi coast in Maharashtra in January–February 1993. The courts subsequently awarded the death sentence to Yaqub Memon, who was found guilty of conspiracy and of financing the blasts, along with 30 life imprisonments and sentences of varying terms of imprisonment to 46 others (including a Bollywood film star).[1] But, the principal conspirator—and now India's most-wanted terrorist—Dawood Ibrahim, still remains at large, widely believed to be based in Pakistan with the support of Pakistan's security establishment.

Yet, seven years after the March 1993 attacks, it seemed no lessons had been learnt nor any serious attempt made to overhaul India's coastal security. In a damning indictment on the state of coastal security, the Group of Ministers (GoM) report on "Reforming the National Security System"of the previous Bharatiya Janata Party (BJP)-led National Democratic Alliance (NDA) government noted (in February 2001) that "India's long coastline and coastal areas have remained largely unprotected and unguarded".[2] It went on to say that "little has been done over the years to understand or take action to create the infrastructure for the protection of India's vast coastal areas".[3]

The GoM report also explicitly stated that

> trained saboteurs and terrorists are prevailed upon to carry drugs for sustenance and operational expenses from the sale proceeds. Passage to couriers of contraband is often conditional to carrying and delivering of arms and ammunition. Smugglers are given assistance and facilities, in exchange of services for organising infiltration of terrorists and saboteurs and landing of explosives, arms and ammunition. A smuggler-drug trafficker-militant nexus engaged in anti-national activities has emerged.[4]

It also noted the need for greater clarity in the role of the state governments vis-à-vis the coast guard for "shallow water surveillance of the coasts".[5]

As a result, the GoM report recommended the strengthening of the coast guard and the establishment of a specialised marine police in all the coastal states and island territories, which was approved by the Cabinet Committee on Security (CCS) on 11 May 2001.[6] Yet, implementation was mixed and following the election of the new Congress-led United Progressive Alliance (UPA) government three years later in May 2004, these reforms did not appear to have the requisite political support.

It was under these circumstances that India's second maritime terror attack took place again in Mumbai from 26–28 November 2008, when ten terrorists of the Pakistan-based Lashkar-e-Taiba (LeT), linked to Pakistan's Inter-Service Intelligence (ISI), used the sea to kill 166 people. With nine of the terrorists killed in the ensuing firefight, the tenth, Ajmal Kasab, was found guilty of murder and waging war against India, and hanged in Pune in November 2012.

Soon after the 2008 Mumbai terror attacks, the UPA government undertook a major overhaul of India's coastal and maritime security, whose inadequacy enabled the terrorists to reach Mumbai's shores. Facing considerable criticism for the lack of coastal security, Indian naval chief, Admiral Sureesh Mehta, acknowledged a "systemic failure" but maintained that neither the navy nor the coast guard had received any actionable intelligence from the country's intelligence services. Subsequently, on 28 February 2009, the then Defence Minister, A.K. Antony announced five key steps to bolster coastal security.

First: The navy is now designated as the nodal authority, responsible for overall maritime security, both coastal and offshore. The navy is to be assisted in these tasks by the coast guard, the state marine police and state agencies.

Second. The coast guard is to be additionally responsible for security in the areas patrolled by the marine police, from the shoreline to 12 nautical miles. The Director General, Coast Guard is to be designated as Commander, Coastal Command, and responsible for the overall coordination between the central and state agencies in all matters relating to coastal security. A new coast guard regional headquarters in Gujarat, under the newly-created post of Commander Coast Guard, North-West, has been established to look after the surveillance of the coastal state. In addition, nine coast guard stations have been set up at Karwar, Ratnagiri, Vadinar, Gopalpur, Minicoy, Androth, Karaikal, Hutbay and Nizamapatnam, integrated with coastal police stations and police check posts.

Third: In order to coordinate the navy–coast guard functions better, Joint Operation Centres (JOC) have been set up at Mumbai, Visakhapatnam, Kochi and Port Blair under the charge of the existing naval commanders-in-chief, designated as commanders-in-chief of coastal defence. These centres are jointly manned and operated by the navy and coast guard with inputs from the central and state intelligence and other agencies, with the navy controlling all the joint operations with the coast guard.

Fourth: The coast guard and marine police are being strengthened and expanded. A new air squadron with Dornier maritime surveillance aircraft has been activated in Porbandar in Gujarat. The navy has been provided a new specialised force, the *Sagar Prahari Bal* (Maritime Protection Force), comprising 1,000 personnel and 80 fast interception craft for protecting naval assets and bases. The coast guard is acquiring additional ships, aircraft and helicopters, as its fleet is inadequate for its tasks. The intelligence set-up of the coast guard has also been improved.

Fifth: A national command, control, communication and intelligence network for real-time maritime domain awareness between the operations rooms of the navy and the coast guard has been established (see below). A chain of radar stations is being set up on the coast and island territories to include sensors for the identification of vessels near the coast. A vessel and air traffic management system for all offshore development areas is being carried out.[7] In August 2009, the Indian navy's official Maritime Doctrine therefore incorporated new constabulary missions for the navy, including counter-terrorism and anti-piracy operations.[8]

Nonetheless, in a reminder of India's continued maritime vulnerability, in late December 2014, a Pakistani fishing boat believed by the Indian government to display suspicious activities and to carry explosives, was intercepted by the Indian coast guard and navy near the India–Pakistan maritime border. After a chase, there was an explosion and the boat sank; an internal Indian Defence Ministry enquiry is ongoing over the circumstances of the sinking. The Indian Defence Minister said that the four men on the boat—all reported to have died—were suspected terrorists and not smugglers at sea.[9] In late April 2015, the Indian Navy and coast guard in a joint operation seized two suspicious Pakistani boats off the Porbandar coast, one of them allegedly carrying over 140 kg of heroin.[10]

Continuing Concerns

India continues to remain highly vulnerable to another maritime terror attack due to the growing complexity of the maritime security environment as well as the continuing concerns over state-sponsored cross-border maritime terrorism. India shares maritime boundaries with seven countries: Pakistan in the Arabian Sea; the Maldives and Sri Lanka in the Indian Ocean; and Bangladesh, Myanmar, Thailand and Indonesia in the Bay of Bengal. India also has a long coastline reaching deep into the Indian Ocean.

The dominance of an experienced maritime community could provide the potential for the next terror attack against India, amidst state support and the rise of religious extremism. While security threats from Pakistan continue, Bangladesh is currently seeing the rise of Islamic extremism alongside the anti-India Bangladesh National Party (BNP)–Jamaat-e-Islami (JeI) opposition alliance, despite Prime Minister Sheikh Hasina's best efforts. The Maldives is also witnessing Islamic radicalisation and extremism.

As the most effective "non-state" navy, the Tamil Sea Tigers have shown that technological developments have made it possible for even a small group to acquire "asymmetric" capabilities at relative modest costs. Fast boats, global positioning system (GPS)-based navigation, inexpensive maps and charts are today within easy reach.

Maritime Domain Awareness

Yet, new and emerging opportunities to counter maritime terrorism need to be exploited. Maritime Domain Awareness (MDA) is fundamental. This essentially relates to the development of a comprehensive operational picture in near-real time to allow the control of surveillance and response assets and rapid response to events. There has been considerable progress on this issue, but far more still needs to be done.

Late last year, the Indian Navy set up the Information Management and Analysis Centre (IMAC) with the coast guard, to function under the National Security Advisor (NSA). This joint operations facility is the nodal centre of the National Command Control Communications and Intelligence Network (NC3I Network), which links 20 Indian Navy and 31 coast guard stations located along the coast and on island territories, providing coastal surveillance information.[11] Transponders for identification are now mandatory for all merchant ships above 300 tonnes, through the Automatic Identification System (AIS) and the Long-Range Identification and Tracking System (LRIT)—a satellite-based, real-time mechanism for reporting the position of ships. There are 74 AIS receivers along the Indian coast capable of tracking 30,000 to 40,000 merchant ships transiting through the Indian Ocean.[12] There is now a compulsory identity card for fishermen; registration of over 2,00,000 fishing boats has begun; security awareness programmes are being held and joint navy-coast guard exercises to counter terrorism have taken place with the involvement of local fishermen.[13] The navy also plans to fit transponders on the boats that sail on the waters along the Bangladesh coast for real-time locations tracked by the IMAC, along with the provision of biometric cards to fishermen for security purposes.[14]

Another key aspect of MDA is the analysis of trends, operating patterns and target behaviour by expert intelligence staff. This requires far greater civil–military cooperation, especially among their intelligence agencies. How does one, for example, characterise unusual or suspicious movements and activities at sea? How does one best and quickly differentiate between smugglers and terrorists?

In essence, far more needs to be done to ensure the effective surveillance of India's coast and Exclusive Economic Zone (EEZ). The electronic tracking system for merchant vessels needs to be widened as well as deepened to provide a more comprehensive picture, including crew detail. This could take place through the exploitation of new and emerging commercially available technologies. AIS systems are vulnerable to "data manipulation", with a notable increase in the number of ships reporting false identities. Some 40 per cent of ships do not report their next port of call.[15] Moreover, as many as 3,00,000 fishing boats operate off the Indian coast.[16] Coordination among India's maritime state governments and marine police also needs to be bolstered.

International Cooperation

There is also scope for a wider and deeper international cooperation. India is currently in talks with some two dozen countries for the exchange of information on shipping.[17] Significantly, a trilateral agreement on maritime security cooperation was signed in July 2013 by India, Sri Lanka and the Maldives. Focusing on counter-terrorism, it significantly enhances cooperation in the MDA, strengthens mechanisms for EEZ surveillance and enhances the sharing of intelligence on illegal maritime activities. India is to share with Sri Lanka and the Maldives its Long Range Identification and Tracking (LRIT) data services for both countries to monitor and track their own flagged merchant vessels, along with the provision of the MDA training and Merchant Ship Information System (MSIS) software. At the same time, both Sri Lanka and the Maldives have agreed to share intelligence on illegal maritime activities on a regular basis.[18]

The Indian Navy's electronic surveillance network also remains connected to the radars installed on 26 atolls in the Maldives. Both Mauritius and Seychelles, which had attended the March 2014 trilateral meeting as guest countries, could also be formally brought into such a cooperative arrangement. But, the effective implementation and expansion of this cooperation inherently requires strong bilateral relations. It was notable that Indian Prime Minister Modi cancelled his scheduled visit to the Maldives in mid-March due to political differences with the Maldivian government.

Conclusion

India remains highly vulnerable to another maritime terror attack. The maritime security environment in both the Arabian Sea and the Bay of Bengal has become more complex, and concerns over state-sponsored cross-border maritime terrorism continue. Yet, new and emerging opportunities to counter these threats need to be exploited. National Maritime Domain Awareness (NDMA) is fundamental. Coastal security needs to be enhanced through improved and coordinated marine police, navy-coast guard and centre–state interactions. Commercially available technology and commercial sources of data need to be further utilised. There is scope for greater international cooperation. But, all this can only be effective if there is better sharing of information and intelligence, as well as coordination on operational matters, among the Indian civilian and military organisations and agencies.

NOTES

1. India Abroad News Service, "1993 Bombay Blasts: Supreme Court upholds Death for Yakub Memon", 21 March 2013, at http://www.ndtv.com/india-news/1993-bombay-blasts-supreme-court-upholds-death-for-yakub-memon-516893
2. Recommendations of the Group of Ministers, "Reforming the National Security System", February 2001, Declassified Version, p. 61.
3. Ibid., p. 70.
4. Ibid., p. 61.
5. Ibid.
6. Press Information Bureau (PIB) Release, 23 May 2001, at http://pib.nic.in/archieve/lreleng/lyr2001/rmay2001/23052001/r2305200110.html. Group of Ministers' Report on "Reforming The National Security System"
7. Rahul Roy-Chaudhury and Antoine Levesques, "India's Concerns and Responses to the 'War on Terror'" in Rachel E. Utley (ed.), *9/11 Ten years After: Problems and Perspectives*, 2012, Ashgate, Farnham, pp. 129-130.
8. The International Institute for Strategic Studies, *The Military Balance*, Volume 110, Issue 1, 2010, Taylor & Francis, Abingdon, p.336.
9. Rajat Pandit, "Parrikar on Pakistani Boat Evidence shows Suspected Terror Link", http://timesofindia.indiatimes.com/india/Parrikar-on-Pakistani-boat-Evidence-shows-suspected-terror-link/articleshow/45756430.cms, 5 January 2015.
10. Press Trust of India, "Two Suspicious 'Pak' Boats with Heroin seized near Gujarat, 8 Held", *Indian Express*, 21 April 2015, at http://indianexpress.com/article/india/india-others/pakistani-vessel-with-8-smugglers-intercepted-off-porbandar-coast/
11. Dinakar Peri, "IMAC will Help Navy Step Up Coastal Surveillance", *The Hindu*, 22 November 2014, at http://www.thehindu.com/news/national/imac-will-help-navy-step-up-coastal-surveillance/article6622612.ece
12. Vijay Sakhuja, "India Reinforces Maritime Domain Awareness but Challenges

Remain", 6 January 2015, at http://isnblog.ethz.ch/security/india-reinforces-maritime-domain-awareness-but-challenges-remain

13. Ibid.
14. "Navy Plan for Fisherman", *The Telegraph*, 19 May 2015, at http://www.telegraphindia. com/1150519/jsp/bengal/story_20876.jsp#.VW7KeqNwaP8
15. Vijay Sakhuja, op.cit.
16. Ministry of Shipping, http://www.iss-shipping.com/Microsites/Document%20Library/Navigating%20off%20the%20Indian%20Coast%20-%20Transgressing%20of%20Fishing%20Nets%20-%20Mistaking%20Fishing%20Boat%20with%20Pirates%20Skiffs.pdf, 7 March 2012.
17. Vijay Sakhuja, op.cit.
18. See NSA-level meeting on trilateral Maritime Security Cooperation between India, Sri Lanka and Maldives, at http://www.mea.gov.in/pressreleases.htm?dtl/23037/NSA+level+meeting+on+trilateral+Maritime+Security+Cooperation+between+India+Sri+Lanka+and+Maldives, 6 March 2014.

13

Talibanisation of the Pakistan-Afghanistan Region:

State Sponsors and Non-State Actors

Christian Wagner

After more than 20 years of Talibanisation of the Afghanistan–Pakistan region, there are many indications that the strategy has failed in various ways. The support of the Pakistani army and its Inter-Services Intelligence (ISI) for the Taliban may have brought some short-term success, for instance when the Taliban took over Kabul in 1996. But the long-term effects and repercussions on the global, regional and national levels have largely been counterproductive.

The process of Talibanisation was the outcome of two developments. First, the process of Islamisation in Pakistan that started after the military defeat of 1971 under the Bhutto government and which was intensified under the military rule of Zia-ul-Haq after 1977. The second thread was the strategy of the Pakistani armed forces to use non-state actors as part of its military strategy against India. This started in 1947 when tribal warriors were led by Pakistani officers in Kashmir. The strategy failed in 1965 but was successfully applied in the fight against the former Soviet Union in Afghanistan in the 1980s. It reached a new momentum in the 1990s when the Pakistani military tried to transfer the strategy as an instrument in its struggle against India over Kashmir. But the military planners have never been able to control the different militant groups and have underestimated the repercussions on Pakistani society. This has led to various negative effects for Pakistan on the global, regional and national levels.

The Global Level

Since the mid-2000s, it became clear that Pakistan and the international community were pursuing different strategies in the war on terrorism in Afghanistan. The International Security Assistance Forces (ISAF) that intervened in Afghanistan after 9/11 and the Afghan National Army (ANA) targeted all militant groups, whereas Pakistan differentiated between "good" and "bad" Taliban. The "good" Taliban included Mullah Omar and the Quetta Shura, the Haqqani network and warlords like Gulbuddin Hekmatyar. The Pakistani army regarded these groups as assets through which it aimed to secure its strategic interests in Afghanistan. The "bad" Taliban included different armed groups that formed the Tehrik-e-Taliban Pakistan (TTP) under the leadership of Baitullah Mehsud in December 2007.

In August 2007, President Musharraf conceded some support for the Afghan Taliban in Pakistan whereas the Taliban commanders and NATO have reported direct links with the ISI. The differentiation between "good" (Afghan) Taliban who serve Pakistan's interest in Afghanistan and "bad" (Pakistan) Taliban who fought the Pakistani forces and who wanted to establish an Islamic State has been artificial because the different groups entertain various organisational and ideological linkages.

Pakistan's double game has contributed to a loss of trust especially vis-à-vis the Western countries. Moreover, the deteriorating security situation in Pakistan has created the image of a failed state. Although Pakistan has faced Western sanctions because of its nuclear programme since the early 1990s and because of Musharraf's military coup in 1999, the United States continued their military cooperation. Pakistan remained an important ally because the major supply lines for Western troops in Afghanistan went through Pakistan. Moreover, the security of the nuclear assets remained an overarching security concern for the United States in its relationship with Pakistan. With the dismantlement of the A.Q. Khan network in 2003–04, the danger of nuclear proliferation from Pakistan became a serious concern for Western security experts.

Pakistan's "state of denial" regarding the Taliban may have also affected the country's credibility in another more important field of its foreign policy, i.e. Kashmir. Pakistan has always tried to internationalise the conflict with India and wanted the international community to intervene. But all great powers, including Pakistan's all-weather friend China, have made it clear that they see bilateral talks between India and Pakistan as the only way to solve outstanding issues.

The Regional Level

The support of the Taliban has served several purposes for Pakistan. In the beginning, the main goal was to achieve "strategic" depth vis-à-vis India. Another aspect was that the Taliban should curb Iran's influence in Afghanistan. Finally, there was the expectation that the unsolved border question, i.e. the recognition of the Durand Line by Afghanistan could be settled with the Taliban. The governments in Kabul had never recognised the border, have vetoed Pakistan's entry into the United Nations (UN) and had repeatedly raised territorial claims on the Pashtun areas in the north-western part of Pakistan. But even during their rule in Kabul between 1996 and 2001, the Taliban refused to recognise the border. Therefore, Pakistan and Afghanistan could never agree on an effective border management.

The porous border was used by all the conflicting parties. The Afghan Taliban groups used their safe havens in the tribal areas in Pakistan for their attacks in Afghanistan. The TTP established sanctuaries in the Taliban-controlled areas in eastern Afghanistan and started to attack the Pakistani forces from there. This has further increased the mistrust between both countries.

Pakistan also could not prevent India gaining influence in Afghanistan despite various attacks on Indian installations by the Lashkar-e-Taiba (LeT). India became the largest bilateral donor in Afghanistan after the Western countries and has supported the reconstruction of the country with USD two billion. Moreover, it has intensified its political and economic relations with the newly elected Afghan government. The Strategic Partnership Agreement (SPA) between India and Afghanistan in 2011 has further strengthened the bilateral relationship. Surveys in Afghanistan showed a very positive image of India as compared to Pakistan which received the lowest ratings. In Afghanistan, there is a strong consensus among the leading political elites that India is a much more "trustworthy partner" compared to Pakistan. Instead of strengthening its position, Pakistan's policy has contributed to a weakening of its stance in Afghanistan. The Pakistani military has changed its motivation from acquiring strategic depth to the prevention of an Indian encirclement.

The National Level

Pakistan paid the biggest price on the national level. The creation of the TTP in 2007 established a Frankenstein monster that has turned its head against the Pakistani state and its civil society. The Talibanisation backfired on Pakistani society and led to an enormous increase in violence. Pakistan rightly deplores that it is among the countries that has suffered the most under terrorism. Besides the fighting in the tribal areas, most of the terrorist incidents are connected to domestic conflicts that have been lingering since many years, for instance in Baluchistan, the political unrest in Karachi or the sectarian clashes between the militant Sunni and Shia groups that had started in the 1980s.

The creation of the TTP added another dimension to the complex security constellations and created new alliances. Several reports indicated that factions of the TTP cooperated with militant Sunni groups like Lashkar-e-Jhangvi (LeJ). These groups targeted the Pakistani state institutions and the armed forces, members of minority groups especially the Shias, and moderate Sunni groups.

In 2014, there were 7,655 deaths because of different forms of terrorism and security operations which was a major increase from 2013 when 5,687 fatalities had been counted. The main increase resulted from the security operation in North Waziristan that started in the summer of 2014. The operation Zarb-e-Azb was intended against all militant groups which seemed to be a major departure from the traditional stance of the Pakistani military. While the operation was welcomed by the Western states, it should not be overlooked that the real touchstone will be the course of action against the Kashmiri groups like the LeT whose leaders still operate unharmed.

The attack on the Army Public School in Peshawar seemed to be a turning point. The killing of 141 people including 132 school children has changed the public discourse in Pakistan. One immediate outcome was the 21st amendment of January 2015 which established Anti Terror Courts (ATC). The law suits of 3,400 persons were subsequently transferred to these new courts. The amendment faced opposition by religious parties which criticised the linkage between religion and terrorism. Members of the civil society criticised the amendment because it strengthened the role of the army through the back door whereas civil institutions like the judiciary and the police remained weak. In January 2015, there were around 60 banned organisations operating in Pakistan. The government watch list showed around 5,400 terror suspects.

Prospects

Talibanisation as a political ideology and as a military strategy has failed on all levels. The use of non-state actors has not helped Pakistan's interests on the global, regional or national levels and has proven to be counter-productive. The international reputation of Pakistan has suffered because of its double game with the Taliban. Regionally, Pakistan became even more isolated among its neighbours, except for China, although the government has often emphasised the need to expand relations with the neighbours in order to make full use of the country's geostrategic location between the South, West and Central Asia.

Militarily, the non-state actors have proved to be hardly controllable. The ideological, personal, tactical and strategic rivalries have caused various splits among the different groups and created new groups that have begun to operate outside their previous military control.

Politically, the vast majority of the Pakistani population has refused the ideology of the Taliban. One indicator is that the religious parties have never attracted many voters and have never achieved more than 3 to 6 per cent in the elections, with the exception of the Muttahida Majlis-e-Amal (MMA) which gained more than 10 per cent in 2002. Moreover, the Taliban ideology was attractive only to a very tiny section of the Pasthun society.

Pakistan has started various actions to get rid of the menace of terrorism. Politically, the 18th amendment of 2010 may have a positive effect on the Baluchistan issue and may offer new opportunities to give FATA a better legal structure and administrative system in order to fight Talibanisation. Since several years, the government is trying to register the madrasas and to reform their curricula. Militarily, the changes in the high command of the army and the ISI led to the operation in North Waziristan in summer 2014. The military has publicly declared that it was targeting all militant groups in the area so that the previous differentiation between "good" and "bad" Taliban seems to have ended. The Peshawar school attack of December 2014 has also changed the public discourse. Today, the negative effects and repercussions of state support for Taliban is being openly acknowledged in Pakistan. This is a great difference to the situation some years ago when the "state of denial" on the Taliban was far more dominant.

It is a well-known fact that the war against terrorism can only be won politically. Terrorism is a strategy and instrument, but not the root cause. The attractiveness of militant movements and terrorist organisations has benefited from the failures of governance. The biggest weakness of the state comes from its failure to provide public goods like education, health, security and justice. The weakness of the state, especially its judicial system and the police force, is probably one of the most crucial factors that helps the militant groups and their ideology to recruit new followers. It should not be forgotten that the Taliban started their career as a local militia in southern Afghanistan in the early 1990s to bring some idea of peace and justice to the areas they controlled. The Taliban were also in the beginning being welcomed in Swat because they provided justice to the people.

The policy of Talibanisation, i.e. the use of non-state actors as an instrument in foreign policy, has also been an indicator of the power constellations in Pakistan's foreign policy decision-making. The operation in North Waziristan may indicate a change but it should not be overlooked that the armed forces are still the most important actor in shaping Pakistan's foreign policy especially vis-à-vis the neighbours.

India and the Western governments should welcome these steps but should also be aware that they are only a beginning. As long as militant groups like the LeT and their welfare organisations can operate freely in Pakistan, the change will remain incomplete. In January 2004, President Musharraf declared that no terrorist attack should be allowed on Pakistani soil. This self-proclaimed benchmark should remain the yardstick for the evaluation of Pakistan's anti-terrorism policies.

14

Confronting Talibanisation in Pakistan and Afghanistan

Marvin G. Weinbaum

As familiarly conceived, Talibanisation refers to the attempts by armed groups in Pakistan and Afghanistan to wrest political power for the purpose of implanting their particular brand of Islamic government. Talibanisation in the two countries has already taken away from the state its monopoly over the use of violence and frequently assumes many of the normal functions of government. Conceived more broadly, Talibanisation is also a process of spreading by whatever means, a view of the political world that reflects a system of values most associated with the Deobandi school of Islamic thought. The Taliban insurgencies in Afghanistan and Pakistan may not capture state power anytime soon but they have succeeded to the extent that many of their ideas have entered the mainstream and their narratives have become part of the national discourse.

Whereas, the Afghan insurgents are largely nationalists and have carefully avoided joining the anti-state activities inside Pakistan, Pakistan's Taliban together with the country's jihadi groups have regularly lent assistance to the Afghan cause. Differences in their agendas notwithstanding, they share similar beliefs in wishing to replace their respective political and constitutional systems with a Sharia-compliant governance. Both also, if in varying degrees, employ terrorism as a tool. Talibanisation is thus ultimately convergent across the two countries, and their futures are largely interlocked.

This paper examines the extent of Talibanisation in Pakistan and Afghanistan and the ways its challenge is both military and ideological. The paper then posits that Pakistani–Afghan reconciliation offers what is probably the best hope for overcoming the threat that Talibanisation poses to both countries. It suggests that rapprochement may be a requisite for achieving a military success or finding a compromise political settlement with the Taliban forces. A reset of relations between the two countries is also seen as promising to result in regional economic and security gains across the region.

The Challenge in Pakistan

Pakistan's Tehrik-e-Taliban Pakistan (TTP) is mostly a confederation of tribal militias that while sharing common goals often disagree on strategic priorities and tactical objectives. As an insurgency, it draws strength from the decades of government policy that has failed to integrate the country's tribal agencies politically and economically into the rest of Pakistan. Antiquated laws have resulted in poor governance and neglected economic development. But the Taliban insurgency is also reflective of the social disruptions and radicalisation of tribal areas resulting from being on the front lines of the anti-Soviet jihad of the 1980s, the Afghan civil war of the 1990s and the influence of the displaced Afghan Taliban, al-Qaeda and other foreign fighters after 2001. Despite the operations of the Pakistan military, most recently in summer 2014 to defang the TTP, its campaign in the tribal areas appears only to have dislodged its fighters, as large numbers have been able to take refuge across the border in Afghanistan.

In a broader sense, the threat of Talibanisation in Pakistan comes from an almost seamless alliance of militant groups, some of which are at least partially controlled by the state and others, like the TTP, which are at war with the state, attacking both civilian and military targets. These groups draw on a vast network of supporters and believers across Pakistani society and most have links to the Afghan insurgent groups. Potentially, the most serious threat of spreading Talibanisation comes from the jihadi groups located in the country's heartland, the Punjab Province—particularly its southern Saraiki areas. Several of the dozen or so of the most active groups were created by the Pakistan military to serve as surrogate forces for them in Kashmir and Afghanistan.

Many of these extremist organisations have deep roots in a Pakistani society where, in the absence of reliable government-provided programmes, they offer basic social services. The popular influence of jihadi groups through mosques and madrasas and their ability to freely recruit members and raise funds makes them particularly formidable. Even while the public strongly rejects the acts of violence by the extremist groups, an often uncritical media and the near-absence of strong counter-narratives from elected officials and civil society ensure that a political radical and socially conservative Islamic worldview gains a wide following.

And yet the Peshawar school massacre in December 2014 has forced the country to face up to as never before to the threats posed by domestic extremism. Both the military and civilian leaderships now repeatedly insist that Pakistan will no longer have its "good" and "bad" militants. The adoption of a National Action Plan, a civilian-led initiative, is designed for the first time to forge an overall strategy. So far, however, there has been murky and inconsistent policy implementation of the NAP. Little progress has occurred in bringing the madrasas and their curricula under control. The Pakistan army, though pursuing the TTP in the tribal areas, is reluctant to confront directly, the militants in Punjab and in Karachi. The country's religious parties have thus far been unwilling to cooperate with the counterterrorism efforts. Most tellingly, the leaders of major extremist groups like the Lashkar-e-Taiba continue to avoid arrest and enjoy virtual impunity as they speak out against the government's anti-terrorist policies. The most concrete change to date has been the 21st amendment that transferred power in the terrorist cases from intimidated, ineffective civilian courts to military tribunals. However, it also marks the loss for a civilian government of one of its most fundamental responsibilities.

The Challenge in Afghanistan

The Taliban is an outgrowth of years of Afghan conflict that placed great strains on the traditional tribal leadership and allowed for the emergence of a previously unknown experience of warlordism in Afghanistan. So, too, the Taliban movement introduced Islamic doctrines at odds with many of the country's traditionally more relaxed religious practices. The catalyst for the movement's rise was the bitter civil war among the mujahideen parties from 1992 to 1996 that saw the near total breakdown of law and order nationwide within a disintegrated Afghan state. The Taliban filled a power vacuum, aided in no small way by the backing of Pakistan's premier security agency, the military's Inter-Service Intelligence.

As an insurgency, the nearly 14-year effort to forcefully restore the Taliban reign in Afghanistan appears to be centralised under the leadership of Mullah Omar—whom the TTP also nominally recognises as its spiritual guide. In reality, Omar's Quetta Shura is increasingly challenged from within where among the Pakistan-based Taliban leaders there has emerged a range of views on the insurgency's strategies and priorities. The Quetta Shura's influence is most questionable inside Afghanistan as most Taliban missions are believed to be planned by the regional and district commanders. By some contrast, the Haqqani Network is a more tightly organised group that, while claiming allegiance to Omar, is operationally separate. Even more independent of the mainstream Afghan insurgency is Gulbuddin Hekmatyar's Hezb-e-Islami, an armed opposition that through its political wing also exercises influence on the Afghan political process. All of these groups are loosely connected to the al-Qaeda and not infrequently, conduct joint operations together with Pakistan's jihadi organisations.

Most discussions of the Taliban in Afghanistan are focused on its military prospects in the coming months and years, especially following on the sharply reduced levels of the international forces and finances. But while the Taliban and its allies ostensibly hold no territory in Afghanistan, the minds of many Afghans have already been effectively Talibanised—a process actually begun with the return of the Mujahideen parties in 1992. Popular Taliban narratives about the West as occupiers and exploiters of Afghanistan's strategic location and natural resources are widely shared. Ethnic and religious tolerance has deteriorated, and many Afghan social traditions and cultural icons have fallen victim to the more austere beliefs of the Taliban and other religious conservatives.

For most Afghans, the Taliban stands as a default option. There is no wide yearning to have it restored to power or appeal for its social and political agendas. Certainly, there is no expectation that the Taliban are the answer to Afghanistan's economic woes. The Taliban's gains have come mainly as a result of a loss of confidence in the government and built-up resentments against the international forces. The Taliban, seen as less corrupt and providing a more reliable and equitable system of justice, stack up well against the Afghan state. That leaves many Afghans, especially ethnic Pashtuns, ambivalent in their loyalties.

The success of the national unity government to undertake reforms and the performance of its military are critical to preventing any further Talibanisation, both military and ideological. Everything rests on the ability of the government to gain the confidence and trust of the public through its progress in delivering basic security and in bettering the life of the ordinary Afghans. This requires that there should be enough political stability to buy time for the unity government to establish that the future does not lie with the Taliban. Undoubtedly, its chances for success depend on the continued international support, wisely employed.

While many in Afghanistan favour a political outcome to end the conflict, an agreement with the Quetta Shura and other groups is probably beyond reach any time soon despite concerted efforts by the Kabul government to begin peace talks. At present, neither the Afghan nor Pakistani Taliban seem able to accept the prevailing constitutional system or show a willingness to participate in a democratic political process. It is a widely held view in Afghanistan that Pakistan could help deliver a negotiated settlement in Afghanistan if it really so desires. Pakistan indeed has influence over the Afghan Taliban and can pose serious obstacles to the reaching of an agreement that fails to give recognition to its perceived national interests. But, Pakistan's ability to get the Afghan Taliban to compromise on its demands for an undiluted Sharia state has been overestimated.

A more realistic means of achieving a political outcome is through the reintegration of those insurgents who have concluded that their interests are better served by a central government that is succeeding and is willing to respond to their grievances. Reintegration involves a peeling off many insurgent commanders and their followers in local agreements occurring across the country—not through a grand bargain struck with the hardcore Taliban leadership. For the time being, the dominant view among these leaders remains that a military victory is possible, hastened by the eventual departure of all foreign troops and a failed Kabul government.

Joining Against Talibanisation

The best hope of addressing the threat of Talibanisation, both as an armed movement and a body of ideas, rests on reconciliation between Pakistan and Afghanistan, two nations that have been in an adversarial mode for nearly seven decades. Improved relations could go far in bringing the close cooperation needed to overcome their insurgencies or, as in the Afghan case, in possibly forcing the Taliban's top leaders to rethink their views towards seriously negotiating with Kabul. With more normal ties between the two countries, Afghanistan would have less reason to see India as providing a counterweight to an imperious Pakistan. Once less suspicious about India's supposed nefarious activities in Afghanistan, Pakistan would also feel freer to cut ties to its Afghan Taliban surrogates and may also be encouraged to confront those domestic extremist groups that military and political leaders have increasingly come to admit are the chief sources of threat to national security.

Few Pakistani policymakers would welcome the restoration of Taliban rule in Afghanistan. This contrasts with the 1990s when Pakistan, engaged in helping the Taliban achieve a total military victory, was not confronting an insurgency of its own. Today, there is reason to fear that a Taliban regime restored to power would almost inevitably energise ideologically-alike militant elements in Pakistan. The idea of a subordinated Afghanistan that could provide strategic military depth is outdated in an age of nuclear deterrents and is, in any case, unachievable. Many in Pakistan seem ready to settle for a government in Kabul that is, at least, not unfriendly. Pakistan has also apparently come to realise that it cannot rely on the Pashtuns alone to secure its interests in Afghanistan but must adopt a more inclusive approach that reaches an understanding with all other ethnic communities.

Although once thought as highly improbable, Afghanistan and Pakistan have recently taken actions that while tentative, represent progress toward a more cooperative, trusting relationship. Clearly, none of this would have been possible without the presidency of Ashraf Ghani. Many in Pakistan in policymaking positions have concluded that they have in Ghani someone sincere about wanting to explore ways to work together in breaking down barriers. Unlike his predecessor, the Afghan President is seen as not viscerally anti-Pakistan.

There appears to be an increased appreciation in Pakistan that aside from serving Pakistan's security concerns, a stable, peaceful and independent neighbour can serve other interests as well. Perhaps the most obvious is the promise of expanded bilateral trade and greater access to markets in Central Asia for Pakistani traders. Agreements on agriculture and irrigation would be in the interests of both countries. A peaceful Afghanistan can also revive the long-discussed building of a gas pipeline from Turkmenistan through Afghanistan that could help relieve Pakistan's severe energy shortages.

Similarly, the growth of the Afghan economy and many of President Ghani's plans for his country's development hinge on greater cooperation with Pakistan that involves freer trade and investment. Afghanistan might also then be in a better position to press for an end to Pakistan's ban on transit trade from India. Although the Kabul government cannot expect from Pakistan the level of development assistance it has received from India, there are many areas where the country could benefit from the opportunities being made available by Pakistan, including the training for civil servants and technical education.

No one should underestimate the difficulty of overcoming the deeply embedded suspicions in Pakistan and Afghanistan and the tendency to blame the other country for its problems. For Pakistan to turn a new leaf on its relations with Afghanistan will take, above all, a change in attitudes among those in the military who have always portrayed Afghanistan as a pawn of India. Government officials, on the other hand, seem largely sold on the idea that they can work with the Kabul government.

In Afghanistan, President Ghani has a steep climb in winning over public opinion and in convincing politicians and the members of the country's intelligence service that Pakistan can be trusted. To overcome doubts, Ghani must be able to counter the growing beliefs that Afghanistan has thus far given more than it has received from his diplomatic initiatives with Pakistan. Yet the Afghan hand in negotiating with Pakistan has never been stronger, and the opportunity for cooperation in jointly confronting the two insurgencies has never been greater. There exists the basis of a trade-off with Pakistan now that the TTP fighters, under pressure from the Pakistan army's attacks on their tribal strongholds, have sought refuge on the Afghan side of the border.

Many Indian observers are understandably uneasy about a warming of Pakistan–Afghanistan relations. It has not been forgotten as to how in the post-Soviet period, Pakistan facilitated the shift of militants from Afghanistan to Kashmir. But unlike that period, Pakistan's unrestrained support for jihadis took place when neither Pakistan nor India had yet become a full-fledged nuclear power. In the 1990s, Pakistan also did not have to consider what impact its Indian and Afghan policies would have on its own insurgency. Importantly, international concerns about state-sponsored terrorism have strongly grown since the 1990s, as has the ability of the United States and other powers to pressure Pakistan against facilitating a large jihadi intervention in Kashmir.

Possibly, in the anticipation that attempts at a reconciliation between Pakistan and Afghanistan will probably fail of their own accord, India thus far at least has displayed no signs of panic and has in fact shown forbearance while the Afghan government has explored areas of cooperation with Pakistan. India can also appreciate that if improved relations with Afghanistan make it easier for Pakistan to live up to its pledge to no longer distinguish between "good" and "bad" terrorists, this may eventually force Pakistan to reconsider its protection of terrorist groups like the Lashkar-e-Taiba.

The regional threat posed by Talibanisation hinges greatly on the outcomes in Afghanistan and Pakistan. Improved relations between the two are welcomed by all the regional country actors, none of which stand to benefit from the Talibanisation of South Asia. Several broad regional conferences have identified projects that would strengthen the economies of all the countries in what has become known as the Heart of Asia. An ungoverned space with the return of Afghanistan to civil war could provide the launching pad for radical fighters from Uzbekistan, Tajikistan and elsewhere to revive insurgencies and spread Talibanisation in their home countries.

The future of these Taliban movements as the leading forces for radical change is under some pressure with the appearance of the IS or Daesh. The IS has thus far drawn affiliates from among the Taliban dissidents in both Pakistan and Afghanistan. For the present at least, the appeal of the IS and its pan-Islamic agenda is limited. There are restraints on its growth in South Asia, where most militant groups in Afghanistan and Pakistan still swear allegiance to Mullah Omar and have ties to the al-Qaeda and Deobandism. But should factionalism continue to grow within both, ideological and other differences with the IS could be readily bridged.

The window for realising a Pakistan–Afghanistan rapprochement will not stay open for long without any tangible progress. The most convincing evidence that Pakistan has come to terms with having an independent, stable neighbouring government would be its eviction of the harboured Taliban and other Afghan insurgent groups. This may be possible only within a larger effort by Pakistan to sever ties with the domestic extremist groups. Pakistan's military and civilian leaders explain that these actions are likely to be deeply controversial and possibly destabilising, and must be phased in over time. The problem for the hard-pressed Ghani government and a fragile Afghan state is that they may not have much time to wait.

15

The New Caliphate in West Asia:
Impact on the Al-Qaeda's Core, Global Jihad and Jihad in South Asia

Thomas F. Lynch III

I propose to present my preliminary conclusions from an ongoing research, begun six months ago, aimed at capturing the unique and not-so-unique features of the Islamic State of Iraq and al Sham (ISIS), alternatively known as the Islamic State of Iraq and the Levant (ISIL) or Daesh. It focuses upon the impact the ISIS—and its June 2014 declaration of a caliphate in Iraq and Syria—has had upon the al-Qaeda and the global jihadist milieu. It also discusses the major implications of the IS caliphate in South Asia. It has been researched with a primary reference to the Middle East and South Asian news report sources and jihadist website postings regarding the interplay between the Islamic State, al-Qaeda and the other multiple Salafi jihadist groups in the international terrorist space. The sources originate in Arabic, Hindi, Urdu and English. A more detailed set of these findings would be published in the next couple of months. These are some of the key findings in four areas:

- The essential features of the Islamic State as it has arisen in Iraq and Syria.
- How the Islamic State has caused a substantive and significant rupture in the global jihadist constellation—directly challenging al-Qaeda's longstanding ascendance in that space.

- The Islamic State's accelerating challenges in establishing a durable and pernicious terrorist organisation beyond its present reach.
- The manner in which the Islamic State matters in South Asia—and how this differs greatly from its relevance in the Middle East and North Africa, and what that means to policymakers here in the region.

What is the Islamic State (IS) Caliphate

The Islamic State in Iraq and al Sham (ISIS) rose rapidly in prominence during 2013 and 2014 as the major Sunni insurgent and terrorist group in eastern Syria and western Iraq. The rapid and overwhelming success of the ISIS during this period came as part of a carefully planned and executed expansion that made good on the group's namesake goal—the creation of an Islamic State in Iraq and the Levant or a Islamic State (IS) Caliphate.

However important its military successes were in 2014 and 2015, the ISIS's real growth came from its exploitation of the massive political and social discontent among the Sunni Arabs on both sides of the border. The ISIS's 2014 capture of most of western Iraq was abetted by a tepid resistance from the alienated local Sunni population, and in some cases, the active assistance from local Sunnis, including other Sunni insurgent groups like Jaysh Rijal al-Tariqa al-Naqshabandiya and Ansar al-Sunna. Its loyalty badly compromised by the sectarian politics practiced by Prime Minister Maliki, the top Iraqi military leadership in Mosul during June 2014 fled north to Kurdistan via helicopter and many of the remaining Iraqi soldiers shed their uniforms and blended into the populace.

The jihadist core of the ISIS arose from those hardened jihadi terrorists and militant Sunni leaders who had been all but broken by the American military surge of 2007–08 and the corresponding Sunni "Awakening" that witnessed a critical majority of the Iraqi Sunnis joining forces with the US and the Iraqi national military in return for American cash and the prospect of a meaningful place in the new Iraqi political order. In 2010, most of the ideological cadre of what later became ISIS was in hiding or incarcerated–including the ISIS's spiritual leader Abu Bakr al-Baghdadi who was imprisoned for terrorism in the US-run Camp Bucca. But from 2010–12, the Iraqi government released—and then the ISIS sympathisers began to break free—thousands of prisoners throughout Iraq. These unrepentant jihadists took strides at organising and radicalising the Sunni tribes and cities of western Iraq for an armed struggle. The trend continued into 2013–14, culminating in the liberation of thousands of jihadists and unrepentant former Baathist leaders from four prisons in Mosul and one in Tikrit.

Yet for all of its successes up and through mid-2014, ISIS quickly confronted daunting challenges. By early 2015, ISIS faced a two-front war with a vast array of enemies within and outside of its contiguous spaces. In Syria, ISIS is not only battling pro-Assad forces, but it is fighting sister extremist groups such as the Jabhat al-Nusra (or the al-Nusra Front), the al-Qaeda affiliate it once tried to subordinate; Kurdish groups in north-eastern Syria that are vying for control of the resource-rich al-Hasakah Province, and other Islamic and Syrian nationalist opposition groups.

Islamic State (IS) Caliphate as a Phenomenon of Salafi Jihadist Fragmentation

ISIS did not materialise from thin air in 2011–12. Its main Salafi jihadist leaders, including its spiritual and corporate leader, Abu Bakr al-Baghdadi, were either members of or affiliated with the mid-2000's Iraq Sunni terrorist group and al-Qaeda affiliate in Iraq (AQI), occasionally referred to then as the Islamic State of Iraq (ISI). Led by the infamous Jordanian jihadist, Abu Musab Zarqawi, this Salafi terrorist organisation rose and fell in a spectacular fashion during the vicious Iraq civil war of 2003–08. Before his death in a combined US Special Forces' airstrike in June 2006, Zarqawi's AQI first pleased but soon confounded the global jihadist standard-bearer, the al-Qaeda (AQ) led by Osama bin Laden and Ayman al-Zawahiri from their refuge in Pakistan/Afghanistan.

Abu Musab Zarqawi's jihadist roots were with that AQ core. Zarqawi spent time with the mujahideen in Afghanistan during the war against the former Soviet Union there, reportedly meeting with Osama bin Laden on at least one occasion. After a decade of ultimately unsuccessful efforts to organise a successful jihad in Jordan—half of those spent in a Jordanian jail—Zarqawi returned to Afghanistan in 1999 to train members of his Jordan-based jihadist group, Jund al-Sham. After briefly fighting against the US invasion of Taliban Afghanistan, Zarqawi fled through Iran into Iraq in December 2001. Zarqawi found his way into northern Iraq in late 2002 or early 2003. With the encouragement from the AQ leadership but less than formal direction for his efforts, Zarqawi established sleeper cells in Baghdad to resist the coming American invasion.

Beginning in March 2003, Zarqawi organised the long-suppressed radical Islam in the Saddam-less Iraq, finding points of convergence with the newly displaced and fearful Iraqi Sunni tribal leaders and with Sunni Baathist leaders—ironically, the same Baathists who had brutally suppressed radical Islam under Saddam. Zarqawi's terrorist outfit took centre stage in the Iraq violence. His AQI was blamed for thousands of acts of terror in Iraq from 2003–06, including some of the most heinous ones against the coalition forces and the Iraqi Shi'ites.

Yet, Zarqawi did not remain a loyal affiliate of the AQ. In 2004, the AQ designated Zarqawi's outfit as its new affiliate, al-Qaeda in the Land of the Two Rivers, expecting Zarqawi to operate as a faithful emir to the preferences of the AQ's leadership core. But Zarqawi had other ideas. By late 2004, we know that the AQ number two, Ayman al-Zawahiri, dispatched at least one messenger to chastise Zarqawi for too much brutality and too little fealty to al-Qaeda's core leadership aims. Among Zarqawi's divergent aims was the seminal Salafi jihadist issue of where and how to best strike against the Western "far enemy" of Islam. For bin Laden's AQ, the correct priority focus was to plot, plan and execute catastrophic strikes against America and the West in Western lands, and where they were vulnerable in the Muslim lands. Bin Laden's AQ also believed that it was wasting energy in focusing violence against the Shi'ites of the Muslim world, arguing that the first priority was to drive off the "far enemy" infidels who propped up illegitimate Sunni Muslim regimes. Zarqawi's AQI differed in objective and he was unwilling to step back from a full-bore terror against the Iraqi Shia targets, catalysing a national Sunni–Shia war that bin Laden's AQ wished to put off.

Zarqawi's 2006 death masked the serious jihadist feud between bin Laden's AQ and Zarqawi's AQI. And yet the seeds of jihadist schism did not die with Zarqawi in 2006 or with bin Laden in 2011. Instead, these seeds lay dormant in the minds of the one-time Zarqawi followers hiding in Syria or imprisoned in Iraq. Among them was the Iraqi-born Ibrahim Awad al-Badry (aka: Abu Bakr al-Baghdadi). Like al-Baghdadi, who became the leader of AQI in 2010, most Iraqi jihadists had languished in Iraqi prisons for several years before gaining release as the American military left Iraq during 2010–11. For these ideologues, the dawn of a war in Syria—a movement to overthrow the Shia Alawite Syrian President Bashar al-Assad—was a godsend.

By late 2011, Abu Bakr al-Baghdadi was sending hundreds of Iraqi jihadists into Syria to advise and assist the many Sunni groups joining the fight against President Assad's military. But they did not come to join with the others; they came to form their own ascendant jihadist outfit. By mid-to-late 2013, al-Baghdadi's ISIS expanded by exploiting and victimising fellow Syrian revolutionary militias, gaining weapons and material after clashes with and outright predation of fellow Syrian revolutionary groups. Most importantly, ISIS gained control of Syrian territory.

Observers of the jihadist milieu in Syria reported that soon after Baghdadi's declaration in April 2013 of ISIS, open competition broke out between al-Baghdadi's ISIS and the groups anointed to be the vanguard of the al-Qaeda-endorsed revolutionary vanguard against Bashar al-Assad. Tensions between ISIS and the AQ-endorsed Syrian al-Nusra Front became a full-blown feud. Al-Baghdadi considered himself as the rightful heir to a Sunni Islamic caliphate because his bloodlines made him a descendant of Prophet Mohammed's family; he chafed at any requirement to suborn his fighters to the al-Nusra Front in Syria. In early 2014, Osama bin Laden's successor, the AQ leader Ayman al-Zawahiri, made a personal appeal to Baghdadi to have ISIS abandon its role in Syria and to remain in Iraq alone, where its roots were. Al-Baghdadi rejected this appeal, and Zawahiri's AQ general command formally disowned ISIS in February 2014.

As AQ had banished ISIS from its constellation, ISIS declared itself to be separate from AQ—an open rupture in the Salafi jihadist universe now laid bare. Thus, the seeds of a formal schism within the Salafi jihadist movement were sown in Iraq in the mid-2000s and blossomed into full rupture during 2014–15. Although there are many important dimensions of this rupture, the three major disagreements separating ISIS from AQ are:

The "far enemy first" thesis: AQ believes that Americans and Westerners must be driven from Muslim lands as a first priority, including in this construct the husbanding of territory and energy to enable a vanguard of expert jihadist operatives to plot and plan catastrophic attacks in the Western lands. ISIS does not share this view, focusing upon attacks against the local foes and opposition groups as its first objectives.

The use of indiscriminate violence: ISIS, as did Zarqawi's AQI before it, believes in the power and absolute necessity of indiscriminate and graphic violence to establish the ascendance of jihad and is unwilling to tether or temper that violence in an effort to attain other goals. With a hard-won knowledge from slumping popular opinion after several years of indiscriminate terror, the AQ believes in tempered violence—acknowledging violence as the primary agent of change in a world where force is the most powerful weapon, but practices managed violence in an effort so as to not alienate the Sunni Muslim umma in a revulsion to the excesses of violence.

The sequencing of adversaries: Laid bare in Zawahiri's July 2005 letter to Zarqawi, the AQ sees risk in battling its many enemies at the same time, preferring to focus first on driving off foreign infidels and then toppling the apostate Sunni Muslim governments before moving onto the elimination of Israel and any wider clashes with Shia Muslims or Hindus. ISIS is indiscriminate in its clash with a multitude of enemies, taking on all adversaries at once in a conspicuous and incredibly risk-tolerant manner that is anathema to the AQ.

Abu Bakr al-Baghdadi's June 2014 declaration of a Salafist caliphate formalised a dormant schism into an open rupture in the Salafi jihadist community. ISIS has established an alternate vision for the future of Salafi jihadism and introduced a formal competition into the jihadist space that is being played out across several important dimensions.

The IS Caliphate and the Icarus Effect: Burning Brightly but near the Sun

The IS Caliphate is very dangerous in western Iraq and the ungoverned spaces in Syria-a regional phenomenon. However, ISIS's prospects for becoming a durable and pernicious leader of a global Salafi jihadist terrorist movement remain dubious. While its expansive aims may be genuinely representative of its ideology, its methods have yet to muster the affiliations or the capabilities necessary in order to meet them. Moreover, the very successes that have marked ISIS's rapid ascent also make it highly vulnerable to an equally rapid fall.

First, it has rapidly generated a constellation of sworn and committed national enemies on all of its borders. As of late November 2014, the US-organised anti-IS coalition included 62 member countries, with major military contributions coming from the US and including: France, Kuwait, Jordan, Lebanon, The Netherlands, Qatar, Saudi Arabia, Singapore, Spain, Turkey, the United Arab Emirates and the UK. Not a member of the coalition, Iran has made substantial contributions of materiel and manpower, reportedly including two brigades of "volunteer" Revolutionary Guards units and a large number of the Guards' officer leadership cadre. No major jihadist outfit has inspired such a comprehensive set of encircling state adversaries in such a short time.

Second, ISIS's feud with AQ has made it a pariah in the global jihadist marketplace, sparking a number of direct clashes over manpower, finances and other resources, including an overt confrontation over the jihadist affiliates, individual recruits, sources of jihadist financing and an ascendance in the jihadist multimedia and social media space. Each of these confrontation areas merits evaluation.

ISIS's 2014 appeal for other jihadist groups to formally align has received a splashy but very uneven response. As of March 2015, the IS

Caliphate claimed a relationship with forty separate jihadist groups. Twenty-eight of these groups have pledged a formal affiliation with ISIS; while twelve have taken a lesser pledge of "support". Generally speaking, the jihadist outfits pledging affiliation are those with little to no pedigree, with severe organisational problems or those that have been shunned by the al-Qaeda over time as being too undisciplined for any incorporation into the AQ constellation. Those pledging a mere "support" for the ISIS tend to be more established jihadist outfits with ongoing or past affiliations with the AQ—like the Islamic Movement of Uzbekistan (IMU), Saudi Arabia's Islamic State in the Land of the Two Holy Mosques, Libya's Islamic Youth Shura, Pakistan's Jundullah and the Abu Sayyaf Group in the Philippines—and thus unwilling to formally sever ties with a long-standing force for leadership, seemingly hedging bets.

Within the Middle East and North Africa, ISIS has established loose linkages with multiple Salafi jihadist groups that its leadership speaks about as "governates" or "wilayats." A majority of these three-dozen declarations have been from the relatively new jihadist groups without any prior allegiance to AQ, and only those in North Africa seem to have a meaningful level of violent activity to date. These affiliations have provided a measure of prestige to the local jihadist outfits. In return, these groups have facilitated a significant flow of jihadist fighters into Syria along lines of infiltration very similar to those used by the scores of Libyan, Tunisian and Moroccan jihadists who came to Iraq via Lebanon and Turkey through Syria for jihad against the American military forces from 2004–09.

Two groups in Yemen and one in Saudi Arabia have declared themselves onside with ISIS. But to date, there is little evidence that any meaningful group formation has taken place in these countries against the stern resistance from AQ affiliates in each nation, and, in Saudi Arabia, from a vigorous and ongoing internal intelligence campaign to identify, disrupt and defeat any attempt by ISIS to build on the general Wahhabi sympathies for the Salafists in Syria and Iraq to distill into a viable Salafi jihadist organisation in the Kingdom. When compared to the Salafi jihadist groups in the Middle East and the Gulf States that remain affiliated with AQ—the al-Qaeda of the Arabian Peninsula (AQAP), the al-Qaeda of the Islamic Maghreb (AQIM) and the al-Shabaab, among others—it is hard to argue that AQ has lost any significant ground to IS in the very important Middle East and North Africa jihadist space.

Outside of North Africa and the Middle East, ISIS's year-long quest for significant jihadist group affiliates has fared little better, and arguably done worse. In Yemen, Afghanistan and Pakistan, IS has attracted a hodgepodge of minor splinter groups. These groups have supported the flow of but a few fighters to the Syria–Iraq battlefields and have not generated any real counterweight to the dozens of Salafi jihadist outfits in the region with stolid ties to AQ, including those like the Harkat-ul-Mujahideen, the Pakistan Taliban, the Afghan Taliban, the Jaish-e-Muhammed, the Jamaat-e-Mukharat or the many others found in Pakistan.

In Central Asia and Russia, the IS did garner an early assistance and a major declaration of support that conveyed an immediate operational impact. The Islamic Movement of Uzbekistan (IMU), with a leadership lodged in Afghanistan and Pakistan, declared itself to be in support of the IS Caliphate in September 2014. The IMU's pledge of support was quickly followed by the enhanced flow of often quite skilled fighters into Syria and Iraq from IMU recruiting nodes in Central Asia and its increasingly troubled training bases in South Asia. These IMU cadres added to those already flowing from a half-dozen other smaller jihadist groups, thickening the Central Asian contingent in ISIS. London's International Centre for the Study of Radicalisation and Political Violence (ISCR) estimates are that over 2,500 jihadist fighters came to Syria from the IMU and other jihadist outfits in Central Asia and Russia during 2014 and early 2015, placing this wider region of Central Asia as a most significant contributor to IS's foreign fighter pool (see Figure 1).

In South-East Asia, ISIS's attractions have come from jihadist groups with little capability and waning relevance in the jihadist global arena. And in Africa, the press-friendly, early 2015 declaration of formal affiliation by the Nigerian Salafi jihadist group Boko Haram is the exception that confirms the rule of less-than-substantive jihadist group affiliations with IS. In a precipitous early 2015 decline from its mid-2014 successes that led to the declaration of a "caliphate" in August—losing 80 per cent of its once-held territory and an estimated 2,800 militant fighters in five weeks of intense attack from a four-nation military offensive that the Nigerian government claims will prove a knock-out blow—the Boko Haram began to conduct increasingly desperate and unpopular actions like suicide bombings using young children, kidnapping to gain recruits, using livestock as shields when fighting authorities, and brutal public executions. Boko Haram lacks funding sources to benefit ISIS, and its role in providing fighters to the latter is unlikely to amount to much because the group's ethnic profile travels poorly through the Arab nations enroute to Syria, Iraq or the Levant; Nigerians making it to do jihad there would not fit well into the dominant Arab, Central Asian and Middle Eastern makeup

Figure 1: Estimated Foreign Fighters' Flow to Syria and ISIS (as of January 2015)

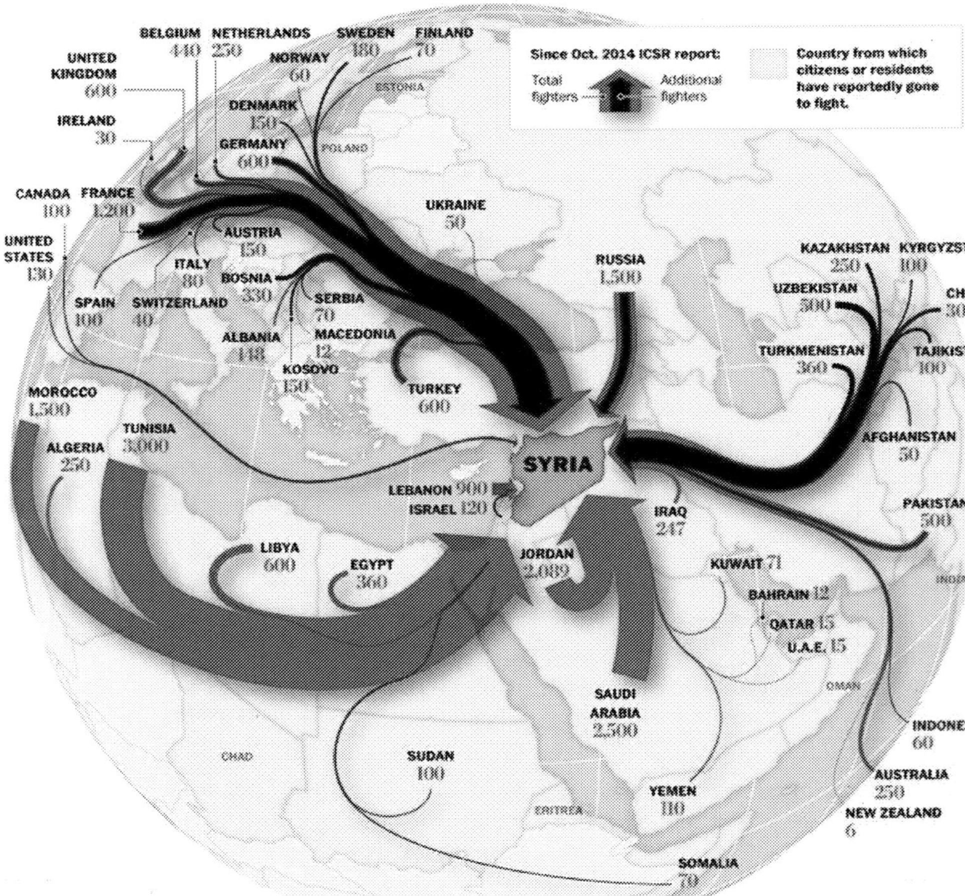

Note: Figures of fighters from Western Europe are from the ISCR high estimate category. All other numbers are from the Soufan Group. Pre-country fighter estimates determined from a date range of December 2013 to the second half of 2014.
Small numbers of fighters are also reported to have come from Bangladesh, Chile, Ivory Coast, Japan, Malaysia, Maldives, New Zealand, Philippines, Senegal, Singapore and Trinidad and Tobago. These countries are not shown because they are off the map.

of the ISIS foreigners in the fight. This allegiance pledge appears to be little more than symbolism, devoid of any meaningful exchange of fighters, funding or enhanced training, and it may actually represent the Boko Haram desperation as it faces a large-scale military setback.

Assessed closely, most of the international groups declaring support for or outright affiliation with the ISIS to date tend to be minor splinters from the standing affiliates with AQ or "undesirables", that, is jihadist outfits long-deemed as too undisciplined or too broken by successful national counter-terrorism operations to rate incorporation into the AQ-affiliate constellation. None are really the mainstream groups within the global Salafi jihadist movement. In contrast, the AQ retains very tight affiliations with three dozen Salafi jihadist outfits possessing name-brand cache and substantive capabilities in their regions of principal operation.

At the same time, ISIS has undertaken a broad, multimedia campaign to recruit and employ individual jihadist fighters from the Muslim diaspora of Western and non-Muslim states. These efforts have been substantive and produced measurable, and often worrisome, results. The ISCR estimates that ISIS's massive and broadly aimed recruiting campaign at this target audience has induced some 20,000 foreign fighters to join in jihad and jihad-supporting activities from 2013–15. These individual jihadists have come most prominently from the North African countries, from west European nations, from the Gulf Arab states and then from Australasia (see Figure 1).

While a worrisome story, ISIS's notable successes have an increasingly prominent countervailing effect. For the most part, recruits gained in IS's individually-focused social media messaging arrive as an indisciplined and largely untrained rabble that is addicted to multimedia activities in an ironically similar way. In addition, the flow of foreign fighters has begun to produce antibodies in both Iraq and Syria. In Iraq, tensions between foreign fighters and the local Iraqi Sunni militia fighters began to show up in February–March 2015, indicating a growing incidence of guerrilla attacks against the Islamic State foreigners. In Syria, ISIS lost significant ground in the north to Kurdish forces backed by coalition air strikes, reportedly losing control of 215 villages and over 1,000 militants killed by Kurdish and other Syrian rebel forces during January 2015 alone. Civil rights groups working in Syria began reporting in February 2015 that ISIS foreign fighters were being killed by rival groups and suspected would-be defectors by ISIS itself in Raqqa, the de facto capital of IS in Syria.

Third, ISIS has a narrowly constructed financial base—one where initially visible riches have masked long-term financial liabilities that have proven fatal to other would-be terrorist organisations. ISIS built up cash coffers from a combination of resource extraction of the Sunni-area hydrocarbon production and export, from extraction of ransom for foreign hostages and from the toppling of multiple financial institutions in western Iraq. Visually impressive, its funding sources are not durable and will be insufficient to sustain the IS caliphate into the future. Durable sources of funding from reliably sympathetic local and regional smuggling networks, from diaspora contributions and from other wide-ranging money-making activities are invariably necessary for sustaining the durable and sufficient sources of terror finances. IS has not established itself well in any of these fiscal areas, and is facing active resistance in them by al-Qaeda and its supporters.

Surrounded by enemy governments, IS's hydrocarbon production facilities and smuggling operations are under serious duress. Anti-IS military operations by US/Coalition aircraft and on-the-ground actions in late 2014 and early 2015 have destroyed dozens of IS-held oil and gas production, refinery and transit facilities across western Iraq and northern Syria, severely constraining its financial prospects. One-time sympathetic government and religious leaders in the wealthy donor countries like Saudi Arabia, Qatar, Kuwait and the UAE have banished IS from their business interactions and charitable contributions, severely constraining this source of finance. Finally, IS's feud with AQ has—in conjunction with these other activities—placed it in a spot where it cannot compete well for the traditional sources of fundamentalist, Salafi charitable and covert-funding mechanisms. Taken together, IS's current position of wealth can only begin to erode, and will rapidly become a severe constraint on its abilities to govern or to stave-off counter-attacks. In March 2015, some analysts reported that IS may have already lost up to 75 per cent of its revenues, making it increasingly hard for the group to provide sufficient goods and services to the nearly 8 million people living in its "Caliphate".

Fourth, ISIS's clash with all the neighbouring states and its schism with AQ has made it a jihadist pariah to a degree never before witnessed in the global jihadist milieu. Appalled by IS's barbaric tactics and reckless campaigns, Jordan, Saudi Arabia and Kuwait have quietly encouraged—the point of direct sponsorship—the activities of long-time state enemy Salafi jihadist leaders willing to denounce ISIS and to organise fighting groups to go to Syria and confront ISIS there. In the summer of 2014, Jordan seemingly cut a deal with two longtime "state enemy" Salafi leaders, Abu Muhammad al-Maqdisi (Zarqawi's former spiritual mentor) and Mahamad Shalabi (leader of Jordan's banned Salafi jihadist movement). Al-Maqdisi was liberated from long-term incarceration and Shalabi had his prosecution for terrorism stayed after each declared ISIS to be illegitimate. Later, they were reported as organising jihadist outfits to confront ISIS in Syria, doubtlessly under the watchful eye of Jordan's intelligence service, the GID.

Finally, ISIS has practiced indiscriminate recruiting and messaging in a manner that makes it seem spectacularly successful for a time, but that enables outside intelligence agencies and law enforcement agencies terrific insights on its organisation, structure and aims—enabling a more precise and effective targeting by the military and human intelligence assets. Its reliance on radical violence in its dominant messaging has left it with no core base of empathy in a cohesive international diaspora—something vital to the historically successful terrorist groups.

All these factors indicate that the IS Caliphate of early 2015 appears much akin to Icarus of the Greek legend. It is burning brightly but in doing so has flown dangerously close to the sun, where the wax on its "wings" is melting and it is courting a dramatic fall.

The IS Caliphate: Impacts and Implications in South Asia

The IS Caliphate's impact in South Asia has been most interesting and highly illustrative of the degree to which ISIS represents a rupture with AQ for the leadership of the international jihadist space. The AQ response to the ISIS challenge in South Asia has been both vigorous and important. The limited appeal of ISIS for the long-established South Asian jihadist outfits is also indicative of the inherent strengths of AQ and the weaknesses of IS in the wider struggle for ascendance in the Salafi jihadist arena.

AQ's response to the IS Caliphate's challenge was the most powerful and vigorous in South Asia. On September 4, 2014, AQ Emir Ayman al-Zawahiri formally declared there to be an al Qaeda of the Indian Subcontinent (AQIS). In this September announcement, Zawahiri reminded the jihadist faithful that AQ understood its issues in South Asia and was prioritising jihad to resolve these issues. He appealed to the faithful to ignore wider distractions and to focus on the South Asian jihad against the infidels and apostates in Afghanistan, exploiting the projected departure of the Western military forces from that country. He called the civilian government of Pakistan as apostate and an enduring target of mujahideen in the region. He also spoke about AQ dedication to jihadist causes in Bangladesh, amongst Indian Muslims, and with the Rohingya Muslim minority and refugees from Burma. In each of these message components, Zawahiri made it crystal clear that South Asia was inherently the AQ's jihadist space, that ISIS was not resonant or welcome, and that AQ would vigorously pursue a "hands-off" policy against ISIS in South Asia.

Just over seven months later, Zawahiri's message seems to have worked. By reinforcing several other trends of Islamist exceptionalism in South Asia, the declaration of AQIS seems to have blunted most of the appeal established by ISIS in several other parts of the world. The IS Caliphate's impact in South Asia has been conspicuously less than in the other regions of the world.

As documented earlier, its appeal for jihadist group affiliations has gone poorly in South Asia. Only three splinter groups in Afghanistan along with a handful of disgruntled Tehrik-e-Taliban Pakistan (TTP) commanders and the Jundallah terrorist group in Pakistan have pledged allegiance, or support in the case of Jundallah, to ISIS since mid-2014. Dozens of other long-standing jihadist outfits in Afghanistan, Pakistan and Bangladesh have remained firmly in the AQ camp, or, in cases like those of the Lashkar-e-Taiba in Pakistan, remained most-affiliated with the nationalist–Islamist aims of the security and intelligence services.

ISIS's pull on individual fighters from South Asia has been equally lukewarm. Independent estimates from the IRCS and the private Soufan Group record no more than 50–60 fighters from Afghanistan, 500 from Pakistan and at most a handful from India and Bangladesh moving from South Asia to Syria in response to the IS call (see Figure 1). Given these estimates, the entirety of South Asia has reported the number of jihadists going to the ISIS fight as less than those from the UK alone, less than Germany alone and dramatically less than the flows from North Africa or Central Asia—especially when assessed on a per capita Muslim basis. This conspicuously underwhelming South Asian response to the IS Caliphate's initially intense global appeal seems paradoxical. Precise reasons for this South Asian exceptionalism merit a more detailed study. However, there are at least four important hypotheses that when taken together, help explain why South Asia remains disproportionately unaffected by the ISIS appeal for the leadership of the global jihad.

First, the AQ senior leadership remains in the region and has vigorously defended its space against IS encroachment. Zawahiri's September 2014 declaration of an al-Qaeda of the Indian Subcontinent (AQIS) was a keenly calibrated announcement that warned off ISIS as an outsider outfit with no real understanding or true concern about the Muslim aims in South Asia.

Second, South Asia already has had a robust array of options for those wishing to do jihad—options tolerated by certain regional states and ineffectively countered by others. Unlike jihadi aspirants in North Africa, Australasia, Central Asia and western Europe who are often alienated from their surrounding society and lack places to go and train for jihad in a tolerated framework of recruitment, vetting, training and operations, the constellation of the active jihadist groups in Bangladesh, Afghanistan and Pakistan continue to provide a place where radicalised Sunni Muslim groups or individuals might go to pursue jihad.

Third, India, with the region's largest Muslim population, uniquely benefits from a history of pluralism and tolerance toward those of its citizens that practice Islam. Unlike Muslims in a constellation of other nations who often believe themselves ostracised, misunderstood or alienated from their own governments, Indian Muslims continue to be a group with a generally positive relationship with relatively robust and inclusive social, political and economic frameworks provided by the state. Only a handful of Indian Muslim youth have been reported as making the trek to do jihad with ISIS in the Middle East.

Finally, there may be a not-so-insignificant impact from the fact that the Gulf Arab states have sworn to destroy the ISIS threat and prevent any blowback into their own countries. As part of their anti-ISIS campaign, these Arab governments have signalled that Muslim immigrant workers from places across South and Southeast Asia will be carefully scrutinised and banned from the vital economic opportunities in the Gulf if they or any members of their families are determined to be participating in the jihad with ISIS. Although uneven in application, this general approach by the Arab Gulf states' migrant worker agencies impacts over 20 million migrant workers and their families across South Asia—and accounting for some $12 billion in annual remittances back to the home countries—placing a reinforcing, if not decisive, wet blanket on the South Asian aspirants who might otherwise consider joining ISIS to do jihad.

Combined, these four hypotheses appear to explain a lot about the uniqueness of South Asia when it comes to the pursuit of jihad. They emphasise that the long-standing patterns of Muslim inclusivity in India coupled with the three decades of established jihadist, and AQ-invested militant outfits in other South Asian states, have placed unique barriers to ISIS' appeal within the region.

While no state in South Asia should be comfortable that it may not suffer a greater penetration from ISIS in the coming few months—mandating vigilance—the factors in play across South Asia suggest that this region will remain the most dominated by AQ's version of global jihad. In turn, that AQ ascendance means that the priorities established by Ayman al-Zawahiri for jihad in his September 2014 message should remain the top drawing concerns for the South Asian policymakers: Conclusion of a successful jihad on behalf of the Taliban in Afghanistan; support for the Tehrik-e-Taliban campaign to topple the civilian government in Pakistan and support for the persecuted fundamentalist Muslims in Bangladesh and in solidarity with the discriminated Muslim Rohingya refugees from Burma.

ISIS's use of social media for a broad array of purposes—radicalisation, recruiting and resourcing—is both unique and far more penetrative into South Asia than as seen from AQ over the past decade. ISIS has even promulgated a significant number of original messages in Hindi—a language seldom if ever used in AQ jihadist propaganda. Thus, it will behove all regional governments—and especially India—to up its game in terms of social media monitoring to keep at very low levels the appeal of these ISIS messages.

It will also be especially important for India to have its Home Ministry work closely with the Gulf Arab States. New Delhi can better inhibit the radicalised subcontinental youth from transiting the Gulf States enroute to do jihad in Syria or Iraq by assuring intelligence-sharing and persistent cross-talks with the intelligence and police services in these governments—services also working to disrupt and eventually eliminate IS recruiting.

Summary and Conclusions

Since early 2014, the formal fight is "on" in the Salafi jihadist global space. Like Icarus, ISIS has burned brightly in the early sun, going through a brash and high-risk strategy that has exposed it widely and made it many enemies.

It is still early, and the jury is still out, but the intra-jihadist struggle pits the long-established global entity of al-Qaeda with a clear and disciplined approach to terror and the establishment of an Islamic Caliphate—even though one that may be fatally flawed—against an incredibly active and seemingly reckless ISIS with lots of multimedia appeal but no time-tested financial or organisational affiliates; and one that is now battling a daunting constellation of secular and Salafi jihadist adversaries sworn to see to its demise. Nowhere are ISIS's struggles more visible than in South Asia. There, ISIS has made minimal inroads against the AQ ascendance despite the fact that countries like Pakistan,

Afghanistan and Bangladesh are hotbeds of Islamic radicalism ripe with seemingly many recruits. A curious combination of pre-established pathways for those aspiring to jihad, a relatively unreceptive Muslim community in India and a cunning AQ messaging, combine to form a barrier to ISIS aims. Could this be a pattern that gets repeated in other regions of the world as the novelty and the momentum of ISIS in Syria and Iraq slows?

This struggle between the IS Caliphate and AQ will continue a lot longer before the results become clear. Yet one thing is clear already: It is far too early to bet against AQ making an ultimate successful stand against this stern but troubled challenge from ISIS.

16

The Caliphate and the Future of the Al-Qaeda and Other Global Jihadist Groups

Waiel Awwad

The objectives of this paper are to highlight the plight of the Arab world, the rise of political Islam, the competition between al-Qaeda and ISIS and the follies of external intervention. Finally, it will deal with the implications, expectations and suggestions on how to defeat ISIS.

The year 2015 marks the 12th anniversary of the Bush–Blair invasion of Iraq. The war in Syria has entered its fifth year and the Moscow talks are underway for breaking the jinx; Boko Haram has declared allegiance to the so-called "Islamic State". The Israeli elections have taken place with the victory of the Likud Party; a series of suicidal bombings have rocked many countries including Yemen, Syria, Kenya and Iraq. Preparing a compilation of regional "jihadist" groups and the global al-Qaeda group will pave the way for Western countries and their regional allies to better understand the phenomenon.

If these incidents have one thing in common, it is that terrorism will continue to spread and to counter it will be a long-haul process. The most worrying thing is that there are people in the Islamic world who still believe that ISIS is not a terrorist organisation. In Saudi Arabia, 92 per cent believe that ISIS is compatible with Islamic teachings and with Sharia. Saudi nationals are second largest after Tunisians among those who join ISIS, which has more than 20,000 Wahabbists as its cadets, while 53 per cent in Turkey believe that ISIS is not a terrorist organisation. There are presently at least 12,000 Turks who have joined ISIS. This is worrisome and we need to reform our thoughts. The fault lies in those Muslim believers who have wrongly understood the message and values of our faith.

Plight of the Arab World

The current situation and turmoil in West Asia is nothing but a manifestation of Western policies and their thirst for capturing the natural resources of the Arab world. This is a never-ending saga for superpowers for the last more than a thousand years. After the fall of the Ottoman Empire, the blood map of the Arab world was divided into 19 small countries by Britain and France (the Sykes–Picot Treaty) in order to retain their influence and dominance over the region. In the middle of the last century, a "colonised enclave", Israel, was created by the colonial powers to ensure that this rich region remained under the influence of the colonists.

World War II left weakened European countries and the spread of communism imparted fear; most West Asian countries gained independence. This led to a transformation of the Arab world similar to that in Europe in the eighteenth and nineteenth centuries. It was a transformation from a feudal agricultural society to a modern industrial society and a struggle in the realm of ideas. Leaders were installed, autocratic regimes encouraged and opponents simultaneously supported secretly and then encouraged to take their resentments to the angry street. This led to mob rule; the mob which comprised of unemployed educated youth, low-wage workers, ill-treated victims, criminals and bystanders. The state collapsed and non-state actors prevailed, which led to military intervention, which in turn invited the international community to help manage the mess. Iraq presents the best example of being a fertile ground for the growth of fascism and recruitment of suicide bombers.

The European intervention in the Arab world, under the pretext of stopping the spread of communism and Soviet threats, was evident in its encouragement of coups against the regimes opposing European policies and replacing them with unpopular figures. The Europeans encouraged internal conflict in the Arab countries, which had gained independence and had started political and economic reforms and an inward restructuring so that they could stand up once again as independent and sovereign nations. This led to the birth of the pan-Arab movement that was challenged by the UK, France and US which encouraged and supported autocratic regimes, monarchies and even dictators. A heavy militarisation of the region was one of the top priorities of the West, so weapons poured into the support of the puppet regimes. The Eisenhower Doctrine stated that the United States is "prepared to use armed forces to assist" any Middle Eastern country "requesting assistance against armed aggression from any country controlled by international communism". The English translation of this was that no one would be allowed to dominate, or have exclusive influence over, the Middle East and its oil fields except the United States, and that anyone who tried would be, by definition, "communist" (William Blum, *Rogue State*, Common Courage Press, 2000, pp. 131–132).

The Rise of Political Islam

The birth of Israel in the heart of West Asia fuelled conflict between the new state of Israel and the newly independent Arab countries. In 1917, the British Foreign Minister, Lord Arthur Balfour, issued a declaration (the Balfour Declaration) that announced the British Empire's support for the establishment of "a Jewish national home in Palestine". While the European nations ensured the birth of Israel, the US protected it, ensured its expansion and the annihilation of Palestine. The continuation of the annexation policy, de-Arabisation and the expansion of Israel at the cost of the Palestinians is considered by many as a perpetual provocation for permanent wars.

The political reforms in the Arab world were minimal; many political parties were barred, especially those with a pan-Arab slogan. The gathering of people was allowed only in mosques. This hardened the stand of those movements in the Arab world that stood for any reconciliation with the ruling elite and led to the belief that all the suffering was because of one individual, the head of the state, and hence all their angst was focussed on the regimes, leading to calls for regime change. The US invasion of Iraq led to more resentment in the Arab street which was aggravated by the global financial crisis, economic recession and rise in prices of essential commodities. The US's intention for occupying Iraq was never because of the weapons of mass destruction, but for the natural wealth of Iraq—a fact admitted by US decision-makers. Hence, it sounds naïve to speak of the US pulling out after the occupation and spending trillions of dollars. The current situation in Iraq and Syria is a culmination of the Pentagon policy of spreading anarchy and sectarian democracy and of nourishing radicalism. This has led to the birth of the terrorist organisation, ISIS—a product of the al-Qaeda that was itself created by the Saudi-ISI-USA nexus.

During the Islamic tsunami "Arab Spring", supported by Qatar and

Saudi Arabia, the ISIS in Iraq formed the al-Nusra front in Syria. They recruited locals and Turkey's Erdogan government opened its 940 km border with Syria to allow the entry of mercenaries—Libyans, Tunisians, Saudis, Chechens, Caucasians, Af-Pak Taliban, Uzbeks, Malaysians and Indonesians—to name a few. The US's dissolution of the Iraqi army, security apparatus and the Baath party provided conditions that contributed to the recruitment into the ISIS. The border crossing between Turkey and Syria was under the control of foreign mercenaries with the help of intelligence agencies (US, UK, France, Turkey and Israel), which ensured that the flow of arms reached the anti-government militant groups in Syria. Turkey's sole ambition of reviving the "Ottoman Caliphate" era led it to support the Muslim Brotherhood and later supplemented the "Mujahideen" to gain ground and topple the secular regimes. They were sheltered, trained, armed and extended logistic support from its soil. According to sources, there are more than 12,000 Turkish nationals who are members of ISIS. US Senator John McCain was a frequent visitor to the training camps near the borders with Syria and met with ISIS commandos many times. In Aaron Klein's report "Blowback! U.S. trained Islamists who joined ISIS", a secret base in Jordan was the site of covert aid to the insurgents targeting Assad. In February 2012, World Net Daily (WND) was the first to report that the US, Turkey and Jordan were running a training base for the Syrian rebels in the Jordanian town of Safawi, in the country's northern desert region. A source told WND that at least one of the training camps of the group, the Islamic State of Iraq and Syria (ISIS), was in the vicinity of the Incirlik Air Base near Adana, Turkey, where American personnel and equipment were located. According to American experts, a quarter of a million mercenaries were in Syria from 83 nationalities. A threat of danger from the returnee jihadists reached Europe and the US, with more than 10,000 blue-eyed mercenaries joining the al-Qaeda affiliated groups to fight in Syria. Israel has joined this group and admitted that 10 Israelis had joined the ISIS.

The capture of Mosul city in Iraq and the surrounding areas in June 2014 attracted the world's attention to the sudden rise of Islamic State of Iraq and the Levant (ISIL/ISIS/IS). Ever since, this monster has been allowed to grow rapidly and extend its influence into large areas of Iraq and Syria. But when it closed on Erbil, the US and allies intervened to halt the ISIS advance. This ensured the safety of almost 3,500 American marines stationed in the US consulate there and of the personnel of the giant US oil companies (Exxon Mobil and Chevron) drilling in Iraqi Kurdistan. ISIS carried out a massive ethnic cleansing campaign against the Yazidi, Shia Turkmen, Chabak, Christians and even Sunni Muslims.

Hence, the emergence of ISIS was not a sudden phenomenon, but a meticulously planned project, which led to it controlling territories and then claiming al-Baghdadi to be the "Emir of Muslims" and calling upon Muslims from all over the world to join hands and declare their loyalty to his leadership.

The government of the US and of some Western countries, controlled by the arms industry, not only allowed this terrorist group to utilise the social media like YouTube, Twitter and Facebook to spread the horrors committed, but were also helped by the corporate media in this. These warmongers made it clear that this demon was here to destroy not only the Middle Eastern countries, but also the "whole world".

Al-Qaeda and ISIS

If the creation of the al-Qaeda in Afghanistan by the US-Saudi-ISI combine was to topple the Soviet Union as admitted by Hillary Clinton in her testimony (https://www.youtube.com/watch?v=4nsQ5POIRUI), then the creation of ISIS was nothing but old wine in a new bottle. The ISIS succeeded in gaining ground in Iraq, only in areas that were under the influence of other militant groups that were sheltered, armed and trained by the West and US. According to Snowden, the "Hornet's Nest", Daesh/ ISIS was created by the US (CIA), Britain (MI6) and Israel (Mossad) combine. Of course, the "Coalition of the Willing" contributed to the success of this project. The release of a classified document from the Central Intelligence Council (CIC) of the US clearly exposed the Project Caliph 2020 (http://www.futurebrief.com/project2020.pdf).

After the invasion of Afghanistan, a Jordanian fanatic and highly violent militant named Abu Musab al-Zarqawi was appointed as the leader of the al-Qaeda in Iraq (AQI). He was active in the al-Anbar province (Fallujah, al-Ramadi). Brig. Gen. Mark Kimmitt, believed "The Zarqawi PSYOP program is the most successful information campaign to date". The political pandering by the countries involved in inciting wars in the region is meant to turn it into stateless, failed states with non-state actors that ultimately would lead to intervention because of the growing sectarian fighting and hence divisions within the unstable new regional order.

The social uprising that erupted in the Arab world under the banner of the Arab Spring, was hurriedly hijacked by radical Islamists, which led to the initiation of "tribal regional warfare" (e.g. Libya and Yemen). The overseas "barbaric killers" were trained in Turkish bases and allowed to fly into Syria and Iraq, remotely controlled by intelligence agencies similar to Afghanistan in the eighties.

The credit for the formation of ISIS goes to the CIA, as most of the top leaders were born in the US training camps of the al-Qaeda in Afghanistan. The spread of ISIS was only possible with the US–UK occupation of Iraq. In his article, "How America made ISIS", Tom Engelhardt states:

> When the U.S. was done, when it had set off the process that led to insurgencies, civil wars, the growth of extremist militias, and the collapse of state structures, it had also guaranteed the rise of something new on Planet Earth: ISIS—as well as of other extremist outfits ranging from the Pakistani Taliban, now challenging the state in certain areas of that country, to Ansar al-Sharia in Libya and al-Qaeda in the Arabian Peninsula in Yemen.

In 2007, former NATO Director, General Wesley Clark, expressed neocon plans that NATO was planning to occupy seven countries in five years including Libya, Yemen, Somalia, Sudan, Syria and Iran. Even Wikileaks revealed the US plan for a military coup in Tunisia and Egypt in order to gain logistic support to invade Libya. Before the inception of ISIS, as far back as 2007, the Pulitzer Prize-winning veteran journalist, Seymour Hersh, had portended the creation of just such a terror group in his 9-page report in the *New Yorker* titled, "The Redirection: Is the Administration's New Policy Benefitting Our Enemies in the War on Terrorism?"

As part of the "Constructive Chaos" project in the Arab world, Balkanisation started in Sudan, which is now divided into two, and regimes were overthrown in Tunisia and Egypt. But, eyes were on Libya which was attacked by the France-led NATO forces under a "Humanitarian Intervention" that compounded the problems. This prompted other superpowers to prevent a similar action in other countries like Syria. In fact, even Silvia Berlusconi, the former Prime Minister of Italy, accused French President Sarkozy of initiating a war on Gaddafi who was loved by his people, on the request of his friend, Bernard Livy Henry.[1] This was done even though Libya was peaceful and there was no revolt against the Libyan President.

There is no doubt that the sectarian policies followed by the U.S. after the Iraq occupation were meant to institutionalise and destroy decades of nation-building; policies that entailed ethnic cleansing, marginalisation, tribal representation and encouraged widespread corruption. Radicalisation was encouraged by focusing on the people who were anti-establishment, socially alienated, rejected by society, with criminal backgrounds, petty criminals, those previously jailed and those who had nothing to lose, wanting to be somebody and/or to take "revenge" against parents or the West. All these factors helped in making a "good terrorist", radicalised by the sermons from the clergy in the Wahabi-run mosques and through charities active in the poor urban localities among small isolated minority communities.

Anger was created against the central government by creating a "Sunni victims"-like situation in Iraq, through the use of torture, sectarian killings, bomb blasts and ethnic cleansing. These helped the rise of insurgent groups opposed to the Maliki government and made recruitment and support initially easy for ISIS to launch its attack on the Iraqi government forces.

Funding and Self-Reliance: According to "A Nation on the Brink: How America's Policies Sealed Iraq's Fate", Dahr Jamail wrote:

> Funded by Arabian Gulf petrodollars from Qatar and Saudi Arabia, other places, and for a long while supported, at least implicitly, by the Obama administration, radical Islamist fighters in Syria opposing Bashar Al-Assad have been expanding in strength, numbers, and lethality for the last three years. This winter, they and their branches in Iraq converged, first taking Fallujah, and then moving on to the spring and summer debacles across Sunni Iraq and the establishment of a 'caliphate' in the territories they control in both countries...Today, Washington's policies continue in the same mindless way as more fuel is rushed to the bonfire that is incinerating Iraq.

Xe Services: Blackwater, the largest private military training company, was formed by Erik Prince, a former member of the Navy SEALS, in 1997. In Abu Dhabi, Erik Prince, without appearing in person but through the joint-venture Reflex Responses, signed a first contract of $529 million on July 13, 2010. According to the *New York Times*, "the secret army trained in the UAE would conduct special operations to put down internal revolts, like those sweeping the Arab world this year". Blackwater later became the Xe Services. According to Manlio Dinucci, "the US-NATO military alliance was planning to use the secret army of mercenaries, whose underlying objectives were to:

- Protect the oil facilities of the American and European oil companies.
- To eliminate their opponents.
- To keep the country weak and divided."

Such are the "innovative solutions", which the Xe Services was to provide to the US government. The Xe Services that operated in the Zayed Military

City (UAE) was "a secret army in the making". The UAE's deal was to establish a military camp for the training of mercenaries, which was signed in July 2010, nine months before the onslaught of the wars in Libya and Syria.[2]

The Spread of an Extremist Ideology

Clergies in Saudi Arabia, Qatar, Kuwait, UAE and other Salafists and Wahhabi centres kept on promoting jihad and called for the toppling of the "kafir/infidel regime" in Syria. The release of criminals and of those undergoing life imprisonments from Saudi and other countries's jails was allowed on one condition: to go and fight in Syria.

ISIS is a well-trained, well-financed and militarily proficient force, equipped with modern vehicles and weaponries. During the occupation of Iraq, the US formed two camps, Camp Cropper and Camp Bucca (al-Qaeda School), in Umm Qasr between 2007–09. Most of the released Guantanamo detainees found their way into Syria and Iraq to join the ISIS or the al-Nusra Front. According to Dr Michael Night, al-Qaeda in Iraq benefited from the unprecedented infusion of a trained terrorist manpower which was detained, tortured, brainwashed and released with a more ferocious intention of killing back with vengeance. During the occupation of Iraq, the majority of the suicide bombers were foreigners from Saudi Arabia, Kuwait, Syria and Egypt. In 2008, the US was holding 257 foreign fighters. The terror project expanded and the Pentagon secretly opened prisons in many places and flew detainees to different countries for tortures and imprisonments. In Libya, the two main hardcore al-Qaeda cadres were sent by a secret CIA plane to Gaddafi who jailed, tortured and later released them as requested by the US along with 500 "al-Qaeda sympathisers" on "humanitarian basis".

From the outset of NATO's 2011 "humanitarian war" on Libya, the Atlantic Alliance was working inclose liaison with the "proal-Qaeda brigades" led by the former Libya Islamic Fighting Group (LIFG) leader Abdul Hakim Belhhadj (Debka). Proal-Qaeda brigades controlled Gaddafi's Tripoli strongholds seized by the rebels on August 28, 2011. Abdul Hakim Belhhadj received his military training in a CIA-sponsored guerrilla camp in Afghanistan. He constitutes CIA's "intelligence asset" operating in the Libyan war theatre. A 2011 report suggested that he had around 1,000 men under his command (see "Libyan Rebels at Pains to Distance Themselves from Extremists", *The Globe and Mail*, March 12, 2011). The US acknowledged later that it used them to topple Muammar al-Qaddafi; the rest is history.

Is there any difference between al-Qaeda and ISIS? Well, they are different sides to the same coin. Al-Qaeda was slow in its tactics; it did not kill civilians on a large scale. ISIS on the other hand did what al-Qaeda did not do; it attacked and terrorised all at once. It had no patience, was always in a hurry to kill; it captured and enslaved women and targeted children for recruitment as foot-soldiers. A theocratic and fundamentalist al-Qaeda had, at the beginning, no intentions of retaining territories, as it was unable to sustain itself and did not want to fight with allies. It avoided provoking the enemy prematurely in order to avoid its fire. On the other hand, ISIS has claimed territory; it hardly bothered about retaliation and always used blackmail tactics. It provoked internecine fighting among militant groups so as to claim supremacy. It widened the fight on tribal, sectarian and communal lines by targeting minorities and carried out ethnic cleansing. ISIS does not trust locals; it focuses more on foreign recruits, recent converts and the uneducated youth who lack the historical and cultural dynamics of the Middle East. This has made it easy for the West to frame it in religious, rather than political, terms.

Implications and Expectations

It is not difficult to defeat this phenomenon, though it would happen in time to come. But why is no one willing to eliminate it now? If anybody wanted to eliminate it, then why was it created in the first place? For the US, it needs to secure military bases in Iraq. The main sources for the CIA revenue are oil, drugs and arm sales. Now that the latter source is flourishing, it is a tool to fight terrorism and rally the international community in a global fight against terrorism. So, first it was in Afghanistan, then in the Levant and later in Africa after Boko Haram and other militant groups declared loyalty to ISIS. For the ailing West, it is Islamophobia that prevails and this will lead to the rise of right wing nationalist parties and the fight for a homogenous culture; whereas for Turkey, it is the new Pakistan. It has used propaganda against the Kurdish groups YPG/PKK, and for its lust for the Syrian and Iraqi territories. Saudi Arabia lost ground after the breakthrough in the nuclear talks with the P5+1 and the merger of Iran with the "Gulf Security Belt" like in the fifties. Al-Saud feels threatened by Iran's influence and has moved in to mobilise the Sunni Salafi front against Iran, propagating that Iran was a threat to the West's interest, while actually it was doing so in its self-interest.

According to McGurk, trained fighters shifted from Syria into Iraq in early 2013. They were taught how to break jails and release hardcore terrorists who joined ranks with them to take on the government forces in both the countries. Those responsible for the creation of ISIS are the same who created Mohamed ibn Abdul Wahab (Wahhabism movement), Hasan al-Banna (Salafism) and Osama bin Laden (the al-Qaeda organisation). The developments in West Asia cannot be seen in isolation from the global scenario and the reshaping of the new world order. When the godfather of the al-Qaeda's mentor, former Saudi ambassador to US, Prince Bandar bin Sultan, met with President Putin, trying to buy his loyalty and disown Syria, he threatened Putin with dire consequences if the latter refused. Now the Islamic state is issuing statements against Russia and has vowed to liberate Chechnya and other Muslim-minority states. The Syrian port of Tartus, on the Mediterranean Sea, hosts a Russian military base—so disintegrating Syria and regime changes are of prime importance to US–NATO and Israel, which would ensure that there would be no Russian presence in the Mediterranean Sea. Both the US candidates have stated this during the election campaign. Russia has still held ground on the Syrian front and this has strengthened its belief that the NATO and USA are trying to isolate Moscow and what happened in Crimea and Ukraine was part of this policy of the US and the West against the Russian Federation. Firstly, it was the gas pipeline that triggered the war in Syria. Qatar wanted to extend a pipeline to Turkey and Europe through Jordan and Syria. And secondly, it was the discovery of a large reservoir of gas in the Levant, which is being shared with Syria, Lebanon, Cyprus, Israel and Palestine (Gaza shore).

External intervention in West Asia has been there for decades and has been documented in many released documents like the Israel Strategy for the Nineteen Century (Yinon Oded Plan, 1982) and the Lin Perk Document, 1996 (PNAC—Clean and Break Plan) to ensure the security of Israel. In the Brzezinski project, Richard Perle called for the USA to invade Iraq. Condoleezza Rice announced "The Middle Eastern and North African New Order" after the Israeli war on Lebanon in 2006.

The role of Israel in the ongoing intervention in West Asia had not been limited to Syria and Iraq but extended to Libya, Tunisia, Sudan and Egypt. It intervened repeatedly in the Syrian conflict and kept on attacking Syria's military installations under different pretexts. Its only objective was to tilt the balance of power in favour of the insurgent groups to topple the Syrian government which had extended logistic support to Hamas in Gaza and Hezbollah in Lebanon to foil the US–Israel emergence of a Greater Middle East, without any resistance to the occupation and dominance of Israel in the region. By doing so, Iran, their only ally in the region, would be cut out after the ISIS grows in strength in Iraq and Syria. The US had been planning to intervene in Syrian affairs and topple the government there for a long time now. This was stated by Collin Powell to President Assad when he visited Syria after the 2003 US–UK invasion of Iraq and dictated to him, the White House terms to avoid such an outcome. Both the US Presidential candidates in their debates have stated that a regime change in Syria was one of the priorities of the US foreign policy. This would help in protecting Israel. That is the prime objective of any US President. The "pro-democracy uprising" was supported and "moderate rebels" were trained and armed. Out of the US weapons, 70 per cent found their way into the hands of al-Qaeda in Syria and Iraq. The pretext of intervening militarily under the banner of "humanitarian intervention" was foiled by Russia and China. Now, it is inching closer after President Obama revealed his plans to counter with its own cultivated ISIS groups. This may lead to imposing a "No Fly Zone" in some parts of northern Syria—a devious plan to set up the stage to divide Syria—similar to Iraq and Libya's "divide and conquer policy". The NATO-led US Special Forces, equipped with a global intervention doctrine, will ensure that no peace, prosperity or freedom return to Syria. They will increase the bombing campaigns, military incursion and occupation. The West has made it very clear that it does not require Russian or the Syrian government's help in tackling ISIS. On the other hand, Russia, Iran and Syria's other allies would support the Syrian government's efforts in fighting ISIS,to foil the Western plot of intervention and chaos. The unlikely scenario is a tactical rapprochement between the US and Russia to fight the global threat and the hysteria generated by the brutality of ISIS. There is no doubt, a plan to reshape the Arab world and divide it further under the pretext of humanitarian intervention. What would be the weakness of such a policy, both regionally and globally? It would have a devastating affect regionally, where instability would spread to Jordan and Lebanon, and its global dimension would be of isolating Russia in the Mediterranean Sea and putting pressure on Iran. Whatever the outcome of the war on Syria and Iraq, it would shape the new world order. If you believe that USA and its allies are leaving Afghanistan, think again—because their mission is unaccomplished.

The ISIS can be defeated if the following occur:

- Political will among the international community and permanent members of the UN Security Council.
- Joint military operations in coordination with the forces on ground actually fighting the ISIS like the Syrian army, Iraqi army and the Kurdish forces.

- Spread of democracy and end of support to autocratic regimes.
- A rethinking of the US–West policy towards the region.

Finally, Tel Aviv has to be accommodated as a coexisting state within the region and it has to learn to live at peace with the neighbours and accept an independent Palestinian state. This would end the enmity towards the US and the West. These may sound as a wish list, but it is the only way to defeat terrorism and ensure the spread of democracy.

NOTES

1. http://www.dailymotion.com/video/xhdrv8_l-appel-de-bhl-depuis-benghazi-libye-en-direct-sur-tf1-au_news#.UPOateTBjFk
2. See Manlio Dinucci, "A Secret Army of Mercenaries for the Middle East and North Africa", *Il Manifesto*, 18 May 2011.

PART III

RESPONSE AND COUNTERMEASURES

17

Counter-Terrorism Infrastructure and Capacity:

The Need for Political Consensus and Preventive Steps—Administration, Security and Legal

Lisa Curtis

India and the US continue to face threats from terrorists that seek to disrupt their democratic way of life, undermine economic progress and strike terror among their citizenries. Despite a general convergence of views on the need to contain terrorism, India and the US have not cooperated as closely as they should in mitigating these threats. If they are to gain the full benefit of their counter-terrorism cooperation, Washington and New Delhi must overcome mutual suspicion, deepen their intelligence exchanges and consider the carrying out of joint counterterrorism operations. The US can help India enhance its homeland security by sharing technology and best practices. And India can help the US by sharing more information on terrorists that operate in India and that have global connections.

Following the 2008 Mumbai attacks, several barriers to cooperation were broken down, prompting Washington and New Delhi to work together in unprecedented ways. However, the American handling of the David Headley case revived, to some extent, the Indian mistrust of the US. It took nine months before Indian officials gained access to Headley for questioning. Stunning revelations about the Lashkar-e-Taiba's (LeT) international reach and its close connections to Pakistani intelligence emerged from the trials of both Headley and his accomplice, Tahawwur Rana.

Headley had travelled frequently to Pakistan, where he received terrorist training from the LeT, and provided information to Pakistani intelligence officials about the potential attack sites based on the scouting missions he had made to Mumbai. In four days of testimony and cross-examination, Headley detailed the meetings he had had with a serving Pakistani intelligence officer and at least two retired military officials. The US failure to pursue the arrest and prosecution of the Pakistani officials named by Headley further disappointed the Indian officials.

In the past, the US chose to view the activities of the al-Qaeda and other Pakistan-based terrorist groups, such as the LeT, through a separate lens. US officials approached LeT from an Indo-Pakistani perspective, rather than develop policies seeking to degrade and defeat the organisation like any other international terrorist group. This resulted in a failure to hold Pakistan accountable and created a facilitative environment for the LeT to plan and execute the 2008 attacks.

In recent years, the US has become slightly more serious about convincing Pakistani officials to crack down on the LeT, but so far with little success. In April 2012, the US issued a $10 million reward for information leading to the arrest or conviction of the LeT founder and leader of its front organisation, Hafiz Muhammad Saeed. But, shortly after the Pakistani media reported in late January that Islamabad was freezing the assets of the LeT, Saeed announced his organisation was starting an ambulance service in Karachi, demonstrating that he and the group continued to operate relatively freely in the country. The continuing terrorist challenges in the region demand that New Delhi and Washington build a better foundation of trust when it comes to intelligence-sharing and counter-terrorism cooperation. As the Indian Joint Intelligence Committee Chief N. Ravi, stated, sharing intelligence helps countries understand the challenges in a comprehensive way and increases their individual capacities to fight terrorism.

Capacity Building

Since 9/11, the US has made extraordinary changes with regard to enhancing its capacity to fight terrorism, including the establishment of the Department of Homeland Security (DHS). One important DHS initiative has been the development of "fusion centers" to assemble strategic intelligence at the regional level. The "fusion centers" bring together federal, state and local officials and also involve the private sector. In 2004, based on the findings of the 9/11 Commission, the US passed the Intelligence Reform and Terrorism Prevention Act, which created the Office of the Director of National Intelligence (ODNI), to direct and oversee the 17 different US intelligence agencies. In its findings, the 9/11 Commission determined that a major reason the US failed to detect and prevent the 9/11 attacks was because there was no single entity responsible for coordinating all the American intelligence capabilities.

There are several questions about whether the ODNI is fulfilling the responsibilities it was created to carry out. Many believe the ODNI has become more of a senior intelligence advisor to the US President, rather than the leader of the US intelligence establishment. Critics feared early on that the ODNI would become yet another layer of bureaucracy, and several intelligence professionals argue that this is precisely what has occurred.

There were also major changes made in the Federal Bureau of Investigation (FBI) in the initial years after 9/11. The agency was reorganised for prioritising counter-terrorism and its intelligence analysis capabilities were enhanced. There are now field intelligence groups in each field office, analysing intelligence and running down terrorist threats. Rather than focusing on merely building their own individual cases, the FBI agents are now encouraged to develop information as part of a broader, strategic counter-terrorism effort.

Perhaps the most effective change has been the establishment of the National Counterterrorism Center (NCTC), which brings together professionals from across the various intelligence and law enforcement agencies to coordinate intelligence and operations. The NCTC has contributed to breaking down barriers between the different intelligence agencies and has resulted in an improvement in the analysts' ability to connect the dots of various streams of information.

Enhanced information-sharing among federal, state and local law authorities improved the US ability to thwart dozens of terrorist attacks in the last decade. Some 65 terror plots, including 50 that could be considered as home-grown terrorism, have been disrupted.

India has also sought to make changes in the way it organises its government agencies to address the terrorism challenges. After the Mumbai attacks, it set up the National Investigative Agency (NIA), which gives investigators a unique authority to investigate across state lines, thereby addressing the challenge of separate jurisdictions for Indian states.

New Delhi also revitalised the Multi-Agency Centre to operate much like the NCTC, and developed the NATGRID to integrate information databases to better track terror suspects.

Developing Political Consensus

India and the US have different considerations when seeking to develop a political consensus against Islamist terrorism. In India, 15 per cent of the population is Muslim while only around 1 per cent of the U.S. population is Muslim. Moreover, there is a history in India of Hindu–Muslim communal violence, as well as a history of Kashmiri separatism. Despite these contextual differences, both countries have an interest in ensuring that enhanced anti-terrorism measures do not alienate the Muslim minority community.

As the US has increased its counter-terrorism measures, it has made a special effort to communicate with the American Muslim communities about the changes. This open communication between the Muslim minority communities and local law-enforcement agencies has contributed to trust building and the disruption of terrorist plots through community informers.

The Obama Administration caught flak for hosting the high-profile three-day international Countering Violent Extremism (CVE) conference last month. But as a matter of policy, adopting a CVE strategy is absolutely essential. Such a strategy aims to prevent the radicalisation leading to attacks.

Community interventions to raise awareness about online radicalisation have been particularly helpful. In the state of Minnesota, for example, CVE programmes have become important in preventing Somali refugees from returning to their homeland to engage in jihad.

In August 2011, the US released a plan titled "Empowering Local Partners to Prevent Violent Extremism in the US". The plan outlined how the Federal Government could support local efforts and private organisations in preventing radicalisation. This has become even more crucial as an increasing number of individuals are leaving their home countries to fight with the Islamic State of Iraq and al-Sham (ISIS).

According to a recently released United Nations report, over 22,000 foreign fighters have joined the ISIS in Iraq and Syria. The report calls the foreign fighters "an immediate and long-term threat" and the likelihood of a terrorist strike "growing, particularly with attacks targeting hotels, public spaces and venues". It is estimated that around 180 US citizens,

600 British citizens, and 1,200 French citizens have travelled to Iraq and Syria to fight with the ISIS.

India has a strong counter-narrative by virtue of its robust democratic system. The Indian Prime Minister Narendra Modi played to this strength when he answered a question last fall from CNN anchor Fareed Zakaria about al-Qaeda's launch of a South Asian branch. Modi responded that Indian Muslims would live and die for India and that the al-Qaeda is delusional if it thinks that they will dance to their tune. He rightly said that global terrorism "is a fight between humanity and inhumanity, nothing else."

18

Information-Sharing and Interconnection of Experiences:

The Two Pillars of the Italian Intelligence Service Reform

Andrea Margelleti

Introduction

Intelligence has less to do with information; it is more about knowledge and understanding. Intelligence operators, in every intelligence service all over the world, are very jealous of their sources, which are their assets par excellence, the private window on a specific landscape that could easily turn itself into an invaluable ace up their sleeve. The confidentiality of the sources is an inviolable principle, but the information they provide could increase their importance if shared. Even though it has its own value, each bit of information acquires its proper value only when it is correlated to others, like a small tile of a broader mosaic. The faith in the power of information often brings different branches of security services to shield the data reported and to view the idea of sharing them as a dangerous gash in a painting in a private collection. But sharing doesn't mean losing anything; it actually contributes in creating an informative network that could maximise the efficacy and efficiency of the intelligence system. In Intelligence, quantity is not always the solution, quality is. Sharing means getting the people to help you in rebuilding the puzzle.

Today, the most challenging threat for both national and international security stems from radical Islamic terrorism. Joining data, resources and efforts could be a decisive step for gaining—if not a solution—at least some answers as to how to confront the threat. In Italy, we took this step ten years ago. The long history of fighting terrorism and criminal organisations inside our national borders has forged unity amongst our security forces and prepared them to stand up to such an asymmetric threat. Above all, those experiences have taught them that some wars require more than operations, force and technology to be fought; they require the true understanding of the people involved. But the deep divisions among the different units have sometimes hindered their efficiency. A lack of communication and exchange of data inside the security apparatus has resulted in an underperformance of assets and prevented an appropriate understanding of the specific situation, with an inevitable effect on the alacrity and quality of the response. Redundancy always causes big waste, but the bigger problem is never the waste of money—it is the waste of time. And in intelligence, time is the most valuable variable that could affect the result of an operation, and therefore, the security of the nation.

Aware of this problem, our government decided to address the issue of national security in a different manner and in the process, chose to adopt a cultural approach. It looked squarely at its past mistakes to find the way for a real and successful change and to implement systematic reform. This rethinking meant covering wide ranging aspects of the security apparatus. The solution revolved around intelligence-sharing.

The Italian Information-Sharing Revolution

The reform of the National Security apparatus has been implemented according to a specific idea: to make it an instrument at the service of the government and society by highlighting the importance of strategic information as a common good. This rethinking took place in two big steps: the establishment of the Strategic Anti-terrorism Analysis Committee (C.A.S.A.—Comitato di Analisi Strategica Antiterrorismo) and the approval of the reforming law for the Intelligence Services in 2007.

Born informally in 2003, after the attack on the Italian Carabinieri contingent in Iraq, and institutionalised the following year, C.A.S.A. brings to the same table high representatives of the state police, of the Carabinieri, officials of the Italian finance police, representatives of the penitentiary administration department and the intelligence agencies. It is charged with maximising the synergy among the different entities of the security forces, to evaluate the information fluxes relating to all kinds of terroristic threats—both national and international—and to coordinate interventions. The focus of the committee's efforts is prevention. Specifically, this purpose is achieved through controlling the places of aggregation frequented by foreigners and suspected of being a hub for radical proselytisers, monitoring seditious social media, websites and prisons to detect the proselytising activities of radicals and scrutinising and evaluating the personal data on dangerous subjects to determine whether to proceed with expulsion provisions.

The strength of C.A.S.A. is that it provides a permanent strategic platform for confrontation. Versatile and effective, C.A.S.A. has developed into a precious instrument that allows the security forces to interconnect among themselves, sharing not only information but also experiences and perceptions, and consequently, to ease the evaluation of the threat and to implement the response measures.

The second, and fundamental, pillar of the evolution of our national security apparatus is the creation of an information system for the security of the Republic, institutionalised by the reform law approved by the Parliament in 2007. This process involved a deep rethink of the structure of the Italian intelligence system, to make it more transparent, closer to the people and more suitable to cope with the fast evolution of the national and global scenario. Compared with the previous organisation, in which the two main branches of the service (internal and external) were part of the Ministry of the Interior and the Ministry of Defence, respectively, they now operate under the direction of the Prime Minister, who is responsible for their operations and nominates the director and his deputy for both agencies. These two branches are the AISE (Agenzia Informazioni e Sicurezza Esterna) and the AISI (Agenzia Informazioni e Sicurezza Interna), respectively in charge of all the information needed to protect the Italian Republic from external and internal threats. Their activities are coordinated by the DIS (Dipartimento delle Informazioni per la Sicurezza).This department guarantees the uniformity required in planning, information research, analysis and operations of the AISE and AISI, and to coordinate the information activities for the protection of the critical national infrastructures and cyber-space as well. To complete the architecture, Italy has an inter-ministerial committee for the Security of the Republic (CISR—Comitato Interministeriale per la Sicurezza della Repubblica), in charge of advising, proposing and approving the guidelines of the policies of the intelligence service.

To maximise the interconnection among the different hubs of this system, the reforms have also established an integrated school of thought for enhancing education, updating and specialising the operative training of the intelligence operators, but especially to teach them to work together.

With the 2007 reforms, the system for the security of the Republic has become well integrated in the decision-making process of the Italian institutions. Moreover, the policy of openness and disclosure pursued in these eight years has made the intelligence services closer to the Italian people. The most obvious example of this tendency is the constitution of a Parliamentary Committee for the Security of the Republic (COPASIR—Comitato Parlamentare per la Sicurezza della Repubblica): it is a ten-member (five senators and five MP) bicameral body, chaired by a representative of the opposition party/group inside the legislature. It is charged with controlling all activities of the security institutions, upholding the principles of the Italian Constitution. COPASIR was established for guaranteeing not only political, but especially people's control and accessibility to the intelligence services. To have a parliamentary committee on intelligence shows that intelligence services are not something to hide, but that they have a value to show to the people. And this idea is confirmed by the change in people's perception about intelligence. If in the past, most Italians looked at the secret services with suspicion and prudence, now the AISI and AISE are being considered as crucial players in preventing any kind of threat to national security; an asset that works for the citizens and therefore, something in which to put their own trust. Even though there is a close relationship between the government and the security agencies charged with protecting the security of the Republic, the Italian intelligence services are much more than a mere tool at disposal of the executive power; it is a national treasure.

Conclusion

The Italian experience shows how interconnection and sharing are the keystone in making the intelligence services a versatile reality, able to address in a fast and efficacious way, the hard task of protecting the nation at all times. This approach seems to have been more evident during the recent years, when in addition to the traditional asymmetric criticalities for the safety of the state, a new kind of threat has risen, which is much more integrated and which is regarding the effects of the international crises on national interest. There is still room for improvement in the Italian system, but the direction is the right one for success.

At a time when the international community is getting more and more interconnected and in which the states all over the world have to face common threats, enhancing sharing among the different national security services could create an information network which could be relied upon, not just for the sharing of information but also of experiences, best practices and—above all—understanding. Specifically, a broader understanding would be the fundamental variable for enabling a move forward in those conflicts based on cultural gaps and on the clash between the different systems of values. It is in this context that the Islamic State (IS) in Syria and in Iraq has to be confronted. Italy's Minister of Defence, Roberta Pinotti, would be presenting to the Parliament a new strategy to confront the security challenges, as without a sustainable and inclusive long-term strategic view, the fight against this kind of threat is destined to fail. Since we share common threats, this is the time to find common solutions.

19

Technology and Equipment for Counter-Terrorism

Darko Trifunovic

Introduction

The idea for creating the Terrorist and Organised Criminal (TOC) search database came from a survey conducted among the students of specialised studies in the Faculty of Security Studies, in the Republic of Serbia. The survey showed that only about 5 per cent of the data about terrorism and organised crime in the open sources is located in professional security service databases. The reason is that the problem of terrorism and organised crime is treated locally, not globally. The survey results pointed to the need for a unique database that would include all possible information about terrorism and organised crime from various open sources. The Faculty of Science along with the Faculty of Security Studies, both from the University of Belgrade, formed a joint team to create such a database. The team from the Faculty of Science was in charge of the analysis, architecture, implementation and maintenance of the required software, while the team from the Faculty of Security was responsible for entering data, data classification, analysis and the creation of functional requirements from the user's perspective. The Faculty of Security Studies and the George C. Marshall Center–European Center for Security Studies, in 2007, signed a cooperation agreement, under the framework of which, the development team of the database got access on a weekly basis to the reports on terrorism and organised crime on a global scale drawn up by the graduate students of the George C. Marshall Center, which were based on various open sources. These reports also represent key source information in this type of open basis. The relational data model was designed, and it is characterised by the possibility of reading the various data types such as text, images, audio and video facilities. The main entities this database includes pertain to individuals, groups, organisations, actions and supporters of terrorism and organised crime, as well as their interconnections.

During the development of applications, an incremental approach is used. Larger jobs were divided into smaller units and priorities for specific functions were identified. In this manner, greater efficiency was achieved. Evaluation and useful remarks by the users of a database has led to improvements in the existing database functions and in harmonising the needs of the users. In addition, the database has been upgraded with useful, new features, which enables a constant improvement in applications. The database has already been successfully applied during the 2008 Beijing Olympic Games, the 2010 World Exhibition held in China and the FIFA World Cup 2012.[1] It is used daily by students and researchers from the faculty and the institute as well as security experts from Serbia and abroad. There are, currently, several thousand users.[2]

Summary of the Invention

The TOC search is an interdisciplinary project, a result of cooperation between the Faculty of Science and the Faculty of Security Studies, both at the University of Belgrade, with the support of George C. Marshall Center–European Center for Security Studies. Combining various disciplines such as security and mathematics, framed in a software solution, the TOC database search was created. This unique and publicly available internet service enables users—in only a few steps—to check whether a certain person is under suspicion of being linked to terrorist activities or organised crime.

The TOC search contains information about terrorists and criminals, terrorist and criminal groups and organisations, their supporters, attacks, the locations of terrorist and criminal activities as well as the relationships among all of the above-mentioned categories. Service www.tocsearch.com proved to be a very simple and effective additional tool which improves the security measures at various events and situations of high risk as well as during the training of students, research and practical work.

The details of similar technical solutions in some other parts of the world are as under:

- Worldwide Incidents Tracking System (WITS); wits.nctc.gov
- Naval Postgraduate Scholl Dudley Knox Library; http://www.nps.edu/Library/Research/SubjectGuides/SpecialTopics/TerroristProfile/TerroristGroupProfiles.html
- The Institute for Study of Violent Groups (ISVG) database; www.isvg.org
- Global Security Database; www.globalsecurity.org
- Global Terrorism Database (GTD); www.start.umd.edu/gtd/

In comparison with the existing similar types of solutions, the TOC search offers the following:

- Support for all categories of subjects of terrorism and organised crime.
- Keeping connections (links) between subjects, as well as the characteristics of these connections.
- The evolution and improvement of the entered data—the data is updated over time.
- Care and classifying data from open and confidential sources.
- Support for all data types: text, images, sound and video recordings.
- Different user roles in the database for viewing and managing data.
- Different levels of access to data.

Detailed Description of the Work to Search

TOC search represents a dynamic software designed for searching and browsing data about terrorism and organised crime on a global level. It is intended for researchers, analysts, students, experts and all organs and institutions whose task is to monitor, scrutinise and protect the public from terrorism and organised crime. The idea of the TOC search base is based on the integration of data from different open sources (news, reports, journals, studies, etc.), and also from confidential information related to terrorism and organised crime. Additionally, further information of the above-mentioned entities such as references to data sources, locations, terrorist/criminal activity, background, aliases and more are available. All the data entered from open sources is marked with a blue key and that from confidential sources with a red key. Feature storage is one of the major advantages compared to most other terrorism and organised crime databases that exist at present. The links enables the use of different mathematical methods for modelling events and predicting trends in terrorism and organised crime on a global or local level over time. The advantage of the TOC search base is that the database is dynamic. Once entered, the data can be updated and amended by the user base. The database has currently about 12 thousand entries and the number of entries increases on a daily basis.[3]

Existing Databases

In the world today, there are many databases which contain information about terrorism and organised crime. Almost all professional security organisations have internal databases that are not publicly available. The most famous publicly accessible databases are GTD (Global Terrorism Database) and RAND—a global database of terrorist incidents.[4] The GTD and the RAND Database of Worldwide Terrorism Incidents (RDWTI) are characterised by large amounts of data; primarily on terrorist attacks. It contains data from 1970 to 2010. Information about each incident that occurred is preserved, which includes the date and the location of incident, target of attack, the perpetrator and the victim. There is also the possibility of visualisation of terrorist incidents by geographical location and type of target. It also provides an option to export data for later analysis. The GTD database contains approximately one hundred thousand datasets and it is the largest publicly accessible base, while the RAND DWTI database contains about four hundred thousand datasets. The main disadvantage in both bases is that they are primarily concerned about terrorist incidents; basic information about the other categories is descriptive and not separated into individual entities. In addition, both databases are static, i.e. they do not support updating the data that has already been entered. Since the incidents are only identified separately, these two databases do not support establishing the connections between other entities besides the descriptive-type entities, where their further analysis is not possible. Both databases support only textual data type. Data cannot be separated into open and classified types. Users are able to search only the data, but cannot enter data.

Functions of the TOC Search

To access the database, the user (student, researcher, faculty, institute, governmental bodies or institutions, etc.) log-in using a username and password, and enter certain personal information. After checking the data from the database administrator, the user receives one of the two levels of data access: blue or red key. Blue key allows access to data and functionalities intended for students, researchers or educational and scientific institutions. Red key is reserved for state bodies and security institutions. For the latter, in addition to data from the open sources, they have access to confidential data relevant to the protection and the fight against terrorism and organised crime. The basic functionalities of the TOC search base (Figure 1) are divided into two basic groups: search and review of data and data management and administration of the base.

Figure 1: Diagram of the Zero Level

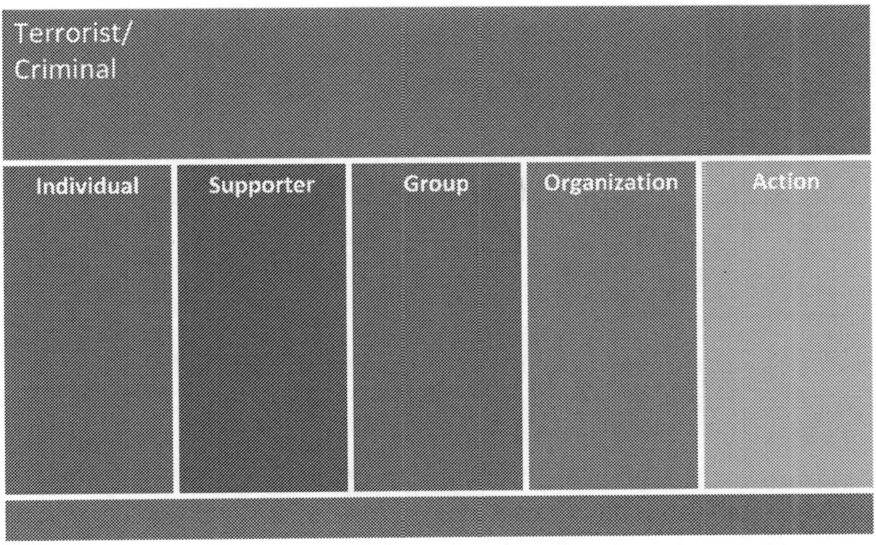

User interface (Figure 2) is designed to be as simple as possible and is user-friendly. It facilitates the user in getting the desired information with a minimal number of steps and has both basic and advanced data search. Basic search means the amount of basic keywords such as name, part of a name or nickname, or pseudonym. Advanced search offers a finer and more precise data filtering in situations when a quick check of several persons is required. These are mainly practical situations such as the control of persons at border and other crossings and mass events (sporting and other). There is also a quick search of the individuals which gives the current information on the entered parties.

One of the most important database functionalities is the ability to enter and modify existing data by the users as well as the administration of the database users, depending on user roles and corresponding access rights (Figure 3). Data management is defined by the role of the facilitator with the blue key or red key. Moderators can add, edit and access data from

Figure 2: The User Interface for Searching Data

the open-source (blue-key data), while the moderators with a red key can, in addition, have access to confidential data (red-key data) and may enter and also change the data.

Data cannot be deleted from the base. For every data entered, the author of the entry or the one making the amendments is known. All previous versions of the data are stored. Administrators have the additional role of managing the users, which includes checking the correctness of the personal data entered, assignment of access rights (red/ blue key) and assigning user roles in the database (external user, moderator, administrator).

The Model of Data of the TOC Search

In order to ensure maximum functionalities and efficiency of the database, special attention is dedicated to the organisation of data (data types, their characteristics, organisation and the way in which the data access is made). According to the nature of the problems being dealt with, the dominant is the textual data type. As mentioned earlier, in addition to textual information, the database also stores pictures, audio and video files which belong to the group of multimedia content.

Figure 3: User Interface for Entering Data into the Database

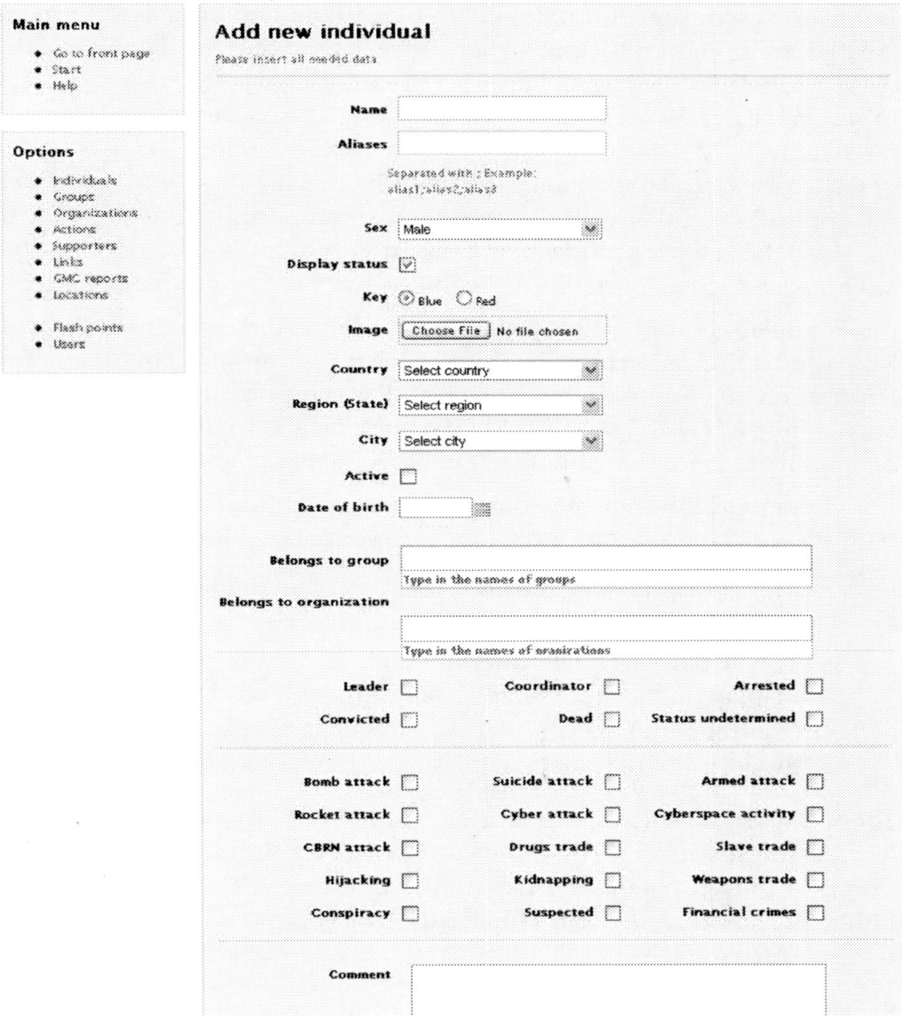

Attributes of each subject are kept as under:

- General information: name, pseudonyms, nicknames, confidentiality of data (red/ blue key) and location.
- Affiliation: The groups and organisations the subject belongs to.
- Relationship status: leader, coordinator, arrested, convicted, status unknown.
- The terrorist/ criminal activity: bombing, armed attacks, arms trade and financial crime, drug trafficking, human trafficking, etc.
- Detailed description of the subject or biography.

Technical Characteristics of the TOC Search

Database search for information about terrorism and organised crime is created as a web application client-server architecture. For using the database, besides the internet browser, no additional software is necessary to access the database at www.tocsearch.com. The entire system is located on a centralised server, in which is located the application part of the database as well as the data itself. The user does not need to know where the application is physically located, nor is that information necessary to use the database. This model of organisation and application has multiple advantages such as portability, flexibility and platform independence.

For database applications, open source tools and techniques were used. The application is written in the PHP 5 programming language. The application runs on Apache 2.2 server. For the presentation part of the application, XHTML 1.0, CSS 2.1 and jQuery JavaScript library were used. The database is implemented in MySQL 5 relational database.

The organisation of the source code is made according to the MVC pattern, which consists of three physically separated layers:

- Model Application: the layer that serves for data management and includes all classes.
- The visual part (User Interface): a layer that is used for the visual display of data and accepts user input and requests.
- Controller: a layer that serves as the link between the application model and the visual part.

Tools Used: The software is written in the PHP programmer language. Net Beans was used for the development of applications (License: The Common Development and Distribution License (CDDL) and the GNU Public License v.2). MySQL Workbench tool (license: GPL Open Source) was used for database modelling.

Security: The base is defined by different user roles to ensure an access control to data and access control to functions. Users are first divided into external and internal and then into users authorised a blue or red key. External users can only view the data, while internal users in addition to viewing, can also enter and modify data based on the type of key they are authorised (blue or red). Although the database is publicly available, a registration is required for its use. Access may be granted by the administrator after checking the credentials of the user, who will thereafter define the role of the user in the database (whether external or internal user) and assigns access rights to the data (blue or red key). Personal data of the users is protected. The data entered by the user is used solely to verify the identity of the users and is not publicly available. No data is deleted from the database and the history of the changes and reference to source is preserved for each entered data. All the entries of the users are filtered several times and the source code of the application is protected.

Besides the security application highlighted earlier, the application has educational utility, and helps students in mastering the practical application of the methods of collection, analysis and data classification, developing research skills and abilities as well as the expansion of knowledge outside of regular curricula at the university. Future developments will be related to the implementation of algorithms for face detection and recognition and for mobile applications for the Android platform in order to take advantage of smartphones. It will also look into modelling events, statistics tests, prediction of trends in terrorism and organised crime on a local and global level and the implementation of software solutions on flying platforms such as drones.

NOTES

1. University of Belgrade, Center for Tehnology Transfer, http://www.ctt.bg.ac.rs/en/available-technologies/the-terrorist-and-organized-criminal-search-database-toc-search
2. The Terrorist and Organized Criminal Search Database (TOC-search) www.tocsearch.com
3. Stanimiroviæ Zorica, Darko Trifunovic, "From Database to Knowledge: The Terrorist and Organized Criminal Search Database", *Social Science Computer Review*, SAGE, Volume 29, Number 4 (November 2011).
4. The Global Terrorism Database (GTD) is an open-source database, http://www.start.umd.edu/gtd/ RAND Database of Worldwide Terrorism Incidents (RDWTI), http://www.rand.org/nsrd/projects/terrorism-incidents.html

20

The Regional Challenge and Cost of Terrorism

Shuja Nawaz

With the change in the geostrategic and geopolitical environment in greater South Asia, following the withdrawal of coalition forces from Afghanistan, a challenge and opportunity have both arisen in the region. Instead of a zero-sum game of political one-upmanship, there is a clear opportunity to alter the traditional paradigms that have shaped thinking in the region. Individual countries in the region are attempting to embark upon socio-economic progress and trying to eliminate the abject poverty that afflicts a vast proportion of their populations. Economics needs to displace politics in the strategic calculus of governance. But, the process of change is not going to be easy. It takes a major effort for politicians and military strategists to revisit and reshape their thinking about regional threats and on how to tackle them. Few appear to have the courage to speak out equally against all forms of militancy and terrorism. But, new elections in the region have produced strong mandates for the current crop of leaders in a number of South Asian countries. If those leaders can stop looking in the rear-view mirrors and look to the future, they may be able to tackle their own countries' problems and perhaps help the region as a whole.

Terrorism and militancy, based on ethnicity, religion or ideology, pose a major threat to all countries in South Asia. Some tentative steps towards the finding of solutions have been initiated. Much more needs to be done. Given the major economic and social challenges facing all countries in the region, it is critical that they find workable solutions for collaborating against terrorism and changing the landscape that spawns terror and militancy. The opportunity cost of conflict is too high to be ignored. Procrastination and complacency are not going to help any government.

Underlying the difficulties facing the military and civilian decision-makers is the effect of the Principal–Agent Conflict that they face. Given the tools at their disposal, they tend to focus on expanding the counter-terrorism operations, rather than changing the environment that spawns and sustains terrorism and militancy. The end result is often to strengthen the militarised response. As India, Pakistan and Sri Lanka have discovered, this ends up becoming a long-term commitment—a veritable quagmire that no country can afford for extended periods.

Despite their different political systems and varying balances between the civil and the military, each country needs to examine the underlying conditions that allow terrorism and militancy to affect the societal choices and disrupt socio-economic development. They need to cast a fresh look at the security issues they face. Instead of relying on stereotypes of internal and external enemies and looking for short-term fixes, they need to cast a farther glance and look over the horizon at their own aims. Given the vast sea of poverty and to lift all segments of their populations above subsistence levels, they need to redefine their objectives and reshape policies to achieve those objectives, even if it means the shattering of age-old images and fears that inhabit their thinking and plans.

It is easy to dismiss such thinking as over-optimistic. But, pragmatism, and not emotion, needs to be the driver of change. To look at the two major South Asian countries, India and Pakistan: both face the challenge of respectively creating some 12 million and 3 million new jobs respectively annually, just to stay even with their population increase and to sustain a gross domestic product development at roughly seven per cent annually. Security expenditures are a drain on those efforts—more so for Pakistan than for India—but a drain nevertheless.

Moreover, each country in the region must acknowledge that the terrorists and militants have an edge over them in terms of their ability to select the time and place of the next attack. The authorities cannot provide 100 per cent security. Hence, they need to become more proactive, using security and politico-economic tools to pre-empt the efforts of the disrupters. When terrorism is cross-border, this may involve cross-border consultation and cooperation, breaking age-old barriers to such collaboration.

Standing in the way of such collaboration is the nexus between the state and terrorism. When a country employs asymmetrical warfare through surrogate means against a neighbour, it increases the chances of international conflict. And it risks the backlash of fomenting terrorism abroad by creating fissures and fault-lines inside its own militarised society. In the past, Pakistan suffered the consequences of such actions both in Afghanistan and Kashmir. India felt the effects of the Tamil unrest in Sri Lanka.

Further, militancy and terrorism are tied to global and regional conflicts that force countries to align themselves with one or the other major power, or become the cockpit for proxy wars, based on ethnic or sectarian grounds. Over time, Pakistan suffered the consequences of its alignments with the Western alliance against the former Soviet Union and later while trying to balance its relations between the Kingdom of Saudi Arabia and the Islamic Republic of Iran. The result was the creation of a highly weaponised and divided society at home and a huge distraction from its development priorities. The re-emergence of new power arrangements in South Asia and the Pacific region are producing similar challenges for the countries in South Asia, as the West tries to contain a rising China by attempting to use a rising India as a surrogate and partner. Other, smaller South Asian nations will have to choose sides over time, reducing their ability to garner resources from both China and the United States for their development efforts.

Meanwhile, global terrorism has been changing its forms and operations. It is no longer operating with a centralised command and control system. Rather, it relies on the spread of ideas and ideologies and uses franchises and networks with local partners as a force multiplier. Small, independent cells, bolstered by local support networks and fed on local grievances, operate under the umbrella of global militancy. This produces a self-sustaining entity that is harder to eliminate with the traditional militarised approaches.

Technologies that once gave governments the edge are now widely available and easily employed by militants and terrorists to communicate and to train and deploy the assets speedily at a time and place of their choosing. Governments will need to outthink these networks and try to stay a few steps ahead of them to forestall anti-state actions. Similarly, terrorist networks rely on technology to raise and distribute funds. But, the government too has the tools to track and cut off such flows, forcing the anti-state networks to resort to a less effective and less-efficient manual transmission of funds. In Pakistan, for example, the State Bank has the ability to monitor such flows and accounts and seal them, if the government so chooses. Moreover, the presence of community-based and regional police entities is potentially an important weapon against such anti-state activities. The presence of the local police person on his or her beat can help block the entry of terrorists and militants. But this has to be rooted in a building up of the confidence of civil society in the police as a protector rather than as a tool of oppression by an over-weaning State. Sharing good practices across national borders will help raise confidence in the ability of the countries to improve their methods and operations. But first, they must remove their political barricades to such traffic of ideas and experience.

Can governments in South Asia face down these threats successfully? May be. The results of their efforts will rest on their ability to change their methods of analysis of these threats and the crafting of suitable operations. More and better communications with the local and regional police officials and civil servants to evaluate conditions on the ground are needed. Drawing these groups and civil society into a discussion prior to the planning of operations and enhancing their ability to support and then take over from the paramilitary and military actors at a suitable time will make the anti-terror operations sustainable. Otherwise, governments risk attacking the symptoms and not the causes of militancy and terror.

Examples from both Pakistan and India can help understand the need to alter the approach towards militancy. Pakistan postponed for six-plus decades the need to integrate its border regions with Afghanistan with Pakistan proper. It also treated Balochistan as a marginal entity because of its smaller population base and failed to involve the local populations in self-government. Civil and military governments at the centre ignored the need for a voice and development of the periphery. Thus was created a breeding ground for militancy and terrorism that threatens the entire country today. Pakistan is now trying a military approach but will need to tie it to greater involvement of local populations in handling their own administration and economic resources. A political solution for the future of the Federally Administered Tribal Areas is still needed to ensure a lasting peace when the military operations cease. Similarly, India's heavily militarised approach in Kashmir has failed to quell the demand for greater autonomy and choice there, while keeping alive a conflict with Pakistan. In Punjab, after an initial military approach, it successfully altered the local economic and political landscape and nearly eliminated all elements of Sikh nationalism. Lessons from Punjab could be transferred to other peripheral regions where insurgencies continue inside India.

The responsibility of political leaders to create the right kind of dialogue in the public sphere remains critical to the success of anti-terror efforts. It is incumbent on political leaders to distance themselves from any alignment with sectarian, religious or ethnic forces that seek to separate populations rather than bring them together. The signalling effect is very important. There have been too many instances of national leaders either remaining quiet or siding with an extremist rhetoric or actions for local or short-term political gains. Especially during election campaigns, political leaders need to be clear about the need to eliminate the possibility of ethnic or religious divisions being used by their partners or own parties. Militants and terrorist use these fault lines to strengthen their hold on the public imagination.

Short-run approaches create a Boomerang Effect. For example, the creation of militant proxies ends up arming more people and creates the possibility of well-armed disruptive forces inside a society over time, as their political allegiances shift. Today's ally becomes tomorrow's enemy. There was a well-articulated debate among the military leadership inside FATA for example, when the idea of arming the local tribal *lashkars* was mooted. *Lashkars* have been used from time to time but they represent a nascent risk and threat to the State and create power imbalances within the tribal societies.

What to do

The South Asian governments need to better assess their own longer-term aims and threats when crafting policies to counter violent extremism and terrorism. This means the crafting of an over-the-horizon strategy that helps create the conditions for the participation of all segments of society in the economic and political life of the country. A greater effort also needs to be made for weaving together the civil society and the police, starting at the local level. A consistent and honest governance is the basis for creating trust between the people and those who are meant to "protect and serve" them, namely the police. Changing the image and the reality of the police will be critical for laying the foundation for creating an impregnable defence against militancy and terrorism. When South Asia eliminates the use of the term "encounter" from its vocabulary, it would have achieved that level of confidence in the operations of its local police forces. More resources for training and equipping the police forces at all levels will be far more effective for fighting terrorism and militancy than in improving the already well-established armed forces.

At a national level, it is necessary to totally eliminate the *rentier* politico-military complex into more egalitarian societies that educate all and provide health, development and access to resources in a more equitable manner. Fighting militancy is not about body counts alone; neither are the body counts an effective metric by themselves.

At a broader level, there is a need to dampen down the regional conflict. India and Pakistan are already suffering heavily due to their ongoing hostility. A study done by Mohan Guruswamy and I for the Atlantic Council on the opportunity cost of conflict between India and Pakistan posited that each country loses up to 1.5 per cent of its GDP growth per annum as a result of the conflict. They could change the conditions for the better by opening up their borders to people and trade and tie the whole region into a single integrated economic zone that would have a tremendous clout on the global scene. South Asia can also benefit from linking itself to Afghanistan, Iran and Central Asia on the one hand and through Myanmar to China and South-East Asia. This would help raise the huge proportions of the poorest into the upper rungs of the economic ladder. And that would blunt the attraction of militancy and terrorism by removing one recruitment tool.

But, challenges stand in the way. Pakistan still has a huge underground economy. Its informal sector continues to outgrow its formal sector creating a vicious cycle in which the government cannot provide services to its people and the people are not willing to pay taxes for those services. Integrating FATA into Pakistan is critical to avoid continuing the conflict that may allow militants to use Afghanistan as reverse sanctuary. Balochistan needs to be given a greater voice and participation. One such idea has recently been put forward in an email by Sherazam Mazari, the son of a famous Baloch tribal leader. It deserves to be read in detail:

> I sat through many intimate conversations between Nawab Bugti, Sardar Khair Buksh and Sardar Attaullah Mengal. I never heard an intent for an independent Balochistan in those meetings. The conversation delved on preserving the Baloch culture, which given the small population of Baloch's within Pakistan was a legitimate concern.

One of the fallouts of Pakistan's identity crisis is a phobia about the elements breaking Pakistan. This has cost us half of Pakistan and today has disenchanted a majority of the Baloch. What is happening in Balochistan today is NOT an insurrection led by the Sardars—it is rather, unfortunately, a middle-class movement. Eighty per cent of the Sardars have been in the past, and also currently, are being supported by the establishment and vice versa. It is Balochistan's people, who are illiterate, poor and marginalised from the mainstream Pakistan and those who are most affected by the current insurgency.

Balochistan will remain an integral part of Pakistan not because of the strong national identity but for the greatest gift Pakistan has—the Indus River. Practically, all of Balochistan's agricultural land is watered by the Indus River from the sources in Sind. The issue today, therefore, is how to bring the Baloch into the folds of a Pakistani identity—and here is a possible proposal. If we could talk with the Taliban, surely we can also with the Baloch people and seek comments on the points suggested by a moderate Baloch Nationalist (not necessarily mine), which are:

- The military operation must stop immediately and all funding to the Sardars should end. A reconciliation commission be established to heal the wounds of decades.
- All those Baloch who have been forcibly taken away and are missing must be released and allowed to re-join their family members.
- Direct compensation in a transparent mode to the families of all those who got killed, kidnapped and tortured.
- Homeless IDPs must be returned to their homes with honour and dignity; rehabilitated and compensated.
- All Afghan refugees living in Balochistan must be returned back to Afghanistan and their names removed from the voter registration lists.
- The Gwadar port and Balochistan's natural resources must be used to uplift the Baloch people. And a plan developed to leverage the recent Chinese investments for the development of Balochistan.
- An independent commission be established to promulgate the steps for preserving the Baloch people's secular identity and culture within the overall Pakistani identity.

There may be other ideas similar to this that are worth exploring. Rather than treat Balochistan as the "other", bring it back into the fold and develop it for all who live within its boundaries. This may also end the heated debate inside Pakistan about the surreptitious Indian support for Baloch separatism. Similarly, a Kashmir solution that rests on the needs and wishes of the people of the region could help eliminate the seemingly unending conflict between India and Pakistan.

India, too, has a vast pool of the poor who need to be brought into the globalised upper rungs of its society. India must not become complacent about its vast Muslim youth population that has recently become the object of recruitment efforts by the militant groups. The reported association of the members of the Indian Mujahideen and HUJI with the planning of the Mumbai attack, and more recently, interviews with Muslim Indians who became disenchanted by the Islamic State indicate that the IS uses the economic plight of the Muslim youth as a means to bring them into its fold. India has the basis for change in the Sachar Commission report that needs to be discussed again, so that progress on the many useful suggestions it made can be measured. The current government may have a good opportunity to build on the work of its predecessor in that regard.

Regardless of the challenges, the countries in South Asia have the means to provide a better governance to their people. Such governance rests on the provision of better services and creation of equal opportunities for their populations, without reference to religion, ethnicity or sect. Building such internal and external bridges in the region will contain and counter terrorism and militancy better than building walls. Indian and Pakistan can lead the way, under civilian governments who have been brought into power with overwhelming public support.

21

The Mumbai 26/11 Attacks:

An Analysis

Rana Banerji

The horrendous attack by ten Pakistani terrorists on several tourist hotels and a Chabad of the Israeli rabbis in Mumbai on 26 November 2008, marked a watershed in India's security paradigm, just as the 9/11 terror attack on the Twin Towers in New York had done for the United States. One hundred sixty-eight persons were killed, of whom 28 were foreigners, including 6 Americans. This was an act of war perpetrated by non-state actors, all Pakistani nationals, one of whom was arrested. Nine others were killed. The evidence of the Pakistani state's involvement was glaring. The Kasab confession, corroborated by the Headley depositions and interrogation by the Indian investigators, brought out how Lashkar-e-Taiba (LeT) leaders like Hafiz Mohd Saeed had supervised the recruitment and training of these ten commandos; how the video-recorded data prepared by David Coleman Headley during his several trips to India was handed over to the handlers of the Inter-Services Intelligence (ISI) Directorate through intermediaries like Sajid Mir and suitably nom-de-plumed serving officers. Headley was given an approver status in the Tahawwur Rana case in the USA, but the access given to the Indian interrogators by the US authorities remained inadequate.

This complicity has now been further corroborated in the Abu Jundal interrogations.With his presence and record of voice transcripts from the LeT control room near Karachi becoming available, Zaki-ur Rehman Lakhvi stands clearly implicated.

Today, the terror threat seems to have turned inwards and seriously hit Pakistan. Peshawar 16/12 was as much a catastrophe, with children of mostly army personnel being hit by the terrorists' strike. Casualties from terrorism in Pakistan since 9/11 have amounted to 16,000 military losses, apart from collateral civilian damage. The question that now arises in the backdrop of the Army's crackdown against the Tehrik-e-Taliban Pakistan (TTP)—is anything going to change? As perceptive media observers in Pakistan like Cyril Almeida (*Dawn* group) have observed, "Is the 'Zarb e Azb' going to prove only a 'temporary smokescreen' and will the Pakistani establishment deal selectively with 'three halves of militancy'—the Afghan Taliban, TTP & Lashkar-e-Taiba (LeT)?"

Failure to Detect Infiltration

The timing of the attack proved deceptive. The original intelligence input indicated that the attack had been planned for September 2008. An alert was given then also. The plan was deferred due to an abortive sea start from Karachi. In November 2008, a fresh alert was given. It was quite specific—but dates were deferred by a few days, possibly due to inclement weather. In retrospect, it can be said that the frequency of alerts given may have bred complacency among the implementing security agencies like the coast guard or the Mumbai police.

The failure to prevent these attacks despite a prior warning, flagged the police unpreparedness and a haphazard coast guard/navy follow up. The recent boat destruction incident of January 2015 reveals a better-preparedness and quick action after an alert, though the incident is mired in some controversy.

The Pradhan Committee findings emphasised the need to dovetail/ coordinate intelligence inputs. It also focused on the long-pending Maharashtra police upgrade requirements and the imperative to institutionalise mechanisms. Since then, action has been initiated to tighten up gaps in the other security domains. Tightening up of maritime security is one such area of attention. Work was taken up for the registration of dhows, the positioning of GPS devices and a centralised monitoring of the equipment installed. All this is work in progress.

Delays in the 26/11 Judicial Process

In Pakistan, only seven people were arrested. They were charged almost a year later. Three others majorly involved were not arrested—Sajid Mir alias Wasi, Abu Qahafa alias Mazhar Iqbal (main trainer) and the mysterious Maj Iqbal (his name was also mentioned in the Tahawwur Rana trial in the USA). Nothing was done about the voice samples handed over to the Pakistani authorities by India, including those of the two identified state agency officials—Maj Samir Ali and Maj Abdur Rahman—ISI handlers who had been named by Headley. The Courts in Pakistan gave several adjournments on flimsy pretexts—eight times between September 2011 and June 2012. There were frequent transfers of judges. The defence lawyers gave pleas of a security threat. Chaudhary Zulfiqar, the main prosecutor, was later murdered, though this could have been connected to the Benazir Bhutto case.

Sebastian Rotella's disclosures in the *Pro Publica*, USA, first revealed how the arrested LeT mastermind, Zaki-ur Rehman Lakhvi, continues to enjoys the best of facilities even while in custody in the Adiala Jail, Rawalpindi. He has access to mobile phones, home-cooked food, visits by relatives as well as cadres and operational aides like Yahya Muzammil, Sajid Mir and ISI officers were able to meet him. He was able to beget a son after a second marriage while in jail. Ironically enough, his son has been named Maulana Adialvi.

The Pakistani establishment's intention became very clear—it wanted to only keep Lakhvi away from the limelight but do little else. Lakhvi's release on bail, which was ordered by the judiciary, caused great embarrassment, revealing delays in forming the Review Committee required under the Maintenance of Public Order Act. Federal authorities were forced on the defensive and faced international opprobrium and diplomatic pressure from the USA and India. During post-mortems, it became evident that all facts were not presented by the prosecution in the bail cases. This may have emboldened his defence, which made attempts recently to deny Lakhvi's very involvement in perpetrating the 26/11 attack.

The Judicial Dilemma in Pakistan

These delays have raised a valid perception in India that Pakistan is not serious about trying the accused in a terrorist strike which has acquired connotations of a war-like escalation through non-state actors. The new-found judicial independence and dumping of the doctrine of necessity by Chief Justice (CJ) Iftikhar Chaudhry's Court during 2007–10 seemed a thing of the past, in so far as this case was concerned. Now, the judiciary seemed most reluctant—even afraid to act. A streak of sympathy surfaced for conservative radicalism. A former Chief Justice of Lahore High Court was defending Qadri, the killer of the Punjab governor Salman Taseer, though the court has now confirmed his death penalty.

Under the newly announced National Action Plan (NAP), nine military courts have been set up. The larger issue that has come up is of the 21st Amendment. Questions have been raised about its constitutional validity and a Bar Council PIL has been filed. Political parties too have questioned its sanctity. Therefore, an observer's question: how long would it take for the consensus for action against the terrorists to dissipate in Pakistan?

Problems of the Judiciary

The lower judiciary in Pakistan finds it difficult to challenge the threat of militancy/terrorism by Islamic fundamentalists. During Iftikhar Chaudhry's tenure, in the "disappearance cases" of the persons apprehended by the security forces, especially in Baluchistan, the CJ confronted the agencies—both the ISI and the Frontier Corps (FC). There have been difficulties also for the security agencies in marshalling sufficient evidence regarding the cases of arrested terrorists, to satisfy the letter of law before "play safe" judges. Witnesses back out due to fear, and criminals fail to get convicted. In Swat, though there was success in military operations and many terrorists were arrested, but very few could be convicted. The statistics are glaring: 282/447 in Punjab only, in 2011.

The Asia Society, USA commissioned a special police reform report in July 2012, associating senior retired Pakistani police officers, which brought out this predicament. This raises the question as to whether the present Pakistan government is at all serious about police/judicial reforms? Recently, a concept of Apex Committees has been started where the police, civilian and military officials sit together to marshal all evidence against the terrorists. Would this approach work in the long term?

Pakistan: Growing Radicalisation

Pakistan has been affected by growing Islamic radicalisation due to the propagation of a convoluted concept of jihad,where "jihad to kill" is justified. There is a continuing commitment of the non-state actors in that country to this ideology. This has been perpetuated by the growth of linkages with outfits like the al-Qaeda. The advent of the Islamic State (IS) signals further ominous portends. The domestic agenda of the adherents to this ideology is the setting up of an Islamic State based on the Sharia. There is an external agenda as well—liberating all other traditional Muslim lands forming part of the Umma, eliminating the influence of the USA,

Israel and *kaafirs*. This has led to the aggravation of anti-US feelings in civil society post 9/11 and especially after Osama bin Laden's elimination in May 2011. Even within the Army, there was the Hizb-ut-Tahrir infiltration. Meanwhile, a splintering of the TTP was reported with pro-IS factions being formed. Sectarian schisms which were already deep in the time of Zia-ul-Haq's Islamisation have now deepened. There are reports of patronage being accorded to the Lashkar-e-Jhangvi (LeJ) by the state, especially in Punjab.

Is the Lashkar-e-Taiba (LeT) on a leash?

A question has sometimes been posed as to why there have been no more attacks against India by the LeT, post 26/11? Partly, this may be due to deliberate pressure from the state, urging it to lie low till international pressure fades and the situation on the Western border improves after a US withdrawal from Afghanistan in 2014. It has not been for want of trying! There are other reasons too.

Historically, the LeT's main utility to the Pakistani state has been as an asymmetric "force multiplier", to spread low-cost, trans-border terror in Jammu & Kashmir and to cause instability elsewhere in India. Now, there is attrition in Jammu & Kashmir and in infiltration across the Line of Control/International Border. A terror fatigue may have set in and a dwindling local support for the "Punjabi outsiders" has resulted in only 80–100 "outsiders" remaining in small pockets in J&K.

However, more militant, younger cadres of the LeT with an ideological motivation—battle-hardened from the camps and from experiences of actual fighting in the Afghan theatre—have been chaffing at bits, as became evident from the Headley interrogation. The spectre of inadequate control by the LeT leadership could be haunting its state handlers. Meanwhile, the LeT has been directed to develop a new strategy which focuses on its networking with the Indian Mujahideen (IM) modules. Safe havens have been offered to the IM leaders who are on the run from arrests in India. Others have been trained and sent back to form sleeper cells inside India.

In the context of the crackdown against terrorists inside Pakistan, it must be realised that the LeT has never attacked the Pakistani establishment so far. Neither has it coalesced with the sectarian Sunni fanatics to attack the Shias—despite its own ideologically (Ahle Hadis) visceral hate for the latter. This has been tellingly exposed in Christine Fair's thesis ("Survival", *IISS Journal*, UK) which contends that the "LeT may be used to challenge Deobandi orthodoxy of other Sunni fundamentalist outfits or militant groups looking to attack the State". This enhances its utility for the Pakistani state

This explains the State's tolerance of, and support to, the so-called philanthropic activities of the LeT's various fronts—the Jamaat-ud-Daawa (JuD), Falah-e-Insaniyat, Hurmat-e-Rasool (students), and Umme Shuhada (mothers), among others. The attempt to project the role and prominence of the Difa-e-Pakistan rallies to divert the energies/occupy fundamentalists such as Hafiz Mohd Saeed, Munawwar Hussain and Maulana Samiul Haq stems from a similar motive and enables the Army/ISI to manoeuvre/control excessive radicalism within the domestic arena. Attempts by the pro-establishment academics to glorify the social work of the JuD and JeI women cadres, especially in the urban areas, falls in the same vein.

LeT's Global Agenda

The LeT does have a definite transnational or global agenda of jihad, delineated in detail in Arif Jamal's recent book, *Call for Transnational Jehad: LeT, 1985-2014*. Its well-trained cadres have regularly been sent for battle inoculation in war theatres like Afghanistan and Bosnia. Networks/linkages have been built up with cells in Australia, USA, Africa, Myanmar and Europe.

Recently, LeT trainers were sent for the training of Rohingya Muslims from Myanmar and Bangladesh in Thailand. A nexus with Sikh terrorists seems to have been forged with the itinerant Babbar Khalsa and the ISYF remnants coming in from Europe/UK for plotting terror incidents inside India. The busting of this module also revealed a continuing ISI involvement in pursuit of this agenda to destabilise India. The aim has not changed; only greater care is now being exercised to avoid international opprobrium by distancing its own complicity.

ISI and the "Rogue Elements"

Sometimes, there is a grudging admission of the involvement of possible "rogue" officials, no longer "authorised" or "retired" but still indulging in the exhortation of non-state actors. The "fate" that befell two of the ISI's most glorified operatives—Sqn Ldr Khalid Khwaja and Col Sultan Mohd Tarar alias Amin—was intriguing. Both of them were killed during the attempts to release a British journalist of Pakistani origin, Asad Quereshi, from the clutches of the TTP in FATA, despite the ISI/Army appeals for release, conveyed to the TTP through various intermediaries. This raises questions about the Army/ISI's ability to control/manipulate non-state actors like the LeT.

Role of Media

In the context of responding to terror incidents spanning the Indo-Pak relationship, the media on both sides needs to act responsibly. There has to be a fine balance between the freedom of the press and objective reporting. In Pakistan's domestic context, there was the sensational Hamid Mir case, where the media and civilian politicians aligned against the ISI and the Army for a brief while, before eating humble pie. We need to know if any lessons were learnt from this chastening experience.

In India, TV channels should look beyond TRP ratings and avoid Pakistan-baiting. They should get sensible, balanced, rational panellists to report from both sides, not rabble-rousers. There may be a need to learn, especially by the vernacular media channels, not to over-hype the situation. One useful step could be to set up consultative media mechanisms in both countries separately, to focus on responsible reporting. The question remains on the issue of media accountability—how to fix it without encroaching on press freedom. Self-introspection could be the way forward.

International Concerns

After the discovery of Osama bin Laden in Abbottabad, not much remained in doubt about the complicity of the Pakistani establishment and its proclivity to "double-deal" with international interlocutors, promising cooperation in the "war on terror" while continuing to abet "non-state actors". This was evident also after the Raymond Davis case in January 2011 where "red lines" of cooperation between the ISI and CIA appear to have been irrevocably transgressed. However, this schism has not led to any major change in the US approach, as its need to keep Pakistan engaged remains a vital strategic imperative. Would this change after the US withdrawal from Afghanistan? Concerns remain though, about the LeT's global agenda.

New factors are discernible, suggesting a change in the Pakistan Army's approach to certain geostrategic policy goals. This became evident after Raheel Sharif's advent as Army Chief as also after the election of Ashraf Ghani as President in Afghanistan. Afghanistan may need to assess though, the genuineness of the Pakistani leadership's assurance to curb the Afghan Taliban resurgence.

China's main concerns are about Uighur Muslims training in FATA but it may be signalling a willingness to come forward in a mediatory role in the Afghan reconciliation. India will remain very much on its own in the context of continuing asymmetric threats coming from trans-border non-state actors and will have to fend for itself.

The Way Forward for Stakeholders

Pakistan's domestic agenda should focus on certain essential priorities if it is serious about enforcing the writ of the state against the insurgency and radicalisation in vast swathes of territory extending from FATA to Khyber-Pakhtunkhwa to South Punjab. In the past, de-radicalisation programmes were taken up by the Army (after the Swat operation) but these have made little impact. There is a need to have a role for police officers as brought out by the 2013 Asia Society report. The army leadership has to understand that Pakistan's main existential threat arises from the internal security situation, not from India.

There is also a need to develop and orchestrate all elements of national power as the military can no longer afford to be seen as the sole custodian of security. Otherwise, Pakistan would be faced with what Shuja Nawaz has termed the *Egypt on the Indus* syndrome—civilian politicians must play a role in the fight against domestic terrorism.

In the long-term, Pakistan requires to invest in education and ensure that the benefits of modern education are made available to the poorer sections of society at affordable costs. Educational curriculum changes would acquire meaning if the Pakistanis learn to lessen their proclivity to remain in a state of denial about the negative actions of the state or non-state actors. This brings up the vexatious issue of madrassa reform, bringing in statutory controls for an oversight of curriculum content and the sources of funding. These reforms should go hand in hand with the efforts to bridle inflammatory oratory rhetoric and in changing the vernacular media narrative. The economic development of FATA and investing in political rights there is another desirable objective.

Relevance of Indian Responses

In India, an urgent step would be to initiate a socio-cultural reaching out to the Indian Muslims. The other most essential requirement would be to strengthen our own homeland security mechanisms through sustained and expedited police/intelligence reforms.

If and when any changing trends in the narrative of stemming terrorism become visible or seem to take root in Pakistan, certain confidence-building measures (CBMs) could be prescribed. The obvious and most reassuring would be the demonstrable punishment of the 26/11 accused, sorting out delays of the judicial process in the connected cases, simplifying mechanisms to make evidence of the ghastly killings admissible in courts and lasting steps for substantive judicial/police reforms.

Sustained institutional contacts between the two armies could be a CBM worth pursuing after more trust is established. These could be done through more frequent contacts in games, training visits, war college courses, military exercises, border/regimental-level hotlines. There could be more contacts of officers of the infantry/artillery/armoured corps units at lower levels. We could set in motion an army-to-army authorised crisis communication channel quickly.

The ruling/opposition political parties of both countries could begin sending parliamentary delegations, state CMs/politicians and other elements of civil society to each other's countries on a more regular basis. In the long run, movement in this direction offers the only way to wish away the hostility bequeathed by history and to restore the inevitable logic of geography for better neighbourly relations.

22

Counter-Radicalisation and De-Radicalisation:

Exploring Approaches and Strategies for Bangladesh

Farooq Sobhan

Introduction

For the last couple of years, Bangladesh has been witnessing a steady rise in radical extremism, especially among the youth. With Bangladesh's considerable successes in terms of counter-terrorism, a new trend in radicalisation has surfaced which threatens to unravel the general peaceful nature of the country's social fabric. However, in comparison to the other countries in South Asia (such as Pakistan and Afghanistan), Bangladesh did not have to confront an acute problem of violent extremism for most of its existence.

As a Muslim-majority country, Bangladesh espouses secularism and this is also enshrined in its Constitution as a basic principle. The current government's zero-tolerance policy against terrorism has largely been very successful. But in order to sufficiently counter the rise of radicalisation, a series of soft measures need to be adopted. A careful analysis of the security trends in Bangladesh suggest that radicalisation is emerging as a larger threat than terrorism.

This paper is divided into three sections. First, it endeavours to define radicalisation and de-radicalisation in the context of Bangladesh. The second section focuses on the various approaches of de-radicalisation as currently adopted by many countries. Finally, it suggests some de-radicalisation strategies for Bangladesh, drawing lessons from the existing practices.

Framing Concepts: Radicalisation and De-Radicalisation

As with many concepts of international relations, peace and security studies, finding an agreed definition of a common concept is often difficult. However, most countries and research institutions construct their own definition of terms taking into account the ground realities. With respect to the definition of radicalisation, the following definition perhaps best reflects the prevailing realities in Bangladesh:

> Radicalisation is a process in which a person gets indoctrinated by others or through self-motivation into a rigid ideology, religious or otherwise, equipped with a set of goals and plans that may eventually lead to extremism, militancy and terrorism aiming at national and/or international systemic change for governance and regulating human lives.[1]

Deconstructing this definition reveals the inherent process of radicalisation. In the process of radicalisation, a person or a group of persons first come into contact with someone who preaches a radical, rigid ideology, often religious, that leads to violent acts of extremism, militancy and terrorism. Recent radicalisation literature suggests that an individual can be self-motivated to follow the path of radicalisation without engaging with any indoctrinator. The ultimate aim of radicalisation, as professed by extremist groups, is to bring about a change in the national or international system, or both systems of governance. The Hizb-ut Tahrir-Bangladesh, for instance, speaks explicitly of its aim of establishing a Caliphate as part of the "Khilafah Islamiyah", with the judiciary functioning according to the Islamic Shariah laws. It even criticises democracy in Bangladesh as the government of devils.[2]

Radicalisation as a process involves a number of steps, although each and every step may not always get equal importance and can continue simultaneously. The process of radicalisation in Bangladesh, generally, includes the following steps: identification, radically motivated "Dawati" activities, testing, influencing, financial inducement and exploitation, recruitment, indoctrination, training, propaganda activities, planning and execution. However, there is ample evidence to suggest that many individuals become radicalised on their own without any contact with the radical extremist ideologues and have travelled to places where violent extremist groups operate. Hence, the phenomenon of self-radicalisation is also a unique aspect of the process of radicalisation. Generally, the process of self-radicalisation involves linkages with the internet and social media.

De-radicalisation, on the other hand, usually denotes programmes to peacefully take the already radicalised individuals and groups away from the radical extremist ideologies and ideas. It is also a process whereby a person or a group of persons are set free, voluntarily or otherwise, from espousing radical extreme views. In devising any de-radicalisation programmes, understanding the different causes and methods of radicalisation are necessary. However, there is a general agreement that social and family ties along with the well-articulated use of the internet and social media can influence positively in bringing the radically motivated people away from the vicious cycle of radicalisation.[3]

Various Approaches to De-Radicalisation

With regard to the ground realities, each country seeks to determine its own approaches to conduct de-radicalisation programmes. These are strategic, intervention-oriented and soft in nature. They aim to reengineer an individual or a group of individuals in such a manner that they feel discouraged and lack any incentive to engage in radical extremist activities. The aim of de-radicalisation programmes also vary. Some programmes aim to encourage radicalised individuals to abandon extreme views, disengage from terrorism, reintegrate into mainstream society, foster family ties, provide a stable support network, use ethical arguments to denounce extremism, cherish religious consciousness, enable a social life and counter the false claims and arguments of the radical extremists.

However, there are some modest objectives of de-radicalisation programmes such as "reducing the number of active operatives; sowing dissent among terrorists; reducing the financial and social costs of imprisonment; boosting government legitimacy; and reducing dependency on repressive forms of counter-terrorism."[4]

Currently, a number of countries run de-radicalisation programmes. Within the limited scope of this paper a very succinct analysis is provided of the de-radicalisation programmes being followed by Algeria, Saudi Arabia and Morocco.[5]

Algeria. The Algerian de-radicalisation programme includes the following measures to discourage members of radical groups:

- Pardons
- Amnesty
- Reduction in sentences

- Dismissing charges (against those persons who give up voluntarily)
- Help with job employment
- Compensation
- Health and educational benefits
- Involving civil society organisations (CSOs) to promote solidarity and cooperation to re-establish trust and tolerance.

Saudi Arabia. One of the most well-known de-radicalisation programmes in the world today is the one run by the Saudi government. Its measures include:

- Counselling programmes
- Broadening political participation
- A balanced curriculum between religious and non-religious subjects
- Giving space to Islamist clerics and preachers
- Greater access to the internet
- Encouraging families to play stronger supportive roles
- Extra-curricular activities: sports
- Payment of a monthly stipend
- Help in finding jobs
- Resume their education
- Facilitating marriages

Morocco. The de-radicalisation programme includes:

- Amnesty and release of political prisoners
- Pardons
- Improving the treatment of prisoners and prohibiting torture
- Advocating the protection of human rights

A close evaluation of these de-radicalisation programmes reveals that most of the countries adopt similar methods to turn the already indoctrinated, convicted individuals away from the radical extremist ideologies and intentions. Most countries place a great emphasis on addressing the economic hardships of the radicalised individuals, invest in education and religious scholarship, involve families and provide a suitable social life as the key approach to de-radicalisation. As far as the Islamist radicalisation is concerned, countries try and engage credible religious clerics and scholars to demystify the false pretences of the extremist ideologies and their appeal. Finally, the skilful use of media, including social media and the internet, is employed as a means of facilitating the de-radicalisation efforts and ensure that they remain sustainable in the long run.

Suggesting Strategies for Bangladesh

Bangladesh is a moderate Muslim country where, as I mentioned before, secularism is one of the key state principles enshrined in the Constitution. Since it emerged as an independent nation in 1971, Bangladesh's society can be characterised by its commitment to religious tolerance and peaceful coexistence among the different religious and ethnic groups in the country. However, like many countries around the world, Bangladesh has to cope with the growing threat of radicalisation and extremism. The activities of a number of extremist groups had risen to such a level that the government was forced to proscribe a few organisations for the sake of the safety and security of its citizens. Attacks by extremists groups on public offices, law-enforcement officials and well-known cultural personalities prompted the government to think about counter-terrorism programmes including those involving both counter-radicalisation and de-radicalisation.

A principal feature of the radicalisation trend in Bangladesh is the overwhelming involvement of the youth. The traditional perception has been that economically and socially, youth from poor backgrounds are more prone to the appeal of extremist ideas but such a proposition is increasingly losing traction. Youth from middle and upper middle-classes, with good educational backgrounds, have also been found to be involved in radicalisation activities. Even girls and women have become key proponents of furthering radical ideas and messages. Another major feature of radicalisation in Bangladesh is the skilful and intelligent use of all forms of media, in particular the internet and social media, in the proliferation and spread of radical extremist ideas. The third and final trend in radicalisation is the subtle and adroit misuse of texts from religious verses and scriptures by extremist ideologues and organisations.

Considering the above major trends in radicalisation in Bangladesh, a multi-pronged strategy encompassing all key aspects of radicalisation and involving all relevant major stakeholders can provide the best defence for Bangladesh against the appeal of extremist ideologies. Bangladesh's counter-radicalisation and de-radicalisation programmes should include, but not be limited to, the following elements:

- A balanced education programme for convicted radicals with the right blend of religious and cultural elements in the curriculum, which enables them to obtain jobs after their release. This should be a key element of any de-radicalisation programme.
- Countering the non-contextual misinterpretation of religious messages by a group of religious scholars, who can run specially

designed programmes to debunk the myths of radical extremist ideology.

- General sensitisation programmes in the mass media for parents to devote proper attention to their children so that they do not give in to the allure of extremist appeal.
- Involving families is also a vital component of any counter-radicalisation or de-radicalisation programme.
- Encouraging radical activists to abandon a path of radicalisation by providing good alternative livelihood options and an opportunity of a proper social life.
- Finally, a carefully crafted politically neutral counter-radicalisation or de-radicalisation policy is essential to guide all relevant stakeholders to do their part in making the policy a success.

However, in view of the growing threat of radicalisation amongst the youth in Bangladesh at the moment, rather than focus on specifically developing a de-radicalisation strategy, what Bangladesh requires most is a counter-radicalisation strategy. Therefore, beginning in 2013, my institute, the Bangladesh Enterprise Institute (BEI), has been working on a three-year project to develop a National Counter-Radicalisation Strategy for Bangladesh.

Developing a National Counter-Radicalisation Strategy encompassing the key areas of concern and involving all the relevant major stakeholders can provide the best defence for Bangladesh against the appeal of extremism. In the development of the National Counter-Radicalisation Strategy, six critical areas have been prioritised. These are:

- Understanding the role of the media in creating awareness and national consensus against threats emanating from radicalisation.
- Exploring the role of civil society in countering radicalisation.
- Conducting a study on the role of the education system in shaping youth perceptions against terrorist ideologies.
- Terror financing in Bangladesh.
- Assessing the impact and role of the Bangladeshi diaspora in Islamist radicalisation in Bangladesh.
- Building a counter narrative vis-à-vis terrorist ideologies and propaganda in Bangladesh.

In addition, the BEI has been undertaking another three-year project on "Conflict Prevention through Counter-radicalisation of Youth in Bangladesh" from 2014–16. The project is intended to support the government's effort in combating militancy and countering radicalisation throughout the country by providing training on peace-building and de-radicalisation tools among the youth and students in the age group of 18–35 years. The BEI has prepared a training manual and is undertaking 28 training workshops in 28 conflict-prone areas in Bangladesh among the youth and students from schools, colleges and madrassas.

Conclusion

De-radicalisation and counter-radicalisation programmes are by no means fool-proof solutions to the problem which many of our countries face today. At the same time, it should be stressed that they can be tremendously effective in countering terrorism. De-radicalisation is a step-by-step approach. Recognising the need for a de-radicalisation programme is essential for a well-articulated de-radicalisation and counter-radicalisation strategy for Bangladesh. Bangladesh's laudable success in counter-terrorism can provide valuable insights in formulating a national counter–radicalisation and de-radicalisation strategy which emphasises non-kinetic measures.

In formulating any de-radicalisation and counter-radicalisation programmes for Bangladesh, all stakeholders need to do their part. Just as the government and law-enforcement agencies have responsibilities to deter the radical extremist motivations and operations, social institutions, community and all sectors of the society have their respective roles to play. Recognising de-radicalisation as part of a holistic policy measure is vital in order to craft a national de-radicalisation and counter-radicalisation strategy for Bangladesh.

NOTES

1. Speech on "Countering Radicalisation in Bangladesh", M. Humayun Kabir, Bangladesh-India Security Dialogue, New Delhi, on 3 April 2014.
2. Hizb-ut-Tahrir Bangladesh: Transnational Islamist Movement, South Asia Conflict Monitor, January 20.
3. "A New Approach?: Deradicalisation Programs and Counterterrorism", International Peace Institute, June 2010, p. 2.
4. Ibid, p. 3.
5. This portion of the paper is based entirely on Hamed El-Said, "De-Radicalising Islamists: Programmes and their Impact in Muslim Majority States", International Centre for the Study of Radicalisation and Political Violence (ICSR), January 2012.

23

De-Radicalisation: Use of the Media and Curriculum: The Way Forward

Sultan Shahin

To radicalise young Muslim children in India, inimical elements exploit all types of media, school textbooks, and madrasas. It is hence important to focus on these elements for de-radicalising those already radicalised and, more importantly, preventing any further radicalisation of our youth.

Most of the radicalisation takes place today in mosques, madrasas, print, electronic media and, above all, in cyber-space. Social media has particularly emerged as a hub of radicalisation. In countries like Pakistan, jihadi print media too plays an important role. One study had found that by 1989, there were 150 jihadi journals in print from Peshawar and Quetta. But while media is used to disseminate Jihadi ideas, those who create this literature are products of the ordinary madrasas, teaching essentially the same textbooks, with minor sectarian differences. While the task of creating jihadi literature was assigned to Deobandi and Ahl-e-Hadeesi madrasas during the Afghan war against the former Soviet Union in the 1980s, Barelvi madrasas too had by and large discarded Sufi literature and adopted a Dars-e-Nizami curriculum long ago. Developed under Aurangzeb, the Dars-e-Nizami had abandoned Sufism and inclusive, pluralistic teachings of the great Sufi saints. Some Sufi–Barelvi madrasas had continued to teach the thirteenth-century Persian poet, theologian and Sufi mystic Maulana Rumi's *Masnawi* and one of the greatest poets of the classical literary tradition Sheikh Saadi Shirazi's *Gulistan* and *Bostan* in their Islamic ethics and Persian classes. But when proficiency in Arabic became linked to jobs in the Gulf, even these madrasas stopped teaching the Persian and Sufi classics. But worse, in the name of teaching Arabic literature, they started teaching even Syed Qutb—considered as the father of modern Islamist terrorism in the Middle East. Introducing young impressionable minds, even in Sufi–Barelvi madrasas, to Qutb in the name of teaching literature, was a very unfortunate decision.Wahhabi–Salafi madrasas have, of course, been teaching Ibn-e-Taimiya, Mohammad Ibn-e-Abdul Wahhab, Qutb, Maududi and other extremist ideologues for a long time.

Thus the media discourse and school curriculum emanate from the prevalent Islamic theology and it is this theology we have to focus on. It is gratifying that even a conservative Muslim scholar like the head of Jamia Azhar, the oldest seat of the Sunni Islamic learning, is now willing to admit a link between terrorism and Islamic education and theology. Jamia Azhar's Sheikh Ahmed al-Tayeb did that recently and, of all places, at a counter-terrorism conference in Mecca. Needless to say, its significance lies in the fact that Saudi Arabia has been the fountainhead of extremist education and the biggest exporter of intolerant, xenophobic textbooks. This is also an admission that a mere tinkering with Islamic textbooks is not working. Saudi Arabia had engaged in some reform of its textbooks in 2002.

Thirteen years after 9/11, in which 16 of the 19 terrorists were Saudis, the world is facing a more complex, more diverse and a more dangerous threat. Part of the reason certainly is that the international community has not clamped down on the Saudi export of the textbooks containing lessons in xenophobia, intolerance, exclusivism, supremacism and hatred of and enmity towards all non-Wahhabis, as mandated by Mohammad ibn-e-Abdul Wahhab. A mere look at some portions of the Saudi textbooks meant for impressionable young minds will tell us as to why so many youths, particularly from Saudi Arabia and other countries where these texts are taught, are leaving their homes and schools for doing what they consider jihad in the so-called Islamic State.

But what did Mohammad ibn-e-Abdul Wahhab teach and what is being taught to our children today across the Islamic world and indeed, even in the West? One of the most important lessons in these textbooks is expressed through the concept of *Al-Walaa' Wa Al-Bara* (which essentially means showing loyalty towards Wahhabi Muslims and bearing enmity towards everybody else). Let me quote from a chapter on Saudi education from a celebrated study of Islamic education titled "Teaching Islam" by Professor Eleanor Abdella Doumato:

It is a law of Tawhid that one should show loyalty to the Unitarian (Muwahhid, Wahhabi) Muslim and bear enmity toward his polytheist (Sufi, non-Muslim) enemies," says the text. "The place of 'Al-Walaa Wa Al-Baraa' has great standing in Islam," the lesson says, as the Prophet said: 'The strongest bond of belief is loving what God loves and hating what God hates' (10b: 110). The lesson elevates enmity for the sake of God above the pillars of Islam (10b: 110).

Who are the polytheist enemies against whom the monotheist Muslim must bear enmity? To MIAW (Mohammad Ibn-e-Abdul Wahhab), polytheist enemies were other Muslims, especially the Ottoman Turks, Shia, Sufis, and anyone who wore amulets or practiced magic. The school text specifies new ways to become an enemy, explaining why Muslims must be alert to show hostility toward the offender (10b: 111).

In the Fiqh and Hadith texts, imitating the Kuffar (unbelievers) is presented as morally corrupting. Women who dress like foreigners, for example, invite temptation and corruption, so the fabric of Muslim women's dress must be thick enough not to show any skin and wide enough to conceal the contours of the body, and the face must be covered to protect her personality. Imitating the Kuffar is an insult to God... (10b: 118). To say Eid Mubarak (happy holiday) to the Kuffar is as bad as worshipping the cross; it's a worse sin against God than offering a toast with liquor; it's worse than suicide and worse than having forbidden sex (Artikab Al-Farj Al-Haram) (10b: 118).

Imitating the Kuffar by using the calendrical designation "A.D." instead of the Hijra year is another problem...as Ibn Taimiyya said, "Agreeing with the Ahl al-kitab (People of the Book) on things that are not in our religion and that are not the customs of our ancestors is corruption.

One should not employ an unbeliever if there is a Muslim who can do the job...(10b: 121). Nor should a Muslim accept employment from an unbeliever, for a Muslim should never be in a position of subservience to the Kuffar.... A Muslim should not live permanently among Kuffar because his faith will be compromised and that is why God required Muslims to migrate from a land of unbelief (Bilad al-Kufr) to a land of belief (Bilad Al-Islam) (10b: 121).

The chapter warns against music, laughter, and singing. The lesson explains that the Kuffar (infidels) assign value to unimportant things because of an absent religious faith, because of which their lives are empty.

"What are these unimportant things? First, there are the performing arts, such as singing and playing instruments, dancing and theatre and cinema, which are visited by people who are lost from the truth. Then, there are the fine arts (Al-Funun Al-Jamila), such as painting, drawing and sculpture" (10b: 124-125).

Forbidding celebrations of birthdays, especially the birthday of the Prophet, and prohibitions against fine and performing arts are all part of the modern fabric and the historical legacy of Wahhabi culture. "It's hostility to any human practice that would excite the imagination or bolster creativity," says (Dr Khaled Abou) El Fadl (2003), which is "perhaps the most stultifying, and even deadly, characteristic of Wahhabism. Anything that suggests a step toward creativity," he says, "constitutes a step toward Kufr [infidelity]."

Saudi textbooks are the most easily available across the world. With the Dars-e-Nizami curriculum being accepted by nearly all the madrasas in the Indian subcontinent, the process of radicalisation started in the seventeenth century itself. Most Muslims are far more attached to their religion and dependent on the ulema (classical Muslim scholars) for guidance in the matters of religion than is realised. So, de-radicalisation essentially means the de-radicalisation of the ulema (plural of *alim*—scholar). This is easier said than done.

Gates of *ijtihad* (religiously mandated rethinking of issues to update Islamic mores) were closed over a millennia ago, in the mid-eighth century CE, at the time of Imam-e-Azam Abu Hanifa. Imam Ahmad ibn-e-Hanbal opened the gate again, but after him in the mid-ninth century CE, it was firmly closed. Imam Ahmad Ibn-e-Taimiya and Mohammad Ibn-e-Abdul Wahhab's work (also considered by some as *ijtihad*) was essentially in the Hanbali tradition. Muslims were asked to blindly follow one of the four imams of *fiqh*, Islamic law, and by and large they have been doing so. Any *alim* (scholar) who dares to claim engaging in *ijtihad* (independent reasoning) is excommunicated. This happens even if the subject of the *ijtihad* is something as inconsequential as the appropriate size of the beard. If an *alim* (scholar) just shows signs of being an *Ahl Al-Rai* (now a derogatory term, used for someone having an independent opinion), he would lose his job and face social boycott.

And yet, an *alim* like Maulana Abdul Aleem Islahi, who is the ideological inspiration behind the terrorist group Indian Mujahedeen, continues to be a respected *alim* in the eyes of the Indian ulema. Not one *alim* has condemned or criticised him—not to speak of boycotting him.

He continues to write his books and run his madrasa for women in the Saidabad area of Hyderabad with aplomb.

Let me give you an example of the perfidy of his work. There is a verse in the Quran that shows that Islam allows complete, unrestricted freedom of belief—"*La ikraha fiddin,*" meaning, "there is no compulsion in religion or way of life (*Deen*)." This is an absolute, clear, unconditional statement. Now see how Maulana Islahi distorts it, with the tacit approval of the other ulema in India:

> To quote, "*La ikraha fiddin*", There is no compulsion in religion (*Deen*). This is an established fact. But it is related only with accepting or not accepting the belief. This does not mean that *ahl-e-Kufr* (infidels) should be left totally free on earth with their un-belief and should not be made accountable. If this were true, what do we mean when we say that the religion (*Deen*) of God has been revealed to dominate the world?" Then he quotes a contextual verse from the Quran and asks rhetorically: "What will this verse mean then and what relevance will the obligation of jihad have?"
>
> In a booklet in Urdu, *Taqat ka Istemal Quran ki Roshni Main* (The Use of Violence, in the Light of the Quran), Maulana Islahi claims that "war has been ordained against those who meet three conditions until they pay *jizyah* (a tax on religious minorities); do not profess faith in God and Day of Judgment; do not accept as *haram* (forbidden) what God and his Prophet have declared *haram*; and do not accept Islam as their religion". It is, Maulana Islahi argues, "the duty of Muslims to struggle for the domination of Islam over false religions, and to subdue and subjugate infidels and polytheists".

Despite his xenophobic, supremacist views, the Maulana continues to be an esteemed member of the Indian ulema community, while the ulema continue to make the repeated claims of Islam being a religion of peace and pluralism, which, of course, it is. However, despite the difficulties involved, the Muslims, who are concerned at the state of affairs, and the humanity at large that has a stake in maintaining peace, will have to take the bull by its horns and rein in this ideology.

It should be no longer difficult to see how jihadis are able to snatch our children away from us, brainwash them and convert them into bombs. Clearly, this happens because jihadi ideology is deeply entrenched in the common Muslim beliefs. Jihadis are not saying anything very different. The Taliban, for instance, were ordinary madrasa students. The relevant question for us in India is: do these Deobandi madrasas in Pakistan that produce Taliban teach anything very different from what being is taught in the original Darul Uloom Deoband or for that matter, the other madrasas in India?

We are horrified by the atrocities perpetrated by Boko Haram. We consider it an African and a twenty-first century phenomenon. But what does the Boko Haram mean? It means, "Western education is sin." Have we forgotten that the Indian ulema are the original Boko Haramists? It was their nineteenth-century fatwa saying "English education is sin" that kept Muslims backward. When Sir Syed Ahmad established a college in Aligarh to teach English, they passed numerous fatwas of *kufr* against him. Of course, the Indian ulema did not go out and kill, but there was no need either. The Muslims fell in line and even Sir Syed could only make a slight dent. This is because of the deep roots of the commonly accepted and commonly espoused Islamic theology that the jihadis are able to convince our children that we, the peaceful mainstream Muslims, are actually hypocrites and cowards, not willing to sacrifice our lives for the sake of establishing an Islamic domination over the world.

There are verses in Quran, revealed to help the Prophet cope with a war that had been imposed upon him. These verses naturally talk of fighting and killing. But no *alim* will say that these verses were only meant for that period in the seventh century Arabia and are no longer applicable to us today in the twenty-first century. Every *alim*, jihadi or non-jihadi, Wahhabi or Sufi, says that the Quran is uncreated, divine, like God himself, and all verses of the Quran have a universal and eternal validity. Why should the jihadi ideologue then not use the contextual, militant verses of Quran to lure our children away to war? The same is the case of the Ahadees, the so-called sayings of the Prophet. These were collected up to three centuries after the demise of the Prophet. What kind of sanctity and authenticity they can possibly have for any rational person? But nearly all Muslims consider them as almost as authoritative and sacred as the Quran. Why is it any surprise then that the jihadis use them to justify their atrocities?

One can see how difficult it would be to de-radicalise our ulema. But this is a task that has got to be done. When the armies of suicide bombers emerge from Muslim societies whenever and wherever needed by the determined Jihadi groups, the Muslims and the world at large cannot afford to remain silent spectators. Now the question is, how do we go forward? If we really want to make a difference, we will have to start a substantive dialogue with the ulema and make sure that they agree to:

- Open the gates of *ijtihad*—rethinking all tenets of Islam in the light of the situation prevailing today. As we have not done our homework for over a millennium, this will have to be pretty revolutionary.
- Declare that only constitutive and essential, not the contextual and allegorical verses of Quran, are meant to guide us today.
- Restore primacy to the Meccan verses that constitute the essential teachings of the Quran, as they can be understood without any need for knowing the context in which they were revealed.
- Declare that the Ahadees cannot be considered as any form of revelation from God. The Islamic State's millenarian thesis is almost entirely based on the Ahadees, though it uses some allegorical verses of the Quran as well. The claim of al-Baghdadi leading an end-time war, *al-Malhama*, just before the final Armageddon, has been a big draw. Some Muslims have come to think that life on earth has no meaning left in the times of the *al-Malhama* and so are rushing to join the war.
- Declare that the Sharia (*fiqh*) is not divine. It was created over a century after the demise of the Prophet by the ulema who tried to codify laws on the basis of the Quranic postulates and Arab cultural practices.
- Declare clearly that Islam believes in coexistence with other religions, not dominion over the world.
- Redefine the commonly used Islamic terms like Muslim, *kafir*, *mushrik*, *ahl-e-kitab*, jihad, *qital*, *farz*, *sunnat*, etc.

I must explain this point a bit. Justice Munir Ahmad of Pakistan, while investigating the anti-Ahmadiya riots in 1954, asked the leaders of all the Islamic sects and schools of thought to define who is a Muslim, in order to determine if the Ahmadiyas could be called as non-Muslims as many ulema were claiming them to be. He found that no two ulema agreed on the definition of a Muslim. Recently, a researcher on the Quran and a regular contributor to the Islamic website NewAgeIslam.com studied all verses in the Quran that have the word *kafir* or its variants. He concluded:

> The Quran does not identify kafir by his/her belief or faith but by certain specific characteristics that make the person an active enemy of religion, God and the people of faith. In Quran, a kafir is one who actively hinders people from practicing their faith, persecutes people of faith, opposes humanitarian practices such as giving of charity, shunning usury, etc. A kafir could be a Muslim, Jew, Christian, polytheist or atheist. The term is faith-neutral.

In a word, we must evolve a truly Islamic and a coherent theology of peace and coexistence, moderation and modernity, to counter the very coherent theology of violence and xenophobia, intolerance and supremacism that the jihadi ulema have created over centuries. All ulema say that Islam is a religion of peace and coexistence. It is time for them to walk the talk. But if they refuse to consider change, we will need to directly reach the Muslim masses.

Finally, the larger Indian community too should introspect. As Daniel Pipes stated, "in this war of ideas, the world should not only encourage and support progressive, modern Muslims but also oppose and refrain from supporting the fundamentalists and extremists". Our national leadership supported Khilafat in 1920s, considering it an essential part of Islamic theology. That was wrong. Now we must repudiate that stance and acknowledge our mistake.

The Muslim personal law in India has not been reformed even to the extent it has been in Pakistan and Bangladesh. This must change. At least, General Ayub Khan's reforms in Pakistan must be introduced and the ulema should be told to accept what their Pakistani and Bangladeshi counterparts did decades earlier. This is not a satisfactory solution but at least, it will be a start and is doable.

The Madrasa education is a serious violation of the human rights of Muslim children. It destroys their lives and fills them with xenophobia and intolerance. Our government not only allows this but partly funds some madrasas. This must stop, unless, of course, the madrasas actually change to become modern versions of what the madrasas used to be like in the so-called golden period of Islam, and produce scientists and philosophers. A secular, democratic government should not be in the business of funding xenophobia and intolerance.

List of Contributors

Yossef Bodansky currently concentrates on research, professional writing and international consulting. Mr. Bodansky was the Director of the Congressional Task Force on Terrorism and Unconventional Warfare at the U.S. House of Representatives between 1988 and 2004, and stayed on as a special adviser to Congress till January 2009. In the mid-1980s, he acted as a senior consultant for the U.S. Department of Defense and the Department of State. Mr. Bodansky has also been the Director of Research at the International Strategic Studies Association [ISSA], as well as a Senior Editor for the Defense & Foreign Affairs group of publications, since 1983. He is the author of eleven books – including Bin Laden: The Man Who Declared War on America (New York Times No.1 Bestseller & Washington Post No.1 Bestseller), The Secret History of the Iraq War (New York Times Bestseller & Foreign Affairs Magazine Bestseller), and Chechen Jihad: Al Qaeda's Training Ground and the Next Wave of Terror – and hundreds of articles, book chapters and Congressional reports. Mr. Bodansky is a Director at the Prague Society for International Cooperation, and serves on the Board of the Global Panel Foundation and several other institutions worldwide.

Lt Gen. Amarjit Singh Kalkat, SYSM, PVSM, AVSM, VSM, was commissioned in the Infantry (8 Gorkha Rifles) in 1955 and is a veteran of the 1965 and 1971 Indo-Pak Wars. He commanded the Indian Peace Keeping Force (IPKF), Sri Lanka, from December 1987 to March 1990, and was awarded the Sarvottam Yudh Seva Medal (SYSM) in 1988, India's highest award for 'Leadership and Command in War and Conflict'. He was the first recipient of this award since its institution in 1981. He served as India's representative on the Indo-Sri Lanka Security Coordination Group along with Sri Lanka Foreign and Defence Ministers for overseeing implementation of the Indo-Sri Lanka Accord 1989-90 and also served as the Co-Chairman with the Sri Lanka Army Chief of Observer Group under the President of Sri Lanka to oversee cessation of hostilities. Prior to his retirement in December 1993, he served as the General

Officer Commanding in Chief of the Southern Command and prior to that of the Army Training Command. A distinguished academic and speaker, he is currently the mentor of Centre for Joint Warfare Studies (CENJOWS), a government sponsored think tank on synergising national capabilities to meet threats to India's Security.

Natalia Tereshchenko is a specialist in security and development in Central and South Asia. She conducts in-depth research and analysis of political, security and military risk in post-conflict settings and provides authentication and risk of return reports for asylum cases. With her experience in project management, she has proposed and implemented innovative projects and assisted in organisation of international high profile conferences. Her thematic experience includes political risk and post-conflict development, human rights, public international law public policy, counter-terrorism, negotiations and conflict termination. A prolific speaker and writer, she is a member of the International Political Science Association, the American Political Science Association and the American Bar Association; 2009 – 2012. She is also a Fellow of the Royal Geographical Society and is on the editorial board, Journal of Mediterranean & Balkan Intelligence (JMBI). She is also the Founder & President of the International Law Students Association, Swiss Chapter: 2009-2011.

Lt Gen. Syed Ata Hasnain, PVSM, UYSM, AVSM, SM*, VSM* is an alumnus of the Indian Military Academy and the Royal College of Defence Studies, London. He was commissioned in the Garhwal Rifles and took part in active operations in Sri Lanka as part of Operation Pawan. Hehas served with distinction in the Army, conceptualising and operationalising the "Hearts Doctrine" while in command of 15 Corps. His unique and innovative approach defined as "Playing Friend Not God" has been widely appreciated as the new HR management mantra across domains in and outside the military. Since his superannuation on 30 June 2013, he has actively pursued intellectual activities and promoted the cause and perception of the Indian Army. He has a postgraduate degree in International Studies from King's College, University of London. He is a prolific member of Track 2 diplomacy with Pakistan, bringing his vast experience of J&K to the meetings. He is a Visiting Fellow of the Vivekananda International Foundation, New Delhi and Senior Fellow with Delhi Policy Group. He lectures at military establishments and training institutes across the country. His writings on strategic issues are widely published in the print media and he frequently comes on talk shows and discussions on television on matters which affect national security.

Ram D Pradhan is an Indian Administrative Service officer of the 1952 batch. He worked with Mr Y.B. Chavan when the latter was the chief minister of Maharashtra in 1960 and subsequently whenMr Chavan became the defence minister of India in November 1962. Thereafter, between 1965 and 1981, he held various posts in Delhi and Geneva and also in the United Nations. Between 1982-85 he was Chief Secretary, Maharashtra and prior to his retirement, served as the Union Home Secretary. He was awarded the Padma Bhushan for distinguished public service for negotiation of peace accords in Punjab, Assam and Mizoram. In March 1987, he was appointed the first governor of Arunachal Pradesh. That enabled him to forge close association with the people of that state and getting first hand understanding of India's border with Tibet. A prolific writer, he has written several books, which include books in Marathi as well.

Rajan Medhekar is a graduate of the Birla Institute of Technology and Science (BITS), Pilani, and a post graduate in Solid State Physics from Bombay University. He joined the Indian Police Servicein 1975 in the Kerala cadre. In his 37 years of distinguished service with the police force, he served in a variety of important and sensitive assignments, both in Kerala and in the Centre. He has also served as the Director General of the elite National Security Guard (NSG), India's premier federal contingency special force for counter terrorism and anti-hijack operations. He has vast experience and deep insight into the functioning of law enforcement, security, intelligence and crime investigation, criminal investigation and prosecution and the Indian legal system. He also has vast experience in implementation of computer applications, cyber security, cyber forensics and software development and he successfully led the computerisation efforts of the Kerala State Police, the BSF as well as the NSG.

John M. Nomikos is the Director at the Research, Institute for European and American Studies and Founding Editor, Journal of Mediterranean and Balkan Intelligence (JMBI). He is Assistant Professor in the Webster University (Athens Campus) in the Department of International Relations. He directed the Greek team in a consortium of five countries (Northern Ireland-UK, Spain, Germany, Bulgaria, and Israel) and completed successfully a two year (2009-2011) European Union-FP7 research project titled: SAFE COMMS on "Counter-terrorism Crisis Communication Strategies for Recovery and Continuity." He is a Certified Master Antiterrorism Specialist (CMAS) and a member of Editorial Advisory Board for the International Journal of Intelligence and Counterintelligence (IJIC) and Journal of Military and Strategic Affairs. His area of expertise is: Transatlantic Relations, NATO Security, Energy Security, Terrorism and Counter-Intelligence, Illegal Migration/Human Trafficking in the Balkan and Mediterranean region, EU Maritime Strategy, Transnational Organised Crime and Islamic Networks in the Middle East, Greek-Israeli Security Relations, Greek and Cypriot Foreign Policy. His most recent publications are: "European Union Intelligence Analysis Centre (INTCEN): Next stop to an Agency?" at the Journal of Mediterranean and Balkan

Intelligence, Vol. 4, No. 2, December 2014. "Balkan-Mediterranean Intelligence Sharing Cooperation and Counterterrorism Policy in Greece" in Denis Caleta and Paul Shemella (eds) Intelligence and Combating Terrorism – New Paradigms and Future Challenges (Published by the Institute for Corporative Security Studies), 2014, Ljubljana, Slovenia.

Amit Kumar is Center of National Policy's Fellow for Homeland Security and Counter-terrorism. His key areas of expertise include the financing, organisation, and evolution of transnational terrorist and criminal networks, both global and South Asian, and development and implementation of international, multilateral, regional, bilateral, and national regulatory Anti-Money Laundering/Countering the Financing of Terrorism (AML/CFT) and counterterrorism compliance measures against such networks through AML/CFT capacity building, and through appropriate legal, policy, and organisational responses; international inspection and oversight; organisational theory; public-private partnerships in critical infrastructure protection; and homeland security. He is also Adjunct Associate Professor in the Security Studies Program at the Edmund A Walsh School of Foreign Service at Georgetown University where he teaches the Graduate Course in Terrorist Financing. He has also taught at the John Jay College of Criminal Justice for several years. Dr. Kumar has a number of years experience working with the Al-Qaida Taliban Sanctions regime at the United Nations. He is currently co-editing a most comprehensive textbook on terrorist financing.

Gp Capt. (Dr) Ajay Lele is a post graduate in Physics as well as Defence and Strategic Studies. Hedid his PhD from the Jawaharlal Nehru University, New Delhi. Post retirement, he is currently working with the Institute for Defence Studies and Analyses (IDSA), New Delhi. His research interests include Weapons of Mass Destruction (WMD), Terrorism and Strategic Technologies. He has authored two books titled Bio-Weapons: The Genie in the Bottle (2004) and Weather and Warfare (2006) and also contributes articles to reputed journals, websites and newspapers.

Jean-François Daguzan is Deputy Director of the Foundation for strategic research (FRS) at Paris; Associated Professor at University Pantheon-Assas of Paris and President of the Scientific Council of the Choiseul Institute. He is also the Chief Editor of Geoéconomie Review and Director of Maghreb-Machrek Review. His publications include: Le dernier rempart? Politiques de défense et forces armées au Maghreb (The Last Wall? Defense Policies and Armed Forces in Maghreb); Guerre et économie (War and Economy, Editor with Pascal Lorot); Le terrorisme non conventionnel (Non Conventional Terrorism Ed. with Olivier Lepick); L'Asie centrale après la guerre contre la terreur (Central Asia after the War against Terror Ed. with Pascal Lorot); Terrorisme(s) abrégé d'une violence qui dure (Terrorism(s) short story of a long term violence); Les Forces armées arabes et Moyen-orientales après les printemps arabes (Arab and Middle East Armed Forces after the Arab Springs Ed. with Stéphane Valter). He has also written a wide range of papers on Maghreb, Mediterranean, Arab World as well as Terrorism issues.

Vice Admiral Shekhar Sinha, PVSM, AVSM, NM* is an alumnus of the Defence Services Staff College, Naval War College and National Defence College, New Delhi. He retired in 2014 as the Commander in Chief of Western Naval Command based at Mumbai and Coastal Security, Western Seaboard. He has also been the Chief of Integrated Defence Staff, New Delhiand Fleet Commander of the Western Fleet responsible for maritime security in the Arabian sea. A recipient of the PVSM and AVSM for distinguished service, the Admiral is also the recipient of two gallantry Nao Sena Medals. He holds a M Phil degree and is a member of IISS (London), USI, IDSA , India Habitat Centre and IIC.

Rahul Roy-Chaudhury is the Senior Fellow for South Asia at the International Institute for Strategic Studies (IISS) in London, where he heads its South Asia programme. Earlier, he served in the National Security Council Secretariat in the Prime Minister's Office in India. Prior to his official appointment, he was on the faculty of the Institute for Defence Studies and Analyses (IDSA) in New Delhi. His research focuses on maritime and naval affairs in the Indian Ocean, India's foreign and security policies, Afghanistan and regional security, and Pakistan's domestic politics and foreign and security policies. He writes for IISS' publications, including Strategic Survey, Military Balance and Strategic Comment. He has written two books on India's maritime security, and is currently completing his IISS Adelphi book on India's Naval Strategy.

Christian Wagner is head of the Asia research group at the German Institute for International and Security Affairs in Berlin. Earlier, he was Senior Research Fellow at the Center for Development Research at University of Bonn 2001-2002 and Assistant Professor at the Institute for Political Science and Administrative Studies, University of Rostock 1996-2001. He was also a Research Fellow at the Center for Modern Oriental Studies, Berlin, an Administrative Officer at University of Mainz and a Lecturer in the Department of Political Science, University of Freiburg. His area of expertise is Bangladesh, India, Indo-Pacific, Nepal, Pakistan, South Asia, Sri Lanka, regional cooperation and alliances, security cooperation in South Asia, democracy/democratisation and minority conflicts. He has a large number of books and publications to his credit.

Marvin G Weinbaum is professor emeritus of political science at the University of Illinois at Urbana-Champaign. He served as analyst for Pakistan and Afghanistan in the U.S. Department of State's Bureau of Intelligence and

Research from 1999 to 2003. He is currently a scholar-in-residence and Director of the Pakistan Center at the Middle East Institute in Washington DC. Professor Weinbaum has his doctorate from Columbia University in 1965, his MA from the University of Michigan in 1958, and his BA from Brooklyn College in 1957. He was awarded Fulbright Research Fellowships for Egypt in 1981–82 and Afghanistan in 1989–90, and was a senior fellow at the United States Institute of Peace in 1996–97. Additionally, Dr. Weinbaum has been the recipient of research awards from the Social Science Research Council, the Ford Foundation, the Hewlett Foundation, IREX, the American Political Science Association, and other granting agencies. After retiring at Illinois, Professor Weinbaum has held adjunct professorships at Georgetown and George Washington universities, and lectures regularly at the U.S. Foreign Service Institute. Dr. Weinbaum's research, teaching, and consultancies have focused on the issues of national security, state building, democratization, and political economy. He is the author or editor of six books, including South Asia Approaches the Millennium: Reexamining National Security, co-edited with Chetan Kumar in 1995, and Afghanistan and Pakistan: Resistance and Reconstruction in 1994. Dr. Weinbaum has also written more than 100 book chapters and professional journal articles, mostly about Pakistan, Afghanistan, and Iran, but also on Egypt and Turkey. He is author of numerous opinion pieces in leading American newspapers and magazines, and many think-tank reports. Among his very recent publications are book chapters in edited volumes dealing with the U.S.-Pakistan relations, Pakistan's political future, and state building and the security challenges in Afghanistan.

Thomas Lynch III is a Distinguished Research Fellow for South Asia and the Near East at the Institute of National Strategic Studies (INSS) at the National Defense University (NDU) in Washington, D.C. He joined NDU-INSS in July 2010 after a 28 year career as an active duty U.S. Army officer, where he served in a variety of command and staff positions. He researches, writes, lectures and organises workshops and conferences for Department of Defense customers on the topics of Pakistan, Afghanistan, India & the Subcontinent, the Gulf Arab States, and the past & future trajectory of radical Islam. He has published widely on the politics and security of South Asia and the Near East, including articles in Orbis, The American Interest, and Joint Forces Quarterly; book chapters in publications by NDU Press and Johns Hopkins University Press; and feature monographs with the New America Foundation, the Combating Terrorism Center at West Point, and NDU Press. He is also regular multi-media analyst and commentator on national and international programs including FOX News television, Chinese Central Television (CCTV) – America, Al Jazeera International television (Qatar), Alhurra television, Express-24/7 television (Pakistan), Voice of America radio and television, and FOX News radio. He is a member of the Council on Foreign Relations and an adjunct professor in the

Security Studies Program in the School of Foreign Service at Georgetown University. He is also a member of the International Institute for Strategic Studies, the International Studies Association and the Arms Control Association.

Waiel S.H. Awwad is a South Asia based journalist since 1979. He has traveled extensively in most of the South and South East Asian countries. As a war reporter, he has covered Sri Lanka, Kashmir, Afghanistan, West Asia and the Gulf Region. He worked as Bureau Chief of MBC (Middle East B'casting Centre)-London, MBC-FM Radio and Kuwait, Oman and Damascus Radio. Prior to that, he ran a special programme: Dateline South Asia in Arabic-the first of its kind with Asian News International (ANI) South Asia Bureau Chief of Alarabiya TV Channel (Dubai Media City), 2002-2012. Much of his writings in English and Arabic have been published in major news papers and magazines. While covering wars in Asia, Dr Awwad was detained in Afghanistan before the fall of Taliban government and also was captured in an ambush during the American invasion of Iraq in 2003 while he was embedded with American troops. He has served as president of the Foreign Correspondents' Club of South Asia (FCC) for two terms 2003-2205 and 2013-2015 and as a President Emeritus for FCC South Asia. He is a recipient of the 5th Rajiv Gandhi Excellence Award, 2014 for the best journalist from overseas.

Lisa Curtis is Senior Research Fellow for South Asia in the Asian Studies Center at the Heritage Foundation. Since joining Heritage in August 2006, Curtis has appeared on major broadcast networks, including CNN, Fox News, PBS, and BBC, to comment on developments in South Asia and testified over a dozen times before Congress on issues related to U.S. policy toward India, Pakistan, and Afghanistan. Her commentary has appeared in The Los Angeles Times, U.S. News and World Report, Foreign Policy, and The National Interest, and in South Asian publications such as The Hindu, India Today, The Friday Times, The News, and Express Tribune. Before joining Heritage, she was Professional Staff Member of the Senate Foreign Relations Committee, handling the South Asia portfolio for then Committee Chairman, Senator Richard Lugar (R-IN). From 2001 to 2003, Curtis served as Senior Advisor in the State Department's South Asia Bureau, where she advised the Assistant Secretary on India-Pakistan relations. In the late 1990s, Curtis served in the Central Intelligence Agency as a political analyst on South Asia. She also served as a political officer to the U.S. embassies in Islamabad and in New Delhi from 1994 to 1998.

Andrea Margelleti was born in Genova in 1966 and is the President of Ce.S.I. (Centre for International Studies). He is a member of the Strategic Committee of the Ministry of Foreign Affairs and a participant in the Observatory on National Security (ONS), of the Institute of Higher Military Studies of the Defence Staff (CASD). Prof. Margelletti has been Strategic Advisor to the Italian

Minister of Defense from March 2012 to February 2014. He is also a member of the Advisory Committee of the International Commission on Non-Proliferation and Nuclear Disarmament and an advisor to COPASIR – Parliamentary Committee for the Republic Security. He teaches at the Advanced Training School of the Italian National Intelligence Community, at the Carabinieri Officer School, at the High Academy of the State Police, at the Institute of Higher Military Studies of the Defence Staff, at the Italian Army's Centre for Post Conflict Studies, at the Centre for Specialised Training of the Italian Financial Police and at the Joint Intelligence Centre of the Defence Staff. He teaches International Relations at the Master in "Peacekeeping and Security Studies" of Roma Tre University and at the course on "Investigative Sciences and Security" at the University of Perugia at Narni. He is also a consultant to various National and International organisations for matters pertaining International Relations, Intelligence and Terrorism and appears regularly as a guest commentator and political analyst on television and radio. Prof. Margelletti has constantly travelled to the main theatres of crisis and conflict in the Balkans, the Middle East, the Far East, South and Central Asia and Africa and is the author of the book "Un Mondo in bilico", published by Eurilink. He is Honorary Academic of the Angelica Costantiniana Academy and a Knight of the Order of Merit of the Republic of Italy and a Knight Commander Pro Merito Melitensi of the SMOM – Sovereign Military Order of Malta.

Darko Trifunovic is a Research Fellow and lecturer at the Faculty of Security Studies-University of Belgrade. A specialist in Counter-terrorism and national and international security studies, Dr Trifunovic has been elected to the position of the visiting professor at the Fudan University in China, Center for American Studies for teaching undergraduate and graduate study programmes. He is former First Secretary of the Foreign Service of Bosnia and Herzegovina at the UN, Adviser to the State Secretary for War Crimes of Republic of Srpska for Terrorism and Violence and (in 2005) Adviser to the Minister of Police of the Republic of Srpska, BIH. He is also the representative of Serbia and Montenegro in the International Strategic Studies Association (ISSA), Defense & Foreign Affairs publications, and the the Global Information System (GIS). The Shanghai Center for International Studies appointed Dr. Darko Trifunovic (RIEAS Senior Advisor) as the first foreign expert for the Olympic Games (2008) security preparation in China. In 2010, Dr. Trifunovic was engaged in World Expo Security preparation. He is Senior Adviser of the Research Institute of European and American Studies, Athens, Greece, as well as member of the Advisory Board of the Institute of Transnational Studies, Munich, Germany. A regular speaker at International Institute for Counter-Terrorism Institute, Herzliya, Israel and member of International Analyst Network, Dr Darko Trifunovic is one of the founding members of ICTAC (International Counter Terrorism Academic Community).

Shuja Nawaz is a native of Pakistan and is currently a distinguished fellow at the Atlantic Council's South Asia Center. Most recently, he was the Center's first director. He is a political and strategic analyst. Mr. Nawaz writes for leading newspapers and websites and speaks on current topics before civic groups, at think tanks, and on radio and television worldwide. He has worked with RAND, the United States Institute of Peace, the Center for Strategic and International Studies, and other leading think tanks on projects dealing with Pakistan and the Middle East. He has also advised or briefed senior government and military officials and parliamentarians in the US, Europe, and Pakistan. He was a newscaster and news and current affairs producer for Pakistan Television from 1967 to 1972 and covered the western front of the 1971 war between Pakistan and India. He has worked for the New York Times, the World Health Organisation, and has headed three separate divisions at the International Monetary Fund. He was also a director at the International Atomic Energy Agency in Vienna 1999-2001, while on leave from the IMF. Mr. Nawaz was the managing editor and then editor of Finance & Development, the multilingual quarterly of the IMF and the World Bank. He served on the editorial advisory board of the World Bank Research Observer. He is the author of Crossed Swords: Pakistan, its Army, and the Wars Within (Oxford University Press 2008). He is also the principal author of FATA: A Most Dangerous Place (CSIS, Washington DC January 2009), Pakistan in the Danger Zone: A Tenuous US-Pakistan Relationship (Atlantic Council 2010), Learning by Doing: The Pakistan Army's Experience with Counterinsurgency (Atlantic Council 2011) and, with Mohan Guruswamy, India-Pakistan: The Opportunity Cost of Conflict (Atlantic Council 2014).

Rana Banerji is an Indian Administrative Services officer of the 1972 batch. He was assigned to the Assam-Meghalaya cadre and after working for the Government of Assam for eight years he was deputed to the Central Government in 1980, from where he retired as Special Secretary, Cabinet Secretariat in October 2009. While at the Centre, he dealt with security and intelligence-related issues impinging on national security policy formulation, with focused expertise on the South Asian region. Post retirement, he headed a task force on intelligence reforms at the Institute for Defence Studies & Analyses (IDSA), and served as Visiting Professor, Pakistan Studies Programme at the Academy of International Relations, Jamia Millia Islamia University, Delhi from January 2012 to January 2015. Currently, he is Distinguished Fellow at the Institute for Peace & Conflict Studies (IPCS), New Delhi. Mr Banerji writes extensively on Pakistan politics and Army. He has been a member of several Track II dialogues and has attended several international conferences and seminars on CBMs, Trans National Crime, Money Laundering & Terrorism, and regional issues.

Farooq Sobhan is a former Bangladesh diplomat and iscurrently the President and CEO of the Bangladesh Enterprise Institute (BEI) which was established in October 2000. He has served as Ambassador/High Commissioner to India, China, Malaysia and the United Nations and as Foreign Secretary from 1995-1997. He was the Special Envoy to the Prime Minister of Bangladesh from 1997-1999. He also visited Washington and the United Nations in New York in May 2007 as the Special Envoy of the then Caretaker Government, with the rank and status of a Cabinet Minister. He served as Chairman of the Group of 77 at the UN 1982-1983, and was Chairman, UN Commission on TNCs 1991-1992. He is a member of the Board of Governors of the South Asia Centre for Policy Studies (SACEPS), based in Kathmandu and was Co-Chairman of the Coalition for South Asian Co-operation (CASAC) from 1994-2001. Mr Sobhan served as a visiting professor at the Elliott School for International Affairs at George Washington University in 2003, where he taught a post graduate course on South Asia. He is the Chairman of the Board of Trustees of the independent Centre for Corporate Social Responsibility (CSR), established in Dhaka in September 2007. He is also the Chairman of an Advisory Committee on Counter Terrorism established in 2006, which includes senior officials of the government. He writes extensively on international affairs and relations and his publications include a book titled "Opportunities for South-South Co-operation" and as co-author, "Shaping South Asia's Future: Role of Regional Co-operation".

Sultan Shahin is an alumnus of Patna University and is the founder and editor of the multi-lingual Islamic website NewAgeIslam.com. His career in journalism spans 40 years during which time he has travelled extensively in India and abroad and has acquired expertise in Islamic theology, politics, and culture as well as an empirical knowledge of the impact of religion and ideology over radicalisation and radicalism. He has written edit-page articles, opinion pieces, special reports, and columns for major Indian publications such as the Hindustan Times, The Indian Express, The Times of India, The Asian Age, etc. as well as for international newspapers such as the Asia Times Online, Hong Kong. His website is aimed at engaging with the Muslim communities across the world, to encourage open debate and to rethink Islam by fighting xenophobia, religious intolerance and gender inequality in Islamic societies. Its main focus is to combat jihadi radicalism at an ideological level by promoting a progressive interpretation of the Islamic scriptures.

Index